Wallace Stevens

READINGS, AN INTERPRETATION, AN

A GUIDE TO THE COLLECTED POETI

Wallace Steven

Musing the Obscure

Ronald Sukenick

NEW YORK
NEW YORK UNIVERSITY PRESS

LONDON
UNIVERSITY OF LONDON PRESS LIMITED

1967

© COPYRIGHT 1967 BY NEW YORK UNIVERSITY
LIBRARY OF CONGRESS CATALOG CARD NUMBER: 67–25041
MANUFACTURED IN THE UNITED STATES OF AMERICA
ISBN: 8147-0409-3 PAPER
SECOND PRINTING, 1971

FOR

Lynn

A MUSER'S MUSE

And of all vigils musing the obscure,
That apprehends the most which sees and names,
As in your name, an image that is sure.

—To the One of Fictive Music

Preface

After all that has been written about Stevens' poetry, its difficulty remains the chief problem. Explication of the kind performed for Eliot has been long overdue for Stevens. Most of the explications that exist, especially of the long poems after *Harmonium*, would be more aptly termed summaries that represent merely the beginnings of the kind of close reading that is necessary. Many of the most important early poems have never had satisfactory explication, and many of the apparently easier poems are still the subject of widely differing and contradictory interpretations. Commentators have been so fascinated by the explanation of Stevens' ideas that they have largely neglected the explanation of his poems, except for fragmentary readings designed to illustrate points which are as often as not incorrect or superfluous. Explication, especially that done by way of illustrating Stevens' theories, has tended to be sketchy, slipshod, and misleading or, often, plainly wrong. Critics, in order to illustrate a point, will use passages that are themselves in need of explanation; they will distort meaning by misleading quotation; in readings they will explain the obvious lines and skip the difficult ones.

Even the better readings that have appeared demonstrate considerable confusion as to how the poems may best be explicated. It is of dubious help to place a poem in a tradition of thought or to trace the influences that bear on it, before establishing what it says—and philosophy cannot serve as a gloss for Stevens' almost impenetrable phrases. Parallels in thought, and even in language, with systematic thinkers, though they may be suggestive, cannot determine meaning in the poem. Explicating a poem by relating it to one of Stevens' general themes, or by comparing it to another of his

poems, can be misleading, and may further obscure the text at
hand. Stevens works through nuance, variation, and sudden
reversal on a theme, requiring on the part of the reader an
absolute attention to the specific text. A term such as "major
man" may signify a complex abstraction in one poem while
in another it merely means "the pick of young men" (*LWS*,
p. 489). Similarly, Stevens' images cannot be frozen into
static symbols: even the color blue, and the moon, which
usually represent the imagination in his poems, do not do so
invariably, or in exactly the same way.[1] Stevens' images must
be understood ultimately in terms of the nuances of context;
an image in one poem does not necessarily mean the same
thing in another—it may mean the opposite. Finally, there is
a kind of explication which, in refusing to read plainly the
discursive content of Stevens' poems, has the effect of render-
ing easy poems difficult, and difficult poems unintelligible.

Doctrinaire objections to paraphrase notwithstanding,
there is no getting around the discursive content of Stevens'
poems, and attempts to do so only lead to further obscurity.
When a Stevens poem is not discursive, when its meanings
are indeterminate, there are ways of handling it that are appropriate (see, for example, my explication of "Thirteen
Ways of Looking at a Blackbird"); there is no reason, on that
ground, for refusing explication of discursive meaning insofar
as it can be explicated. Despite Stevens' insistence that poems
have imaginative and emotional meanings, rather than rational meanings, as of course they do, no one who has looked
at Stevens' explanatory notes to "The Man with the Blue
Guitar" can doubt his cognizance that rational meanings can
be extracted from a poem in order to help understand it. As
to the limits of such glosses, Stevens made the following pro-
viso: "You will understand that in converting a poem, written
and thought out in the peculiar figurations of poetry, into
plain English, one's explanations are bound to call for a certain amount of toleration" (*LWS*, p. 788).

As R. P. Blackmur long ago demonstrated, the obscurity
of Stevens' poetry is different in kind from that of Eliot or
Pound: "Mr. Stevens' difficulties to the normal reader pre-

sent themselves in the shape of seemingly impenetrable words or phrases which no wedge of knowledge brought from outside the body of Mr. Stevens' own poetry can help much to split."[2] The difficulty is with the phrasing itself, which is at a level of metaphor so sustained that it is hard to connect it with the subject of the poem. Stevens' arguments proceed in a sign language of metaphor often remote from the subject matter. What this kind of language unavoidably requires is plain, line by line paraphrase, and though there is, of course, need for further interpretation, it must presuppose such explication. Summary of the arguments is not sufficient, since the difficulty is not primarily in following the arguments but in the reference of the language itself. In explicating such poetry, one is either governed by the strictest detail of the poem, or one is free to give any interpretation at all.

It is perhaps pertinent to say that my choice of poems for full explication is not an attempt to promote a Stevens canon. A poem such as "The House Was Quiet and the World Was Calm," though among Stevens' best poems, is not in need of the kind of reading I am concerned with here. On the other hand, "The Rock," which I do not consider to be one of Stevens' best poems, has been chosen for full explication both because it has become important in critical discussion, and because it is difficult. I have given close readings of most of Stevens' major and best-known poems beyond a certain level of difficulty, and I have tried to establish an approach to the rest. Further readings did not seem sufficiently profitable, even without considering limitations of space.

"The Guide to Stevens Collected Poetry" provides an entrée to a larger body of poetry than could be, and, for that matter, need be, paraphrased. It will be the most effective if used after reading the introductory essay and becoming familiar with the paraphrased poetry. In combination with the rest of the book, it should be adequate in giving cues to the subjects of the poems, and in indicating their frame of reference within Stevens'. thought and poetic practice. The Guide either makes brief comments on the poems, or refers the reader to a section or sections of the book that discusses relevant thematic material. Together with the paraphrases, it covers the complete *Collected Poems*, and all the poetry in *Opus Posthumous* that is of importance.

I would like to express my gratitude to J. V. Cunningham and Irving Howe for their help on an earlier version of my manuscript while I was at Brandeis University and, in particular, my indebtedness to the former for his many detailed suggestions and corrections, both in my essay on Stevens' theory and practice, and in explication of individual poems. Thanks are due to Bell Gale Chevigny for a helpful reading of parts of this manuscript, and to Professor Oscar Cargill, to John Hammond of New York University Press, and to Robert King, formerly of the Press, for their help. I would also like to express my gratitude for a Fulbright Fellowship that provided for a year of study in connection with the original manuscript. Acknowledgement is due to Alfred A. Knopf, Inc. for permission to quote from the following works by Wallace Stevens: *The Collected Poems of Wallace Stevens* (copyright 1954, by Wallace Stevens); *The Necessary Angel* (copyright 1951, by Wallace Stevens); *Opus Posthumous* (copyright 1957, by Elsie Stevens and Holly Stevens); *Letters of Wallace Stevens*, edited by Holly Stevens (copyright 1966, by Holly Stevens). I would also like to acknowledge the permission of Holly Stevens to quote from Wallace Stevens' commentary in *Mattino Domenicale ed Altre Poesie*, edited by Renato Poggioli and published by Giulio Einaudi.

NOTES

[1] See, for example, "The Comedian as the Letter C," V, 15, and my explication of "Esthétique du Mal," II. For an attempt to work out a key to Stevens' use of colors, see George McFadden, "Probings for an Integration: Color Symbolism in Wallace Stevens," *Modern Philology*, LVIII (Feb., 1961), 186–93.

[2] "Examples of Wallace Stevens," *Form and Value in Modern Poetry* (Garden City, New York, 1957), p. 202.

A Stevens Chronology *

1879 Born at 323 North Fifth Street, Reading, Pennsylvania, October 2, to Garrett B. Stevens, lawyer, and the former Margaretha Catherine Zeller. He was the second of three brothers; he had two sisters, one of whom died shortly after the end of World War I, while serving with the Red Cross in France. His father occasionally published poetry and prose in the local papers.

1896 In high school he won the *Reading Eagle* Prize for essay, and the Alumni Medal for Oration.

1897 Graduated with merit from Reading Boys High School. He had worked for the *Reading Times* in the summers. Enrolled at Harvard as a special student (not a degree candidate).

1899 One of Stevens' undergraduate poems at Harvard elicited a sonnet in reply by Santayana ("Cathedrals by the Sea"), who was then teaching there, and whom Stevens knew.

1900 Graduated from a special three year course in English at Harvard. President of the *Harvard Advocate* from March, 1900, to the end of the college year. Between 1898 and 1900, many contributions, both prose and verse, to the *Advocate* and to the *Harvard Monthly*. After graduation he worked on the editorial staff of the *New York Tribune*, and on the periodical, *The World's Work*.

1901 Entered New York Law School.

1904 Admitted to the bar in New York. Began legal practice.

1909 Married September 21, 1909, to Elsie Viola Kachel (who

* Much of the material in this chronology was taken from *LWS* or, when possible, was checked against that volume.

used her stepfather's surname, Moll) of Reading. The Stevenses had one daughter, Holly.

1913 Bust of Elsie Stevens made by sculptor Adolph A. Weinman, the profile of which was later used on the Mercury Head dime and the Liberty Standing half dollar, issued from 1916 to 1945 and 1947, respectively.

1914 At thirty-five, first publication, since his undergraduate work, in *Trend* and Harriet Monroe's *Poetry*.

1915 Publication in the Nortons' magazine, *Rogue,* and in Alfred Kreymborg's *Others,* including "Peter Quince at the Clavier." A version of "Sunday Morning" published in *Poetry,* November issue. In New York he was acquainted with such artistic and literary people as Louise and Allan Norton, Donald Evans, Carl Van Vechten, Mina Loy, Walter Conrad Arensberg, William Carlos Williams, Alfred Kreymborg, Witter Bynner, Pitts Sanborn, Carl Zigrosser, Walter Pach, and Marcel Duchamp—he was, according to Williams, "part of the gang."

1916 Joined Hartford Accident and Indemnity Company, legal staff; transferred to Hartford, which remained his place of residence throughout his life. The one act play "Three Travelers Watch a Sunrise" appeared in *Poetry,* July, as winner of that magazine's prize for a verse play.

1920 "Three Travelers Watch a Sunrise" produced at the Provincetown Playhouse in New York. Won *Poetry's* Levinson prize for the group of poems called "Pecksniffiana."

1922 An early version of "The Comedian as the Letter C" ("From the Journal of Crispin") won first honorable mention for the Blindman Prize of the Poetry Society of South Carolina, judged by Amy Lowell.

1923 Publication of *Harmonium* by Alfred A. Knopf. Stevens was forty-four. The edition sold fewer than one hundred copies, but was praised by such reviewers as Marianne Moore and Matthew Josephson.

1924–1929 Almost no writing; consolidation in the business world.

1930 First periodical publication since 1924.

1931 Second edition of *Harmonium,* dropping three poems from the original and adding fourteen.

1934 Became vice president of the Hartford Accident and Indemnity Company.

1935 *Ideas of Order* (Alcestis Press edition). Stanley Burnshaw's review of that volume, attacking Stevens on grounds of social indifference, to which Stevens responded in *Owl's Clover.*

1936 *Owl's Clover.* Knopf edition of *Ideas of Order.* "The Men That Are Falling" named the *Nation's* prize poem.

1937 *The Man with the Blue Guitar and Other Poems.*

1942 *Parts of a World. Notes toward a Supreme Fiction.* "The Noble Rider and the Sound of Words," after having been read by Stevens at Princeton, was published by the Princeton University Press along with addresses given on the same occasion by Philip Wheelwright, Cleanth Brooks, and I. A. Richards.

1943 "The Figure of the Youth as Virile Poet" was read by Stevens at Mount Holyoke College.

1945 *Esthétique du Mal* published in a limited edition by The Cummington Press (first published in *Kenyon Review,* Autumn, 1944).

1946 Member of the National Institute of Arts and Letters.

1947 *Transport to Summer.*

1950 *The Auroras of Autumn.* Bollingen Prize for 1949. The first book-length study of Stevens: William Van O'Connor's *The Shaping Spirit.*

1951 National Book Award. *The Necessary Angel: Essays on Reality and the Imagination.* Gold Medal of the Poetry Society of America. One of Stevens' several honorary degrees awarded by Harvard at the time of the fiftieth reunion of his class.

1953 *Selected Poems* published in England with the selection made by Stevens.

1954 *Collected Poems.* Declined an offer to be Charles Eliot

Norton Professor of Poetry at Harvard for 1955–1956 because he did not want to retire from business.

1955 Pulitzer Prize. Second National Book Award. Died August 2.

1957 *Opus Posthumous.*

1958–1967 Sixteen books published about Stevens, including several collections of critical essays, a bibliography, a concordance to his poetry, and a number of full-length studies.

Contents

Abbreviations

CP: *The Collected Poems of Wallace Stevens.* New York, 1954.

LWS: Holly Stevens (ed.). *Letters of Wallace Stevens.* New York, 1966.

NA: *The Necessary Angel.* New York, 1951.

OP: Samuel French Morse (ed.). *Opus Posthumous.* New York, 1957.

Poggioli: Renato Poggioli, trans., *Mattino Domenicale ed Altre Poesie.* Torino, 1954. (Contains commentary by Stevens not included in *LWS.*)

Wallace Stevens

I.
Wallace Stevens:
Theory and Practice

i. The Reality of the Imagination

Excessive attention to Wallace Stevens' theory can obscure what his poetry is about. His subject might best be described at the outset, for the sake of simplicity, in terms of the question posed in the early poem, "The American Sublime": "How does one stand/ To behold the sublime/ . . . how does one feel?" (CP, pp. 130–31). This is less an ideological question than it is one of stance or posture: with what tenable attitude may one confront the difficult circumstances of contemporary American secular life and avail oneself of the good possible in it? How, in short, does one get along? Writing poetry was for Stevens a way of getting along. He must be taken seriously when he says that he writes poetry because he needs to (OP, p. xxxvii). The act of composition was for him a way of discovering and crystallizing what he called in one of his last poems, "Local Objects," "the objects of insight, the integrations/ Of feeling . . ."

> That were the moments of the classic, the beautiful.
> These were that serene he had always been approaching.
> (OP, p. 112)

These are discoveries not of the good, but simply of good things—"As when the sun comes rising, when the sea/ Clears deeply" (CP, p. 398), times "when the cock crows on the left and all/ Is well" (CP, p. 386)—whose revelation composes the poet in the composition of his poem.

This composure in face of what Stevens calls "the pressure of reality," this "serene" which is, at its extreme, a highly intense state of mind, stands as a kind of ideal experience which is central to Stevens' poetry. His theories, the heroes and fictions he hypothesizes, are tentative efforts to recapture and formularize it so that the experience may cease to be merely fortuitous. Through it he seeks to achieve a rapport with the conditions of contemporary life within the limits of what that life will allow him to believe, within what is credible. He does not merely evade or condemn what he considers the spiritual and imaginative impoverishment of contemporary reality, but takes it as given and makes of it what he can. Frank Kermode has aptly said of Stevens, in contrast with his "great contemporaries": "In an age of poetic myth-making Stevens is almost alone in his respect for those facts which seem 'in disconnexion, dead and spiritless.' "[1] It is in his willingness to accept the fact of contemporary life that Stevens, as Irving Howe has put it, has begun to move beyond the "crisis of belief" that troubled his contemporaries, to the question, "how shall we live with and perhaps beyond it?"[2]

The desire for faith does not issue for Stevens, as it does for some of his contemporaries, in an attempt to utilize or rehabilitate older belief. The orientation of his poetry is historical, but this awareness of history works toward freeing it from the past for a more acute perception of the present. Myth, once recognized as such, is regarded as at best a noble falsification of the present based on the assumptions of the past or, in other words, as quixotic. The "final belief" in a "fiction" proposed in "Asides on the Oboe" (*CP*, p. 250) is discovered by the end of the poem to be nothing less than a full recognition of our humanity, divorced from such falsification. Stevens' poetry expresses what might be called a nostalgia for perfection, or for an idea of perfection, which sometimes gives his thought a Platonic tone, but like his nostalgia for our religious myth, this is merely nostalgia. Stevens recognizes an innate obsolescence in myth as crystallized perception of reality, and addresses himself therefore to immediate perception of the changing present as the most likely way to discover what we can or do in fact believe. (Although Stevens thought poetry could articulate the "credible," that which it is possible to believe, he did not claim that the function of poetry is the creation of systematic belief: "Poetry does not address itself to beliefs. Nor could it ever invent an ancient world full of figures that had been known and become endeared to its readers for centuries"—NA, p. 144.) Adequate adjustment to the present can only be achieved through ever fresh perception of it, and this is the effort of his poetry. It tries to find what is fresh and attractive in a reality that is frequently stale and dispiriting by way of coming to a satisfactory rapport with it.

In order to arrive at such a rapport it is necessary to satisfy the extra-rational but nonetheless real need for positive belief within the conditions of an indifferent and changing reality, as, for example, the desire to maintain a noble conception of human life. It is the constant irrational force of this desire that Stevens has in mind when he speaks of nobility as "a violence from within that protects us from a violence without" (NA p. 36). But though the need for belief is not rational, it may be rationally understood, as Freudian psychology makes the irrational mechanics of desire available to the understanding and control of the reason. Thus, referring to Freud, Stevens suggests the possibility of a "science of illusions" (NA, p. 139). If one thinks of illusion as that created by the painter as he discovers the beauty of a landscape in his composition, or as that comprised in the poet's rhetorical formulations about reality, it is roughly equivalent to Stevens' idea of a "fiction" in which he resolves the problem of belief. A fiction is not an ideological formulation of belief but a statement of favorable rapport with reality sufficiently convincing that disbelief may be suspended. Stevens defines poetic truth as "an agreement with reality" believed, for a time, to be true (NA, p. 54). The "truth" of a fiction is poetic truth.

Because the fiction mediates between the requirements of desire and the conditions of reality, and because the relation between the two keeps changing, no statement of that relation is final. On the contrary, such statements do and must become constantly outmoded. It is like a game which, lacking any purpose but the playing of it, can only be played again and again. The urbane playfulness of Stevens' wit suggests his consciousness of this. His sense of humor is a way of expressing thought's perspective on its own limitations, its awareness that it must be ultimately outwitted by the extra-rational forces between which it mediates.

ii. Change

Stevens' poetry deals in a series of antithetic terms, such as chaos and order, imagination and reality, stasis and change. The repeated recombination of the terms in each antithesis produces a continual restatement of the shifting relation between them:

> Two things of opposite natures seem to depend
> On one another, as a man depends
> On a woman, day on night, the imagined
>
> On the real. This is the origin of change. (CP, p. 392)

In considering such antithetic terms Stevens will adopt the point of view of one, then of the other, and then that of some nuance between the two. He was a poet who, in this sense, refused to make up his mind because he believed that change was the life of the mind: "It can never be satisfied, the mind, never" (CP, p. 247; compare "An Ordinary Evening in New Haven," X—CP, p. 472). William York Tindall has written that Stevens usually brings conflicts to an end "by an agreement of opposites; for he had looked into Hegel."[3] I do not believe that Stevens was dialectical in this sense, for his syntheses are momentary, unstable, and, instead of advancing his argument, always break down again into the original antithetic terms. That is why the relation between such terms must be continually restated, and it accounts for that constant reformulation of a cluster of ideas that comprises so much of Stevens' poetry. The first stanza of "An Ordinary Evening in New Haven" describes the procedure of the poem: a statement about the nature of reality followed by progressive qualification.

> The eye's plain version is a thing apart,
> The vulgate of experience. Of this,
> A few words, an and yet, and yet, and yet— (CP, p. 465)

The rest of the poem consists of an exploration of the relations possible between the plain view of reality and its opposite, the imaginative view.

It is only another manifestation of this antithetic character that despite his acknowledgement of change, Stevens longed for peace, for stasis, for an unchanging ideal: "He wanted his heart to stop beating and his mind to rest// In a permanent realization" (CP, p. 425). Stevens' poetry gropes toward a final formulation that does not exist, one such as might be given by the tantalizing "impossible possible philosophers' man" who sums us up (CP, p. 250), and hence no single formulation can remain satisfactory. The "philosophers' man" is a fiction which must change as the exigencies which made it necessary change. One might reach beyond the quotidian to some finality, but, as Stevens put it in the early "The Man Whose Pharynx Was Bad" (CP, p. 96), "time will not relent."

In Stevens' conception, history is a process in which no idea of reality is final, poetry is a progressive metamorphosis of reality, and reality itself is an entity whose chief characteristic is flux. Man

> Lives in a fluid, not on solid rock.
> The solid was an age, a period
> With appropriate, largely English, furniture . . .
> Policed by the hope of Christmas. (OP, p. 68)

Verrocchio's statue of Colleoni represents for Stevens the static ideal left behind by dynamic history. The idea of nobility it embodies is no longer appropriate to the changed conditions for nobility in a new historical situation. As a symbol for belief it has failed to withstand the pressure of a new reality and has consequently become incredible: "It seems, nowadays, what it may very well not have seemed a few years ago, a little overpowering, a little magnificent" (*NA*, p. 9). Failing as a symbol of belief, the statue has become a magnificent artifact. Artifacts also are the statues in "Dance of the Macabre Mice" (*CP*, p. 123), in "Lions in Sweden" (*CP*, p. 124), and in the first two parts of "Owl's Clover," where the sculpted group of horses loses meaning in face of the bitter old woman: "The mass of stone collapsed to marble hulk" (*OP*, p. 44). The statue seemed "a thing from Schwarz's" (*OP*, p. 47)—the reference is most likely to F.A.O. Schwarz, the well known toy store—hence, a toy, a plaything, not to be taken seriously. So also, the "great statue of the General Du Puy" in "Notes toward a Supreme Fiction" belonged "Among our more vestigial states of mind" (*CP*, pp. 391–92).

But although no faith is absolute, particular beliefs are credible for particular epochs. Stevens writes out of a situation in which the beliefs that once ordered reality have become incredible; but the soul "still hankers after sovereign images" (*CP*, p. 124). Stevens is concerned with discovering belief that is credible in the American present. The style by which Claude Lorraine achieved serenity is obsolete (*CP*, p. 135), "Marx has ruined Nature" (*CP*, p. 134)—by replacing it as a source of salvation, for such as Wordsworth, with the means of production and distribution or, more simply, with history—and "The heaven of Europe is empty, like a Schloss/ Abandoned because of taxes" (*OP*, p. 53). "The epic of disbelief/ Blares oftener and soon, will soon be constant" (*CP*, p. 122). It is the function of poetry to meet this situation: "It has to face the men of the time and to meet/ The women of the time" (*CP*, p. 240).

In a world whose fundamental condition is change, the only tenable kind of belief must involve an affirmation of change. There is no value in history beyond the content of the present as it comes and passes. In "Owl's Clover" this condition is figured in a "trash can" of beliefs where fragments of the statue are found:

There lies the head of the sculptor in which the thought
Of lizards, in its eye, is more acute
Than the thought that once was native to the skull;
And there are the white-maned horses' heads . . .
Parts of the immense detritus of a world
That is completely waste, that moves from waste
To waste, out of the hopeless waste of the past
Into a hopeful waste to come. (OP, p. 49)

"Nothing is final," chants the sun like Walt Whitman singing, "No man shall see the end" (CP, p. 150), and therefore,
once more in the words of "Owl's Clover," "It is only
enough/ To live incessantly in change" (OP, p. 50).

Stevens' theory comprises more of a mechanics, or psychology, of belief than an assertion of particular belief. His fundamental assumption is that belief is a psychological process
through which it is possible to arrive at an affirmative relation
to one's environment. Like other needs, the need for an affirmative relation to reality, the "passion for yes" (CP, p.
320), has a repetitive pattern of desire, fulfilment, and ennui
in a cycle that generates its own perpetuation. No part of the
pattern is absolutely bad because all the parts are essential to
the continuity of the cycle. Thus in "No Possum, No Sop,
No Taters," when the crow who is part of the sterility and
temporary stasis of the winter landscape rises up, "One joins
him there for company,/ But at a distance, in another tree"
(CP, p. 294). The condition of the landscape is not a good
to embrace but an evil to be tolerated as part of the ultimately benign cycle of change. This is "The last purity of
the knowledge of good" to which the poem refers. Nor, correspondingly, is fulfillment itself absolutely good, as in "Banal
Sojourn" (CP, p. 62), where the fulfillment of summer is described as having become a surfeit. This pattern is repeated in
the cycle of the seasons as they affect the emotions, with winter representing barrenness, spring, desire, summer, fulfilment,
and autumn, the decay of desire, a kind of asceticism.[4] The
beginning of each emotional season is an experience of freshness and the end one of ennui and impatience for change

(the onset of winter is sometimes an exception, an occasion for gloom). The vital point is that nothing should impede the continuity of the process on which the stimulation of desire and its satisfaction depend.

Because of this affirmation of change, the traditional lament of transitoriness is transformed in Stevens' poetry to a hymn of praise. Change is not less destructive, but this destruction is desirable and the imagination must help to execute it:

> The mind is the great poem of winter, the man,
> Who, to find what will suffice,
> Destroys romantic tenements
> Of rose and ice. (CP. p. 238)

The mind reduces belief to the wintery barrenness of disbelief. But what it destroys is belief that is inadequate, and in so doing purges the world of

> . . . an old delusion, an old affair with the sun,
> An impossible aberration with the moon,
> A grossness of peace. (CP, p. 239)

A new resolution in the credible must follow one that is no longer satisfactory, as the satisfactions of one season are replaced by another season with satisfactions of its own:

> The spring will have a health of its own, with none
> Of autumn's halloo in its hair. So that closely, then,
>
> Health follows after health. Salvation there:
> There's no such thing as life; or if there is,
> It is faster than the weather, faster than
> Any character. It is more than any scene. (CP, p. 192)

There is no one relation to, or agreement with, reality that can be called "life," and the many possible relations succeed one another as they are appropriate. To live in the health of change, therefore, is to live always in a present of constant change. Time is

. . . apart from any past, apart
From any future, the ever-living and being,
The ever-breathing and moving, the constant fire.
   (CP, p. 238)

The celebration of time, as in the literal march of time of
"Dutch Graves in Bucks County," is directed to time as it
represents an on-going break from history that frees the mind
to live in an agreement with the present: "And you, my semblables, in gaffer-green,/ Know that the past is not part of
the present" (CP, p. 291). This is the benevolence of time,
that comes with its destructive power: "Freedom is like a
man who kills himself/ Each night, an incessant butcher"
(CP. p. 292). But despite time's purgative function in creating "An end of evil in a profounder logic" (CP, p. 291), its
destructiveness remains:

Men came as the sun comes, early children
And late wanderers creeping under the barb of night,
Year, year and year, defeated at last and lost
In an ignorance of sleep with nothing won. (CP, p. 291)

Within these terms of evil, the good finds its limits:

. . . The assassin discloses himself,
The force that destroys us is disclosed, within
This maximum, an adventure to be endured
With the politest helplessness. (CP, p. 324)

iii. Chaos and Order

The perception of chaos comes for Stevens when reality
seems void of meaning and without emotional connection
with the ego. It is suggested by the sea as in "The Comedian
as the Letter C"; by the barrenness of winter as in the "Nothing that is not there and the nothing that is" of "The Snow
Man"; by the "large" (vastness, or infinitude) as in "the last

largeness" of "The Curtains in the House of the Metaphysician"; by darkness as in "Domination of Black"; by "the blank" as in "Notes toward a Supreme Fiction" (*CP*, p. 397), or by "this blank cold" of "The Plain Sense of Things"; by the decay of autumn that reveals the bare essentials of the landscape, or by a decaying culture whose order no longer seems credible. Chaos is reality apprehended without the projections of the ego, so that we find ourselves in the position of "intelligent men/ At the centre of the unintelligible" (*CP*, p. 495),[5] and thus alienated from the reality of which we are part.

But this indifferent, unintelligible chaos of reality without the imagination, which is what Stevens calls "absolute fact," is also that solid world beyond rhetoric and the imagination in which the ego may uniquely find fulfillment of desire. Thus Stevens qualifies his description of absolute fact as "destitute of any imaginative aspect whatever," by adding: "Unhappily the more destitute it becomes the more it begins to be precious" (*NA*, p. 60). The indifferent reality beyond the ego is the data with which the imagination works, the rock, as "The Man with the Blue Guitar" puts it (*CP*, p. 179), "To which his imagination returned,/ From which it sped." Moreover, when one comes to accept this chaos as the only truth in the sense that it is the only order that exists, it may be brought into gratifying relation with the ego:

> . . . having just
> Escaped from the truth, the morning is color and mist,
> Which is enough. (*CP*, p. 204)

One may then enjoy a pleasurable relation with reality in which the ego demands from the chaos of reality nothing but what it can give, and chaos is therefore adequate to satisfy the desires of the ego. In this state one simply enjoys the sense of one's own existence in a physical reality, beyond any meaning of that existence imposed by the ego:

> It was how the sun came shining into his room:
> To be without a description of to be. (*CP*, p. 205)

Thus, the formulations of "Connoisseur of Chaos" (*CP*, p. 215): "A violent order is disorder" because it is imposed on, and therefore falsifies, the chaos of reality; and "A great disorder is an order" because, although "The squirming facts exceed the squamous mind," although reality proves incomprehensible to the ego, yet beyond the comprehending mind, a sense in this disorder is felt:

> . . . yet relation appears,
> A small relation expanding like the shade
> Of a cloud on sand, a shape on the side of a hill.

In the terms of "The Man with the Blue Guitar" (*CP*, p. 169), the chaos of the storm is brought to bear, is brought into significant relation with the ego. The ego imposes no order on reality, therefore "the structure/ Of things" is accepted "as the structure of ideas" (*CP*, p. 327). Reality is recognized as the unique source of the ego's content, thereby bridging "the dumbfoundering abyss/ Between us and the object" (*CP*, p. 437) that alienates us from it, and allowing the ego to find fulfillment in reality.[6]

It is his poetry that gets Stevens from reality as chaos to reality as perceived in some kind of order by the ego. This may be seen in his use of images:

> When the blackbird flew out of sight,
> It marked the edge
> Of one of many circles. (*CP*, p. 94)

This, from "Thirteen Ways of Looking at a Blackbird," demonstrates the way an image may be used as a principle of order. The blackbird, seen as a point of reference, defines an intelligible area among many possible but undefined intelligible areas. Speaking of "resemblances," the name Stevens gives to the basis of metaphor, comparison, he says: "What the eye beholds may be the text of life. It is, nevertheless, a text that we do not write. The eye does not beget in resemblance. It sees. But the mind begets in resemblance as the painter begets in representation; that is to say, as the painter makes his world within a world" (NA, p. 76). The mind orders reality not by imposing ideas on it but by discovering significant relations within it, as the artist abstracts and composes the elements of reality in significant integrations that are works of art.

It can be seen from this description of chaos and order that, as he presents no particular belief, Stevens presents no particular order but a theory of order, just as one might teach a theory of painting without advocating one style over another. He affirms the chaos of reality and seeks through the imagination for ways to make it tolerable, and even a positive good. This affirmation of chaos may not, in theory, seem an effective means to order, but when one comes upon it in "Sunday Morning" the case is different: "We live in an old chaos of the sun" (CP, p. 70). So stated, chaos seems good and the world seems ennobled by its identification with chaos. This is not a "truth" assumed for its usefulness even though it is untrue. It is a way of thinking about something, a way of thinking about something that promotes a way of feeling about something. Again, the evocation of an unintelligible cosmos is not ordinarily sympathetic. This is "The Curtains in the House of the Metaphysician" (CP, p. 62):

> It comes about that the drifting of these curtains
> Is full of long motions; as the ponderous
> Deflations of distance; or as clouds
> Inseparable from their afternoons;
> Or the changing of light, the dropping
> Of the silence, wide sleep and solitude
> Of night, in which all motion
> Is beyond us, as the firmament,
> Up-rising and down-falling, bares
> The last largeness, bold to see.

This says nothing true or untrue about the chaos of reality in terms of absolute fact, but merely presents a congenial way of thinking about it that we can believe. The statement of the poem compels belief. What I am trying to show is how Stevens' theory issues in poetry, and that chaos is ordered for Stevens not in his systematic thought, but in compelling statements in given poems. It is statements of the order of "The Curtains in the House of the Metaphysician" of which one should think when Stevens speaks of believing in a fiction.

iv. Ego and Reality

The characteristic movement of Stevens' thought as it is engaged in poetry may be described by two points of reference, the first taken from "Notes toward a Supreme Fiction," the second from "The Man with the Blue Guitar":

> From this the poem springs: that we live in a place
> That is not our own and, much more, not ourselves
> And hard it is in spite of blazoned days. (CP, p. 383)

> I am a native in this world
> And think in it as a native thinks. (CP, p. 180)

Between these two points Stevens' thought flows as a current between a negative and a positive pole. It is the gap between them that the poem must bridge and that, in fact, creates the need for the poem. In Stevens' theory it is the idea that after the last negation an instinct for affirmation remains, that impels the movement from the first point to the second (see "The Well Dressed Man with a Beard," CP, p. 247, and "Esthétique du Mal," VIII, CP, pp. 319–20). The movement begins with the ego's sense of disconnection from the absolute fact of reality which is felt as alien to the ego's concerns. As the ego approaches absolute fact it tends to reconcile that fact with its own needs through the imagination, which thus establishes a vital connection between the ego and reality. The absence of the imagination, or absolute fact, must itself be imagined (CP, p. 503), and in the process that fact is brought into meaningful relation with the ego. What seemed inert, insubstantial, and irrelevant will then seem vivid, substantial, and filled with interest. One will be as a native who draws strength from his environment, rather than an alien who is oppressed by it.

This vivid sense of reality is produced by the imagination and captured in some metaphor or description. At this phase Stevens' poetry tends to be in praise and amplification of the reality so imagined. But as the ego's idea of reality imposes itself in our apprehension of reality, it becomes a "violent order," a cliché that distorts reality and is a falsification of it. We then escape solipsism through a desire to return to absolute fact, to forsake our ideas about the thing for the thing itself, which at this point seems like "A new knowledge of reality" (CP, p. 534).

> . . . so poisonous
>
> Are the ravishments of truth, so fatal to
> The truth itself, the first idea becomes
> The hermit in a poet's metaphors,
>
> Who comes and goes and comes and goes all day.
>   (CP, p. 381)

Thus, an imbalance in favor of the imagination is restored by a return to reality, and the see-saw career of our idea of reality starts all over again.

At the heart of this interchange between the ego and reality is the effect of the imagination in bringing the two into vital relation. I suspect that this is not merely a point of theory for Stevens but rather an intensely real experience upon which the theory was constructed. Faced with the depressing prospect of a reality that seems dull, plain, and irrelevant to the needs of the ego, the poet comes to feel that the world in which he lives is thin and insubstantial, so remote from his concerns that feeling he is part of it "is an exertion that declines" (OP, p. 96). When, through the imagination, the ego manages to reconcile reality with its own needs, the formerly insipid landscape is infused with the ego's emotion and reality, since it now seems intensely relevant to the ego, suddenly seems more real.

> It was everything being more real, himself
> At the center of reality, seeing it.
> It was everything bulging and blazing and big in itself.
>   (CP, p. 205)

Stevens expressed this experience several times in more theoretical terms, as the manner in which the exercise of the imagination gives us the sense of a vivid and substantial reality beyond the mind:

> . . . if we say that the space [reality] is blank space, nowhere, without color, and that the objects, though solid, have no shadows and, though static, exert a mournful power, and, without elaborating this complete poverty, if suddenly we hear a different and familiar description of the place:

> This City now doth, like a garment, wear
> The beauty of the morning, silent bare,
> Ships, towers, domes, theatres, and temples lie
> Open unto the fields, and to the sky;
> All bright and glittering in the smokeless air;

> if we have this experience, we know how poets help people to live their lives. (NA, p. 31)

Again, in a passage on the function of poetry, abstracted by Stevens from H. D. Lewis' article, "On Poetic Truth":[7]

> . . . its function . . . is precisely this contact with reality as it impinges on us from the outside, the sense that we can touch and feel a solid reality which does not wholly dissolve itself into the conceptions of our own minds. . . . a quickening of our awareness of the irrevocability by which a thing is what it is, has such [particular] power, and it is, I believe, the very soul of art. (OP, pp. 236–37)

v. The Function of the Imagination

The imagination for Stevens is not a way of creating, but of knowing. The imagination creates nothing, in the sense that it presents us with nothing that is not already in the world to be perceived. He in one place defines it as "the sum of our faculties," and characterizes it by its "acute intelligence" (NA, p. 61). He goes on to compare the imagination with light. "Like light," he says, "it adds nothing, except itself." The imagination, in other words, brings out meaning, enables us to see more. It does not create but perceives acutely, and the object of its perception is reality. What it perceives in reality is the credible. The credible, of course, is that which can be believed, and may be distinguished from absolute fact. The credible must be based on absolute fact, but is perceived by the imagination and may be beyond the range of normal sensibility (NA, p. 60). The nature of poetic truth is not that it is true in the sense that absolute fact is true, but that it says something about reality we can believe— which, of course, is not to say it is untrue. It moves us from a state in which we cannot believe something about reality to one in which we can believe something about reality, and consequently puts us, to use Stevens' phrase, in "an agreement with reality" (NA, p. 54).

Stevens writes that "the poet must get rid of the hieratic in everything that concerns him and must move constantly in the direction of the credible" (NA, p. 58). When a poet gives to us something about reality that we can believe which before had been incredible, he adds, again in Stevens' phrase, to "our vital experience of life" (NA, p. 65). The poem expresses that vital experience precisely because, as I have pointed out, in it the ego has reconciled reality with its needs so that reality is infused with the concerns of the ego. "A poem is a particular of life thought of for so long that one's thought has become an inseparable part of it or a particular of life so intensely felt that the feeling has entered into it" (NA, p. 65). The poet is able to add to our vital experience of life because of the heightened awareness of life that results from the intensity of his thought and feeling. In his essay "Three Academic Pieces," Stevens gives an example in another connection which is applicable here as illustration of the process of the imagination:

> It is as if a man who lived indoors should go outdoors on a day of sympathetic weather. His realization of the weather would exceed that of a man who lives outdoors. It might, in fact, be intense enough to convert the real world about him into an imagined world. In short, a sense of reality keen enough to be in excess of the normal sense of reality creates a reality of its own. (NA, p. 79)

The poet, then, gives us a credible sense of reality which brings us into vital relation with it.

Since the poet's vision is an intensified one, his description of reality in the poem is correspondingly heightened. It is "A little different from reality:/ The difference that we make in what we see" (CP, p. 344). Here there is a pertinent analogy with Wordsworth, for whom the interaction of Nature and the imagination produced a new experience of reality resident in the poem. Stevens' idea is developed in "Description Without Place":

> Description is revelation. It is not
> The thing described, nor false facsimile.
>
> It is an artificial thing that exists,
> In its own seeming, plainly visible,
>
> Yet not too closely the double of our lives,
> Intenser than any actual life could be. (CP, p. 344)

Description is revelation in that it is an imaginative perception of the thing described: it is neither the thing itself, nor a pretended reproduction of the thing. It is a new thing, not reality but a real artifice, so to speak, with its own reality that makes actual reality seem more intense than it ordinarily is. "The poem is the cry of its occasion,/ Part of the res itself and not about it" (CP p. 473). The poem is not about the thing (the "res"), but is the articulation of one's experience of the thing, an experience in which the articulation—the writing of the poem—is itself an essential part. To this should be added Stevens' statement in "The Noble Rider and the Sound of Words": "A poet's words are of things that do not exist without the words" (NA, p. 32).

With this in mind, regard a poem like "The Death of a Soldier" (CP, p. 97). The poem discovers a persuasive way of regarding a random and meaningless death as important and dignified. It perceives something in the soldier's death, not something that was not there in the fact of death, but something not seen except when looked at in a particular way, the particular way the poem looks at it. This is the good of rhetoric, to provide the perception that comes through saying things in particular ways.

vi. The Function of Rhetoric

The sense of reality is given in poetry through what Stevens calls "resemblance," or the similarities between things. The imagination creates resemblance in poetry through metaphor (NA, p. 72). Poetry, through resemblance, makes vivid the similarities between things and in so doing "enhances the sense of reality, heightens it, intensifies it" (NA, p. 77). Therefore, "The proliferation of resemblances extends an object" (NA, p. 78). This is one theoretical source for Stevens' preoccupation, in poetic practice, with variations rather than progressive form, for it follows that saying a thing in another way is not merely repetition but also an extension of the original statement. In his essay "Two or Three Ideas," Stevens translates the first line of Baudelaire's "La Vie Antérieure," "J'ai longtemps habité sous de vastes portiques," in three different ways:

A long time I lived beneath tremendous porches.
 (OP, p. 203)

I lived, for long, under huge porticoes. (*OP*, p. 203)

A long time I passed beneath an entrance roof.
   (*OP*, p. 213)

One of the points he is trying to make in doing so is that our sense of reality changes and that this change is reflected in terms of style by the way we say things about it. "The most provocative of all realities is that reality of which we never lose sight but never see solely as it is. The revelation of that particular reality or of that particular category of realities is like a series of paintings of some natural object affected, as the appearance of any natural object is affected, by the passage of time, and the changes that ensue, not least in the painter" (*OP*, pp. 213–14).

For Stevens, poetry is a way of saying things in which the way of saying yields the meaning and in which the way of saying is more important than, but indistinguishable from, the thing said. "The 'something said' is important, but it is important for the poem only in so far as the saying of that particular something in a special way is a revelation of reality" (*OP*, p. 237).[8] It is not only written language but also its sound that gives us, in poetry, a credible sense of reality: "words, above everything else, are, in poetry, sounds" (*NA*, p. 32). We seek in words a true expression of our thoughts and feelings which "makes us search the sound of them, for a finality, a perfection, an unalterable vibration, which it is only within the power of the acutest poet to give them" (*NA*, p. 32). This kind of truth is that of true rhetoric: the appropriateness of a particular way of putting things is what persuades us of the truth of that way of putting things. True rhetoric, which is the poet's obligation, "cannot be arrived at by the reason alone," and is reached through what we usually call taste, or sensibility; hence Stevens speaks of the morality of the poet as "the morality of the right sensation" (*NA*, p. 58). When the right sound is discovered, it gives pleasure: when Stevens speaks of listening to the sound of words, he speaks of "loving them and feeling them" (*NA*, p. 32). The pleasure given by the right sound, apart from this sensuousness of language, is that of the gratification that occurs when the imagination, through language, brings one into a favorable adjustment to reality. "The pleasure that the poet has there is a pleasure of agreement with the radiant and productive world in which he lives. It is an agreement that Mallarmé found in the sound of *Le vierge, le vivace et le bel aujourd'hui*" (NA, p. 57). Thus Stevens can regard language as a god, a savior, in face of a bitter reality: "Natives of poverty, children of malheur,/ The gaiety of language is our seigneur" (CP, p. 322). For Stevens, "There is a sense in sounds beyond their meaning" (CP, p. 352), and that sense of sound beyond meaning is an essential of language as it is used in poetry.

vii. Obscurity

Stevens does not hesitate to reduce or obscure the discursive meaning of the language he employs in order to get at that sense in sounds. That is why he writes, "The poem must resist the intelligence/ Almost successfully" (CP, p. 350).[9] Again, he writes: "A poem need not have a meaning and like most things in nature often does not have" (OP, p. 177). This line of thought probably came to Stevens from the French Symbolist tradition, in which there is a conscious division between the creative and communicative functions of language,[10] and in which, therefore, the creative value of words depends on their suggestiveness rather than on their strict meaning, so that obscurity and lack of specificity become virtues. "[Poems] have imaginative or emotional meanings, not rational meanings. . . . They may communicate nothing at all to people who are open only to rational meanings. In short, things that have their origin in the imagination or in the emotions very often take on a form that is ambiguous or uncertain."[11] This would account for some of Stevens' obscurity as intentional, as I think is the case in the insistently cryptic "Thirteen Ways of Looking at a Blackbird." Certainly it could account for his freedom in coinage and, further, in his employment of nonsense. "I have never been able to see why what is called Anglo-Saxon should have the right to higgle and haggle all over the page, contesting the right of other words. If a poem seems to require a hierophantic phrase, the phrase should pass" (*OP*, p. 205). Usually Stevens' nonsense, while it has no rational meaning of its own, does create a meaning in its context which it communicates, as in "An Ordinary Evening in New Haven," XXIX, where the sound of the phrase, "the micmac of mocking birds," in description of the lemons, helps to distinguish the character of "the land of the lemon trees" form that of the cloddish "land of the elm trees" (*CP*, p. 486).

Frequently, however, Stevens' obscurity is not due merely to the use of language for effects that exclude rational meaning. Despite Stevens' calculated use of obscurity, his poetry has been from the beginning largely one of thought and statement. "Sunday Morning" is a meditative poem and in it, and in such poems as "The Comedian as the Letter C" and "Le Monocle de Mon Oncle," the initial and perhaps chief problem of explication lies in penetrating the rhetoric to determine the thought it contains. In the volumes following *Harmonium* the poetry, especially in the long poems, is increasingly discursive. It is evident both from his poetic practice and from his prose that Stevens came to hold the poetry of thought as an ideal:

> Theoretically, the poetry of thought should be the supreme poetry. . . . A poem in which the poet has chosen for his subject a philosophic theme should result in the poem of poems. That the wing of poetry should also be the rushing wing of meaning seems to be an extreme aesthetic good; and so in time and perhaps, in other politics, it may come to be. It is very easy to imagine a poetry of ideas in which the particulars of reality would be shadows among the poem's disclosures. (*OP*, p. 187)

In fact, there is a sometimes unresolved division between the discursive and imaginative functions of language that exists throughout Stevens' poetry. "Thirteen Ways of Looking at a Blackbird" represents only one extreme of this division, at which it appears to be assumed that the communication of specific discursive meaning is incompatible with the esthetic effects of language. It is perhaps a sense of strain between the discursive and imaginative functions of language that motivates R. P. Blackmur's comment in his essay, "On Herbert Read and Wallace Stevens": "Does it not seem that he has always been trying to put down tremendous statements; to put down those statements heard in dreams? His esthetic, so to speak, was unaware of those statements, and was in fact rather against making statements, and so got in the way."[12] It is exactly this strain that makes itself felt when the referents of Stevens' language become uncertain, when his syntax fails, and his verse becomes unintelligible. Stevens uses obscurity in order to be suggestive, but he also uses it when the context requires that he be explicit. The blue and the white pigeons of "Le Monocle de Mon Oncle" are intelligible as contrasting states of mind and, though their meaning is indefinite, they suggest certain things about that contrast. But the "Blue buds or pitchy blooms" of "The Man with the Blue Guitar," XIII (CP, p. 172), seem to be specific kinds of intrusion into the blue of the imagination—a specific meaning for the phrase is implied, but is not communicated. The "three-four cornered fragrances/ From five-six cornered leaves" of "An Ordinary Evening in New Haven," VIII (CP, p. 470), is in the same way puzzling rather than suggestive. On a larger scale, explication of section VI of the first part of "Notes toward a Supreme Fiction" (CP, p. 385) is problematic: a specific idea is indicated in the section but the statement fails to communicate it because the referent of the language is unspecified. One must guess at what is "not to be realized," what "must be visible or invisible." Sometimes uncertainty of meaning in Stevens' poems is caused by private reference, as in "The Man with the Blue Guitar," XV (CP, p. 173), which Stevens has glossed as referring to a

popular song (*LWS*, p. 783). License for such private reference, however, comes out of his emphasis on the imaginative
or creative aspect of language. If Stevens uses the phrase
"dew-dapper clapper-traps" (*CP*, p. 182) to describe the lids
of smokestacks (Poggioli, p. 183), it is because he likes the
way it sounds regardless of its obscurity. Unintelligibility in
Stevens' poetry occurs characteristically when the communication of specific discursive content is frustrated by the use of
those effects of language beyond meaning which Stevens
conceives to be most essentially poetic.

viii. Genre

As a poetry of thought and statement, that of Stevens has
been compared with English neoclassical poetry. Stevens'
poetry is not didactic, however, in the sense of arguing or
discursively demonstrating its doctrine. In "The Man with
the Blue Guitar" there is no consecutive argument and,
though there is a kind of finale, no conclusion; and this is
largely true of the long poems in the following volumes.
These are poems that consist of unsequential reflections on
a central theme, in which the point of the poem is in the
sum of the discrete reflections, in which conclusions are unimportant, in which, in fact, since there is no progressive
argument, there can be no logical conclusion. If they may be
said to have a structure, it is fundamentally the structure of
the poet's mind as it is realized in the act of improvisation.
Hence on one hand the loose, limitless variations-on-a-theme
form, as in "The Man with the Blue Guitar" or "An Ordinary Evening in New Haven," and on the other, the symmetri-
cal but arbitrary forms, as in "Notes toward a Supreme Fiction," which serve as a frame within which to improvise.
There is, for example, no formal reason why the three sections
from *Opus Posthumous* (p. 72) called "Stanzas for 'The
Man with the Blue Guitar,'" or even the poem, "Botanist
on Alp (No. 2)" (*CP*, p. 135), could not be inserted in "The
Man with the Blue Guitar" without harm to the whole.

Such poetry may be usefully distinguished from discursive or didactic poetry. In intent its end is not proof but conviction, or persuasion as in rhetoric except that it is as if Stevens were trying to persuade himself; its goal is not to demonstrate truth, but to effect resolution. It is aimed not at distinguishing the objective from the subjective, but at uniting the two (see my explication of "Extracts from Addresses to the Academy of Fine Ideas," VI). It does not attempt to assert fact, but rather seeks to adjust belief to fact, to bring about that "agreement with reality believed for a time to be true" (NA, p. 54), that Stevens conceives to be poetic truth. In other words its area of operation is not that of doctrine, but of psychology. That is why Stevens can write, "It is the belief and not the god that counts" (OP, p. 162), and again, "In the long run the truth does not matter" (OP, p. 180). For the dogmatist, for the philosopher, and for the didactic poet it is the truth that matters, and the adjustment to it is secondary. This is a poetry that adheres to a psychological mode of meditation whose end is resolution, as opposed to the discursive mode of the didactic whose end is demonstrated truth. It is therefore not surprising that Louis L. Martz finds that Stevens' poetry resembles formal Christian religious meditation.[13] But though he places Stevens in the meditative line of Donne, Herbert, and Hopkins, Stevens' resemblance to this line has nothing to do with form or tradition. On the contrary, the meditative character of Stevens' poetry is due to the untraditional ideological situation out of which he writes: he does not start with received truth which is to be justified as in, say, *Paradise Lost*, but from a position of no belief which constantly impels him to resolution in the repetitive search for the credible of which his poetry consists.

ix. The Fiction

Stevens' clearest statement of the idea of a necessary fiction is in "Asides on the Oboe" (CP, p. 250):

> The prologues are over. It is a question, now,
> Of final belief. So, say that final belief
> Must be in a fiction. It is time to choose.

However, in "Men Made out of Words" he writes that "Life consists/ Of propositions about life" (*CP*, p. 355), then goes on to evoke the fear that our fictions, "the sexual myth,/ The human revery or poem of death," are merely fictions, dreams, and that consequently, "defeats and dreams are one." And, in "The Pure Good of Theory" he declares:

> Yet to speak of the whole world as metaphor
> Is still to stick to the contents of the mind
>
> And the desire to believe in a metaphor.
> It is to stick to the nicer knowledge of
> Belief, that what it believes in is not true. (*CP*, p. 332)

One must qualify the necessary fiction as a cardinal point in Stevens' thought with the idea that some such projection of the mind is not so much necessary as unavoidable. A major statement of this is in the Ozymandias fable of "Notes toward a Supreme Fiction": "A fictive covering/ Weaves always glistening from the heart and mind" (*CP*, p. 396). Another is in "An Ordinary Evening in New Haven":

> Inescapable romance, inescapable choice
> Of dreams, disillusion as the last illusion,
> Reality as a thing seen by the mind,
>
> Not that which is but that which is apprehended,
> A mirror, a lake of reflections in a room,
> A glassy ocean lying at the door,
>
> A great town hanging pendent in a shade,
> An enormous nation happy in a style,
> Everything as unreal as real can be. (*CP*, p. 468)

We never see merely what the eye takes in but compose as we see: "one looks at the sea/ As one improvises, on the piano" (CP, p. 233). This, as stated in the poem "Variations on a Summer Day," accounts for such exercises in impressionism as "Sea Surface Full of Clouds." I do not wish to make Stevens consistent in a way in which he is not. With regard to the apprehension of reality, sometimes he says one thing and sometimes he says the opposite. In "An Ordinary Evening in New Haven," for example, he also writes,

> We keep coming back and coming back
> To the real: to the hotel instead of the hymns
> That fall upon it out of the wind. (CP, p. 471)

But in sum it comes to this: we can apprehend the substance of reality through our metaphors of it, but only for a moment; even as we make contact with the real we turn it into the imaginary, which quickly degenerates into cliché (see "Notes toward a Supreme Fiction," first part, II and III, CP, pp. 381–82). Reality is the data of the ego, but that data is transformed by the ego in the version of reality captured by the poem or the fiction:

> It is never the thing but the version of the thing:
> The fragrance of the woman not her self,
> Her self in her manner not the solid block. (CP, p. 332)

"To lose sensibility, to see what one sees," can be for Stevens a matter of spiritual destitution (CP, pp. 320–21). At the other extreme, to see one meaning only through a rigid system of thought is also spiritual poverty. The latter condition is personified in the figure of Konstantinov in "Esthétique du Mal." He is the "logical lunatic," "the lunatic of one idea/ In a world of ideas," whose extreme of logic is illogical (CP, pp. 324–25). Fictions must be credible in face of reality, and in fact the "pressure of reality" demands that we resist it with credible fictions (NA, pp. 22–23).

The fiction, so qualified, is a credible version of reality. It is neither reality itself nor a projection of the ego, but an abstract construction of the relation between the two in which the feelings of the ego are adjusted to the fact of reality. The fiction must be abstract because it must be selective in discovering those aspects of reality which meet the needs of the ego.[14] Thus a fiction is not belief in the ordinary sense but is a crystallized relation to reality which reveals reality as in some way gratifying to the ego—or, as the third subdivision title of "Notes toward a Supreme Fiction" tells us, it must give pleasure. Belief is a matter of "the more than rational distortion,/ The fiction that results from feeling" (CP, p. 406).

We do not depend on poetry or a theory of belief to bring us into this relation with reality, for we are moved naturally into such experiences by fortuitous events in the world around us:

. . . when the sun comes rising, when the sea
Clears deeply, when the moon hangs on the wall

Of heaven-haven. These are not things transformed.
Yet we are shaken by them as if they were.
We reason about them with a later reason.
   (CP, pp. 398–99)

But "The casual is not/ Enough" (CP, p. 397), so Stevens systematizes, through his theory, the specifications for this relation in order to be able to encourage it into existence. The success of this process is described with exactitude in "The Man with the Blue Guitar," XVIII (CP, p. 174), as it occurs "After long strumming on certain nights." A "dream,"—a fiction which is not quite believable—when it becomes credible in face of reality, is no longer merely a fiction, a belief: "A dream no longer a dream, a thing,/ Of things as they are." As a belief it is not held as an intellectual construction, but has a reality like that of the wind whose sensory presence is its only meaning ("wind-gloss"). Thus, the end of belief comes down to a gratifying, sensuous experience of reality, an agreement with life rather than an idea about it, "the mere joie de vivre" (LWS, p. 793).[15] Sometimes in Stevens, belief is put as a vital instinct, a sense of reality we project onto absolute fact in the way that the vegetation of spring grows over reality's barren rock, as if in this respect we mimic the organic processes of nature because we are of its nature (see my explication of "Long and Sluggish Lines" and of "The Rock," I and II). Belief, then, is a sense of reality in which, as in death in "Flyer's Fall" (CP, p. 336), "We believe without belief, beyond belief."

x. "The center that he sought was a state of mind."

In "An Ordinary Evening in New Haven," XXVIII, Stevens writes that, "If it should be true that reality exists/ In the mind," then the theory of poetry—the theory of how to create reality in the mind—would be the life of poetry. One might even, he goes on, extemporize "Subtler, more urgent proof that the theory/ Of poetry is the theory of life" (CP, pp. 485–86). Though we exist in reality we are bound by the mind, and thus it is not the nature of reality that matters so much as our sense of it, the sense of it that the imagination gives us. However, the favorable sense of reality that the imagination can produce, the "agreement with reality," is momentary:

> For a moment final, in the way
> The thinking of art seems final when
>
> The thinking of god is smoky dew. (CP, p. 168)

These moments are for Stevens a radical experience[16] which, it would not be too much to say, all his theoretical poetry merely tries to recapture. In a world without other spiritual center, the occurrence of this experience provides a focus, or a "foyer," as it is put in "Local Objects" (OP, p. 111). It includes "The few things, the objects of insight, the integrations/ Of feeling,"

That were the moments of the classic, the beautiful.
These were that serene he had always been approaching
As toward an absolute foyer beyond romance. (OP, p. 112)

The intellectual content of the experience is no further defined, either in this poem or elsewhere, because it has no definite intellectual content. The experience is fortuitous, since one does not know what objective content to seek: it is comprised of "things that came of their own accord,/ Because he desired without knowing quite what" (OP, p. 112).

This is the same problem of content for a native and contemporary ideal that Stevens raised in the early poem, "The American Sublime": "What wine does one drink?/ What bread does one eat?" (CP, p. 131). The answer is that there is no sacrament because there is no deity, that the ideal has no definite content, and that the "ultimate good" is a certain subjective experience whose only reality is psychological. "The Final Soliloquy of the Interior Paramour" (CP, p. 524) describes the "ultimate good" as the world imaginatively perceived so that one loses consciousness of the self and becomes aware of an order which is in fact that of the imagination ("that which arranged the rendezvous"). The "miraculous" power of the imagination creates a condition that seems to be one of secular beatitude that occurs "Here, now." Finally the imagination is identified with God, without, however, asserting the reality of God. On the contrary, the reality of the experience is entirely psychological, since the power that caused it, the imagination, operates only "Within its vital boundary, in the mind." The "ultimate good" here, the spiritual focus, may be described in the words of the opening line of "Artificial Populations" (OP, p. 112): "The center that he sought was a state of mind,/ Nothing more." This is not an experience that depends on an accession of knowledge, or on an intuition of some known principle, such as diety, assumed to exist beyond the mind. The poem rather describes a state of mind in which the world is experienced in a certain desirable way: "nothing has been changed except what is/ Unreal, as if nothing had been changed at all" (*OP*, p. 117).

Stevens raised another question in "The American Sublime" when he asked with regard to the sublime: "But how does one feel?" (*CP*, p. 131). The question is pertinent since the ideal he pursues is a certain experience, and comes down to a way he sometimes feels. "The Final Soliloquy of the Interior Paramour" describes not a rational but an emotional experience: one has a sense of "a warmth,/ A light, a power," and one "feels" an obscure order (*CP*, p. 524). The language here suggests that in this condition a sensuous experience of reality is paramount. So also in "As You Leave the Room" (*OP*, p. 116), the modification of the ego which is accompanied by an exaltation of mood, "an elevation," is the result of an intensely sensuous experience of reality in which the latter seems "something I could touch, touch every way."

The most thorough description of this central experience, which is in the first part of "Notes toward a Supreme Fiction" (*CP* p. 386), begins by dispensing with that poem's abstract apparatus in favor of purely sensuous description: "It feels good as it is without the giant,/ A thinker of the first idea." Perhaps, the poem continues, a true experience of reality depends not on such abstractions but on that sensuous relation with it during, for example, "a walk around a lake," when one becomes composed as the body tires and physical composure comes to be one with mental composure. At such times one is in an equilibrium, a state of "incalculable balances," that includes both the mind and one's surroundings. This is exactly that resolution through an "agreement with reality" that Stevens' poetry aims to create. It is a radical combination of mood and circumstance that is "Extreme, fortuitous, personal." It involves the beauty of random events in reality, which, in the words of "The Sense of the Sleight-of-hand Man" (*CP*, p. 222), "Occur as they occur": "Could you have said the bluejay suddenly/ Would swoop to earth?" But above all it requires an intense sensuous awareness of reality that is beyond the range of systematic thought. Hence the conclusion of "The Sense of the Sleight-of-hand Man":

It may be that the ignorant man, alone,
Has any chance to mate his life with life
That is the sensual, pearly spouse.

At the same time one has a sense of lucidity, even of clairvoyance, because one grasps the "truth;" one perceives reality in
its sensuous integrity, and is completely satisfied with it.
Compared to this, the truth of intellectual abstraction seems
hazy and remote. So we are told at the end of the description
of the experience in "Notes toward a Supreme Fiction":

We more than awaken, sit on the edge of sleep,
As on an elevation, and behold
The academies like structures in a mist.

What is fundamental in these moments of relation is an
acute awareness of existence itself, the palm, in "Of Mere
Being," "Beyond the last thought," in which the golden bird
sings and which is the end that we desire only for itself: it is
this and "not the reason/ That makes us happy or unhappy"
(OP, pp. 117–18).[17] This is the sense of existence for which
the ghosts yearn in "Large Red Man Reading":

They were those that would have wept to step barefoot
into reality,

That would have wept and been happy, have shivered in
the frost
And cried out to feel it again, have run fingers over leaves
And against the most coiled thorn, have seized on what was
ugly

And laughed . . . (CP, pp. 423–24)

At the same time there occurs an agreement between the ego
and reality in which the separation between the two disappears and they seem one harmonious entity: "The reader became the book," and "The quiet was part of the meaning,
part of the mind" (CP, p. 358).[18] The reconciliation of the

ego with reality produces a vivid and harmonious sense of existence.

Ultimately, one is brought to reality, and consequently brought to life, by one's feeling for reality; in such feeling lies the poem's power to revivify. The poet in "Large Red Man Reading" brings the ghosts to life because he "spoke the feeling for them, which was what they had lacked" (*CP*, p. 424). The possibility of such an experience of revivification, in which "being would be being himself again,/ Being, becoming seeing and feeling and self" (*CP*, p. 255), is described in "Extracts from Addresses to the Academy of Fine Ideas," IV. Section V of that poem considers the possibility of an abstract idea that might make such experience generally available, but VI rejects systematic thought, and the poem finally places faith in imaginative expressions based on feeling, "the heart's residuum," for a positive relation with reality despite its inherent evil.

Since this experience of ideal relation with reality is by nature fugitive, there can be no formulation of it that one can repeat to summon it up; nothing avails but improvisation. And when improvisation fails, when the ego cannot bridge the gap between it and a too alien reality, there is an antithetical experience, a negative counterpart of the ideal one. It occurs when the relation to reality becomes too great a burden, so that "being part is an exertion that declines" (*OP*, p. 96). When this happens, the ego may attain composure by withdrawing from reality into itself, just as it may in opposite circumstances attain composure through heightened experience of reality. Thus in "Solitaire under the Oaks" (*OP*, p. 111), one escapes from reality to "pure principles" and is, consequently, "completely released." The point of the experience described in the poem is release, and though it is achieved through contemplation of principle, the principle is unimportant so long as it is instrumental in bringing about this release. What is desired is a state of mind, a psychological equilibrium without any particular intellectual content, in which one is relieved of the pressures of reality. Whereas the positive counterpart moved toward greater experience of reality, this state of mind seems to move toward exclusion of any experience of it: one exists in an "oblivion," thinking "without consciousness" about arbitrary principle, so that "Neither the cards nor the trees nor the air/ Persist as facts." Instead of a heightened sense of existence, one finds here precisely its opposite: it is

> As if none of us had ever been here before
> And are not now: in this shallow spectacle,
> This invisible activity, this sense. (OP, p. 113)

It is true, of course, that these are all late poems, and may represent a composed withdrawal from life in preparation for death, but one finds among the same group far more poems about the opposite experience, such as "The Final Soliloquy of the Interior Paramour" and "As You Leave the Room" (OP, p. 116), the latter of which seems quite plainly a poem whose occasion is the end of life. This negative experience is epitomized in "An Ordinary Evening in New Haven," XX (CP, p. 480):

> . . . the pure sphere escapes the impure
>
> Because the thinker himself escapes. And yet
> To have evaded clouds and men leaves him
> A naked being with a naked will
>
> And everything to make. He may evade
> Even his own will and in his nakedness
> Inhabit the hypnosis of that sphere.

The thinker may escape the real world ("the impure") for a consciousness pure of reality. But the evasion of any idea of reality creates the need for another to take its place ("everything to make"), unless the thinker manages to exclude all content from his consciousness (which may therefore be described as "his nakedness") and remains in a hypnotic state that, perhaps, resembles the extinction of consciousness in mystic nirvana or, perhaps, merely the point of inanition in revery. But one cannot sustain this state of mind any more than one can sustain its counterpart. There is a "will," a given in human nature that amounts to a necessity, in himself and others, that he must evade in order to enter this state and that he cannot evade for long, that drives the thinker's consciousness back into contact with reality once more. So the succeeding section (XXI) begins:

> But he may not. He may not evade his will,
> Nor the wills of other men; and he cannot evade
> The will of necessity, the will of wills.

When either of these fugitive experiences is consummated, then, one moves toward its opposite. Here, undoubtedly, is a source of the characteristic polar fluctuation of Stevens' thought in its repetitive approach to and withdrawal from reality.

xi. The Importance of Stevens' Art

One of the sayings in the group of comments called the "Adagia" runs as follows: "Life is an affair of people not of places. But for me life is an affair of places and that is the trouble" (OP, p. 158). The remark is apposite to Stevens' poetry. He did not write poetry that had to do with people in social relation. There is little in his poetry of narrative, little that is personal, little that is occasional, nothing that is dramatic. In an age before, as he put it, Marx ruined nature, he might have been a nature poet of the magnitude of Wordsworth. He wrote about his response to place, to objects, to landscape, and he wrote about ideas, and his ideas come down to the importance of an intense responsiveness not to personality, nor indeed to ideas, but to sensuous, physical reality. The essential self is, for him, the body,

> The old animal,
> The senses and feeling, the very sound
> And sight, . . . (CP, pp. 46–47)

In Stevens' vision, that which is beyond the self is a fluid, constantly changing present in which nothing endures and nothing has any end beyond itself:

It is a theatre floating through the clouds,
Itself a cloud, although of misted rock
And mountains running like water, wave on wave,

Through waves of light. It is of cloud transformed
To cloud transformed again, idly, the way
A season changes color to no end,

Except the lavishing of itself in change. (CP, p. 416)

In such a reality the effort of the intellect to discover absolute value seems absurd, and reality itself seems to lose its substance and solidity. Stevens appealed to the senses to give him, through poetry, a feeling of the substantiality of that reality beyond the mind as something pleasurably vivid, fresh, and various rather than same, insipid, and without value.

We do not have to be told of the significance of art. "It is art," said Henry James, "which makes life, makes interest, makes importance . . . and I know of no substitute whatever for the force and beauty of its process." (NA, p. 169)

NOTES

[1] Frank Kermode, *Wallace Stevens* (New York, 1961), p. 92. In this regard, one thinks of William Carlos Williams along with Stevens.

[2] "Another Way of Looking at the Blackbird," *The New Republic* (Nov. 4, 1957), 17 and 18.

[3] *Wallace Stevens*, (Pamphlets on American Writers, No. 11 [University of Minnesota, 1961]), p. 29. J. Hillis Miller denies this, as I do, but develops the point differently: "Wallace Stevens' Poetry of Being," in Roy Harvey Pearce and J. Hillis Miller, eds. *The Act of the Mind* (Baltimore, 1965), p. 146. (This article contains the essence of the longer version published in Miller's *Poets of Reality*.)

[4] For a discussion of Stevens' seasonal cycle, see Kermode, pp. 34–37.

[5] Section IX of this poem, however, reaches in the opposite direction, toward order.

[6] See Northrop Frye, "The Realistic Oriole," *Hudson Review*, X (Fall 1957), 363, who comments that Stevens' poetry tries to annihilate "the sense of contrast or great gulf fixed between subject and object, consciousness and existence." N. P. Stallknecht, "Absence in Reality," *Kenyon Review*, XXI (Fall 1959), 545, notes that Stevens celebrates the unity of mind and nature as in the Romantic tradition.

[7] *Philosophy, The Journal of the British Institute of Philosophy*, XXI (July 1946), 147–66. Essentially the same statement is found in NA, p. 96. See Joseph N. Riddel, "The Authorship of Wallace Stevens' 'On Poetic Truth,' " *MLN*, LXXVI (Feb. 1961), 126–29.

[8] Abstracted by Stevens from H. D. Lewis' "On Poetic Truth." See n. 7. The passage is exactly apposite to Stevens.

[9] "Man Carrying Thing." The same thought with slight variation is found in the "Adagia" (*OP*, p. 171).

[10] See Yvor Winters, "The Hedonist's Progress," *In Defense of Reason* (Denver, no date), pp. 453–54, for a discussion of the history of this distinction in connection with Stevens.

[11] Stevens in *Explicator*, VII (Nov. 1948), Item 18.

[12] *Form and Value in Modern Poetry* (Garden City and New York, 1957), p. 222.

[13] "Wallace Stevens: The World as Meditation," *Yale Review*, XLVII (Summer 1958), 517–36.

[14] In terms of his theory Stevens uses abstraction to mean "a quality of being taken out, abstracted in the root sense" (Martz, "The World as Meditation," p. 531); "artificial in its proper sense, something constructed rather than generalized" (Frye, p. 365). An abstraction in this sense is an artificial construction of elements selected from reality.

[15] Stevens uses the phrase in relation to section XX. See my analysis of that section.

[16] The attempt to define this experience was suggested by J. V. Cunningham, who took note of it in "Tradition and Modernity: Wallace Stevens" (formerly published in *Poetry*, LXXV [Dec. 1949], 149–65), *Tradition and Poetic Structure* (Denver, 1960), pp. 122–23.

[17] See Miller, pp. 157–61, for a discussion of Stevens' perception of being.

[18] For an account of the dynamic relation between these two terms of the experience, see above, section iv.

II.
Readings*

"The Paltry Nude Starts on a Spring Voyage" (CP, p. 5)

The nude is an emblematic figure of spring. There is a comparison between spring, in the first part of the poem, and a similar figure representing summer, in the latter part. Thus spring is "paltry," especially early spring, spring at the start of her voyage, as compared with the fullness of summer described later on. She, early spring, is without pomp—she is not imagined, like Botticelli's Venus, with a shell, but rather embarks on "the first-found weed"; nor is she imposing like an archaic deity, but silent, insubstantial. She, as we with the sparsity of spring, is discontent with her own paltriness: she desires the pomp of "purple stuff" (cloth), and is impatient with the staleness of winter ("salty harbors" as opposed to the excitement of the high sea—"bellowing," and "high interiors" with its suggestion of being enclosed by the sea and by high waves). The goddess of spring, she dominates everything ("touches the clouds") as she runs her seasonal course. But this is still meager compared to the fullness of summer, the nude of "a later day," who is "goldener," a center of pomp. The season is the servant of fate, and summer in particular is a servant who follows spring inexorably, tidying up its "scurry" ("scrurry" in Collected Poems is a misprint) and comparatively wilder, lighter motion, making it "spick."

* The readings follow the order of Collected Poems and Opus Posthumous

"Domination of Black" (CP, p. 8)

The colors cast in the room at night by the fireplace are like the colors of the bushes and the fallen leaves, and turn through the room as the latter turn in the wind. But the dark color of the hemlocks is also in the room; this and the memory of the peacocks' cry add an ominous note.

The colors of the peacocks' tails resemble the autumn leaves at twilight. These same colors, of the leaves, the tails, sweep through the room as they are cast by the fire, in a way resembling the leaves being swept from the trees. It is hard to tell whether the peacocks cry against impending darkness ("twilight") or against one of the other elements of the scene, because one thing in it is so much like another, each so much part of everything else. The cry of the peacocks seems rather to mark, and to be itself part of, the whole process of annihilation exampled by the fire, autumn, impending darkness.

Finally the stars in the night sky, the cosmos itself, is drawn into this vortex of similitudes. The stars too seem part of this process of annihilation, and the speaker, feeling afraid, remembers the cry which marks it.

"Le Monocle de Mon Oncle" (CP, p. 13)

Stevens writes of the speaker of "Le Monocle" that, "I had in mind simply a man fairly well along in life, looking back and talking in a more or less personal way about life" (LWS, p. 251). Like "The Comedian as the Letter C," this poem proceeds from speculation to speculation on the topic at hand, here love at middle age, but the didactic content, rather than being couched in narrative, occurs in the meditative mode that came to be dominant in Stevens' longer poems. The title of the poem may be interpreted as "my uncle's point of view," the attitude toward love of a worldly-wise man of middle age. (Stevens comments that the title means "merely a certain point of view"—LWS, p. 250.) It is

in French perhaps because of that country's reputation for
erotic enlightenment, but also, certainly, for the sake of the
phrase's comic-elegant sound.

The poem is arranged in twelve eleven-line stanzas of
iambic pentameter which accommodates variation freely,
especially in the substitution of an anapest. The most
notable thing about the verse is its extravagance of alliteration
which is sometimes used structurally, like rhyme. End rhyme
is itself not used regularly but as a convenience of structure.
It is used in two ways: to form couplets, and to unify a
stanza by means of sound echoes. The second is the more fre-
quent. The most usual unit of organization within the stanza
is the pair of iambic lines, though in some cases, as in the
last six lines of section I, they are not merely pairs but
rhymed couplets. The pair of iambic lines is the unit of
organization in that the syntax is most frequently arranged
in successive pairs of lines. In addition there is an attempt
to bind pairs of lines together even, occasionally, when the
syntax runs over, sometimes with rhyme but usually without.
The main devices used to this end are multiple alliteration
and balance of units within the pair of lines, as in lines four
and five of section IX:

> Their curious fates in war, come, celebrate
> The faith of forty, ward of Cupido.

Sometimes alliteration is used to connect the terminal feet
of a pair of lines as in,

> And you? Remember how the crickets came
> Out of their mother grass, like little kin, (V, ll. 8–9)

where the lines are held together by the consonance of
"came" and "kin." Repetition is used much like alliteration:

> It stands gigantic, with a certain tip
> To which all birds come sometime in their time.
> But when they go that tip still tips the tree. (X, ll. 9–11)

The intense organization of this verse, like that of the heroic couplet, with its consequent capacity for succinct comment, helps to create the tone of fastidious didacticism (for example, "This trivial trope reveals a way of truth," VIII, l. 4) that is characteristic of the poem. The verse is capable of accommodating epigrammatic generalization at convenience:

The honey of heaven may or may not come,
But that of earth both comes and goes at once.
(VII, ll. 8–9)

The measure of the intensity of love
Is measure, also, of the verve of earth. (V, ll. 4–5)

In this, as well as in its organization, and sometimes even in the movement of a single line, the verse is comparable to the heroic couplet. (Compare, for example, the movement of VIII, l. 3, "It comes, it blooms, it bears its fruit and dies," with "The Vanity of Human Wishes," l. 76: "They mount, they shine, evaporate, and fall.")[1] The verse, then, gives the poem the formal appearance of close, logical reasoning appropriate to its didactic content. But in fact this formal appearance is illusory, for the style only reflects a self-consciousness in the poem's didacticism, and is a way of minimizing the didactic content. That is one reason why the meanings of the poem's lines are so elusive: figures whose sense is almost impermeable to the intelligence are expressed in forms that the intelligence is accustomed readily to grasp. For example, in VII a parable is explained by another parable, and in II, ll. 6–8, a difficult metaphor is offered as a gloss of the preceding lines. What is given is never the line of reasoning itself, but the more or less metaphorical illustrations of the line of reasoning, frequently in the form of obscure illustrative parables. The apparently reasoned, didactic tone of the poem is, rather, mock didactic, and its speaker, described as lecturer, scholar, rabbi, is deliberately pedantic.

The first two lines of section I consist of ironic rhetoric directed to the woman whom the speaker addresses, in the tone of "Who do you think you are?" As the fifth line says, the speaker, presumably the uncle of the title, is mocking her. This woman may or may not be his wife, but there is no reason to believe she is the fictive muse, as Kermode suggests.[2] The sense of the action makes her out to be a real woman who is growing old. Lines three and four indicate that some clash of words has taken place. They may be paraphrased, "There is nothing so painful as an exchange of cutting phrases." Whatever the nature of the argument, one may fairly presume that the speaker's reaction to it triggers the series of reflections on love of which the poem consists. The speaker continues that he wishes he might be without feeling ("a thinking stone"), for he remembers her as she once was (ll. 8–9), and the contrast with what she is now is enough to move him to tears (ll. 10–11). That is why he considers that in mocking her, he mocks himself (l. 6): in taunting her with a magnificence she no longer has he is exacerbating his own painful feelings on the subject.

In II the speaker represents himself as being at an age where each spring is seen marking not a year given, but a year taken away; as the "man of fortune greeting heirs," he is one who greets the passage of time as that which will eventually take away all he has. The first four lines of this section present an image of the coming of spring, abstract and evocative. The colors here create a quality of richness and vividness, as the blue and the white pigeons and the dark and the rose rabbis of the last section merely evoke distinctions in qualities between different states of mind. The evocation of the coming of spring is accomplished by abstracting a few of its qualities and recomposing them in a poetic image that suggests its reality. A vivid bird flies across a rich terrain, seeking his place among the bird choirs that greet the spring. When he finds it he will join the songs of welcome to spring which for the speaker seem to be, on the contrary, songs of farewell. There can be no spring, no bloom of life, for one who has arrived at the middle of his years ("meridian"). The woman he addresses will not accept the fact of aging, but rather persists with a baseless, a fabulous happiness ("anecdotal bliss") in pretending that she has special knowledge, perhaps of the kind derived from 'star-gazing' ("starry *connaissance*"). Rather than accept the fact that in middle years one passes irretrievably beyond the bloom of life, she pretends to know better.

In the third section three images of artifice in hairdress are given. "Tittivating" means making small alterations in one's toilet to increase one's attractiveness. The speaker says that he will not draw out the history of the subject—how in the past women wore ingenious coiffures. Hair is here a synecdoche for physical beauty, not merely for woman's beauty. The barbers are not those who have cared for the present woman's hair, but include all those "studious ghosts" who invented beautiful coiffures in the past, among whom are the tittivating Chinese men. The sense of the second rhetorical question is that the result of such ingenuity in toilet, however elaborate, is transitory: "not one curl in nature has survived." Stevens writes of the last two lines that "the speaker was speaking to a woman whose hair was still down" (*LWS*, p. 251). The lack of coiffure ("dripping in your hair") of the woman he addresses mocks these examples of ingenuity passed away ("studious ghosts") because, though without artfulness, she is nevertheless present and alive.

The first two lines of IV state that the fruit of life, of its own nature, ripens and falls. When she to whom he speaks was without experience, it was sweet; but that was because she had not yet tasted its spicy fruit. An apple serves as well as a skull for a book in which to read a moral: they both, upon meditation, may yield the lesson that all living things must fall and die. But as the fruit of love (in the story of Adam and Eve), the apple is even better than a skull in which to read a moral because one can also read in it a lesson about love: one cannot understand love until after the heat of passion or of youth has passed and one can reflect on it merely "to pass the time."[3]

The intensity of love is an index of youth and verve (section V), which for the speaker no longer exists. He, on the contrary, is conscious of the ebbing of his life. Why will the woman to whom he speaks not, on her part, admit this fact? He reminds her how she had recognized her kinship with that which is ephemeral and will return to dust. "When your first imagery/ Found inklings" may be paraphrased simply as, "when you first imagined."

From the perspective of middle age the nuances of love become indistinct and its sameness becomes apparent (VI). If men at forty persist in sentimental occupations—the rather remote metaphor referring to the poem's amatory theme is "painting lakes"—they will not see the peculiarities of the individual amour, "each quirky turn," but that which all love has in common, the "substance that prevails." They will view love as "introspective exiles," that is, as those who are no longer under the sway of love's sovereignty, as it were, and must look into memory to analyze their experience of it. The more romantic aspect of love is a theme for youth, "for Hyacinth alone."

In VII an image of possible heavenly dispensation is contrasted with an image of undeniable, earthy reality. The heavenly may never get here, while the earthy is here and now. The sense of the parable is that heavenly good ("honey") may come, but earthy good comes as certainly as it goes; its coming is contingent on its going. Line nine may also be a sexual pun in description of copulation: this is the good of earthly love, while that of heavenly love may never be realized. The good of heaven would not be thus uncertain if an indication of divinity were to arrive on earth, but none does (compare *LWS*, p. 464). What, in fact, would be the good for us of a lady "heightened by eternal bloom?" Though she might be eternal, our good would come and go all the same. This section signifies acceptance of whatever pleasure love still may offer in the here and now.

In section VIII the speaker's point of view is like that of one of the "introspective exiles" he described in VI, who no longer attends to the nuances of love. As "a dull scholar" he lectures on what all love has in common. Love here is figured as a predetermined cycle, the stages of which each, in his turn, must pass through, "an ancient aspect touching a new mind." Love at middle age is described as the fruition of a process (the bloom of youth is gone, the fruit of experience and maturity remains); the decay from middle age to death is put, in terms of that process, as an appropriate health and, finally, the comparison of the middle aged lovers to squashes gives the distance of humor. Their end is seen as the joke of nature on man:

> The laughing sky will see the two of us
> Washed into rinds by rotting winter rains.

Section IX celebrates "the faith of forty," an attitude appropriate to love at middle age which can incorporate the kind of conflict that is represented by the initial clashing of words of the poem's opening lines (section I). The verses celebrating "the faith of forty" will include such "clashes"; they will also be smart and accurate, realistic like soldiers fighting. The celebration requires music that is as magnificent or, perhaps, as courtly as that of the paladins. The song must be lusty (ll. 6–8), and hence will call for a good deal of daring ("bravura"). The "oblation" would be more like a toast.

With an appellation reminiscent of "the bawds of euphony" of Thirteen Ways of Looking at a Blackbird," the speaker (section X) rejects the sentimentality of the "fops of fancy" who leave poetic records of their erotic fantasies (l. 2), and whose romanticism is figured in such phrases as "mystic spouts," "magic trees," and "balmy boughs." Line three means that such fantasies nourish the fops' grubby lives in reality. A figure is then presented which attempts to salvage love from such a sentimental point of view while accommodating it to the realistic point of view. Love is not mere sentimentalism like the "magic trees"; it is rather another kind of tree:

> It stands gigantic, with a certain tip
> To which all birds come sometime in their time.
> But when they go that tip still tips the tree.

That is, love has an immutable reality (the "tip" of the tree) to which all come in their turn, but which is beyond its mutability in given lovers; it is, as in VIII, "an ancient aspect" that endures beyond each new lover's experience of it; it is, as in VI, innately part of our substance that prevails. It is possible that the "certain tip" is specifically phallic, depending on the nature of "the thing I have in mind" which it is like. As the plum in "The Comedian as the Letter C" outlives its poems and "survives in its own form," so does love outlive its lovers. The idea is the same as that in the last section of "Peter Quince at the Clavier" (CP, p. 89), where beauty in the flesh, as opposed to its perception in the mind, is attributed immortality through a series of metaphors about things that pass away only to be repeated in the same form.

In section X a psychosexual reality is attributed to love: it is part of our nature to which all come "sometime in their time." In XI a final qualification is made. If love is not merely sentimental, neither is it merely sexual. We play the routines of romantic love, its "doleful heroics," and so on, without regard to sex, the "first, foremost law"; any such note of coarse realism as that of the frog is anguishing and odious to us as lovers beside the romantic pool. We believe in love because it is in our nature, our prevailing substance, to believe in it, whether or not such belief is supported by the physical processes of reality. For Stevens, belief comes about through psychological necessity, and it is the function of the imagination to mediate between that necessity and what he calls the "absolute fact" of reality. Speaking of the glory of the gods of classical mythology, for example, he writes: "Their fundamental glory is the fundamental glory of men and women, who being in need of it create it, elevate it, without too much searching of its identity" (OP, p. 208). So the poem has created an imaginative relation—in Stevens' term, a "fiction"—between the fact of aging and the psychological necessity of affirming love, that reconciles the two or, again in Stevens' terms, brings us into "an agreement with reality" (NA, p. 54). For this reason the final section, by way of resolution, merely notes the imaginative relation that has been created in the body of the poem.

The final section begins with the kind of parabolic utterance that has often served in place of direct formulation throughout the poem. The blue and the white pigeons are abstract qualities representing different states of mind. The dark and the rose rabbis are also such abstract qualities, but the moods they represent are more specific. The former is analytic and reductive, and is that of youth.[4]

> . . . Every day, I found
> Man proved a gobbet in my mincing world.

This is contrasted with the attitude developed in the poem, which is the attitude of middle age—the attitude of "Mon Oncle" of the title, "my uncle's point of view." It represents a willingness merely to note the psychological facts of love, as the poem does, without reducing them through an analysis of their transitory nature. "Fluttering things" refers to the blue and the white pigeons which, as different aspects of love, represent the attitudes toward love distinguished in the poem: that of youth, which is participating, active, and that of middle age, which is more reflective. Lines eight to eleven are a notation of the attitude of the poem—that love appears to be different from these different perspectives.

"The Comedian as the Letter C" (CP, p. 27)

"Thirteen Ways of Looking at a Blackbird" represents an extreme at which didactic content is unusually limited; "The Comedian as the Letter C," on the contrary, is an argument couched in narrative. It is a poem that proceeds by logical discourse, from proposition to proposition modified to proposition further modified. It sets forth doctrine just as does the *Essay on Man*, though in form it is not expository, but narrative and comic: "not doctrinal/ In form though in design"

(VI, l. 73). In kind the narrative is, like *The Prelude*,[5] literary biography, the history of a poet's mind—though the mind of the poet in question is that of the fictive Crispin, Stevens' invention and mask—and the action of the narrative is a voyage and quest for knowledge which deals, like Wordsworth's poem, with the loss of the imagination and the conditions in which it may be revitalized.

The subject of the poem includes the relation of a poet to his art but is not fundamentally that. Crispin's aim is not merely to achieve accurate description of reality in poetry, but, rather, through accurate description of reality to establish satisfactory rapport with it. That is the point of the colony Crispin projects after arriving at his "new intelligence" (IV, l. 15), in which the inhabitants are to be the harmonious articulations of their environment. Hence the crucial propositions of the poem (variations on the initial "man is the intelligence of his soil") turn on man's relation to his environment, not on that of the poet to his art. The narrative, although its hero is appropriately a poet, is basically concerned with the poet as a type of imaginative man, and thus the subject is not quite, as Hi Simons puts it, the relation of the poet to his environment.[6] The denouement may be a defeat of the poet but it represents a reconciliation of the imagination to the quotidian and, therefore, the poem has a happy ending: "what can all this matter since/ The relation comes, benignly, to its end?" (VI, ll. 95-96).

"The Comedian as the Letter C" is conceived as thoroughly comic. Crispin is the comedian, the comic personage of the action. As the letter c, "merest minuscule" (that is, lower case letter), as he is described in the poem, he is both an abstraction representing the comic point of view and an example of comic destiny. (Stevens has also made a point on three different occasions of the c sounds recurring throughout the poem, apparently as a kind of comic emblem for Crispin —see *LWS*, pp. 294, 351-52, 778). He is a valet from Bourdeaux whose name derives from the comic valet of seventeenth-century French drama, and he is associated with a long and various tradition of the figure of the harlequin.[7] As

valet he is servant, knave to reality (I, l. 22), trying to divine
its order and submit to its will; as servant, fit to play the
comic role, he becomes the dupe of reality. But if servant, he
is also freeborn, or the thane (I, l. 22), an apprentice seeking
"the quintessential fact, the note/ Of Vulcan, that a valet
seeks to own" (II, ll. 84–85); if comic, he is also the comic
innocent, "the marvelous sophomore" (III, l. 86), like the
Candide to whom he is at one point compared (V, l. 73),
who learns by dint of experience, and who has in fact set out
to learn.

> . . . Hence it was,
> Preferring text to gloss, he humbly served
> Grotesque apprenticeship to chance event,
> A clown, perhaps, but an aspiring clown. (IV, ll. 88–91)

He is both dupe and philosopher, trying to "track the knaves
of thought" (V, l. 81), and instead getting caught in the very
reality he is trying to comprehend. This irony, treated as
comedy, provides the poem with its perspective toward Crispin and his adventures.

The diction, too, is steadfastly comic. It makes use of absurd comparisons, either too ignoble, such as the world as a
turnip (VI, l. 65), or pronouncedly too august, as in "His
grand pronunciamento and devise" (VI, l. 8). Latin is employed for the irony that its gravity can afford:

> . . . exit lex,
> Rex and principium, exit the whole
> Shebang. . . . (IV, ll. 5–7)

Elegance is intentionally pushed to the brink of preciosity:
"the peach/ When its black branches came to bud, belle day"
(IV, ll. 69–70), so that it calls attention to itself and sets a
tone of both elegance and self parody at once. There is also
exaggerated inelegance, as in the plum described as, "good,
fat, guzzly fruit" (V, l. 33); and abrupt flatness of statement
as in,

. . . earth was like a jostling festival
Of seeds grown fat, too juicily opulent,
Expanding in the gold's maternal warmth.
So much for that. . . . (II, ll. 55–58)

In general there are so many unusual words, even for Stevens,
that the text abounds in eccentricity, incongruity, and its
surface becomes grotesque. It is worth noting how all this
comic machinery permits communication of a mass of doctrine as Crispin's intellectual odyssey proceeds through proposition, theory, and idea. It is a strategy used to communicate
a body of abstract thought in an imaginative form by a poet
who, as seen in "Thirteen Ways of Looking at a Blackbird,"
maintains a distinction between the communicative and
imaginative functions of language.

That reality is subject to man's interpretation, that man
discerns and formulates its laws, renders it intelligible, and in
so doing determines its nature, is the initial proposition of
the poem. "Nota: man is the intelligence of his soil." It is a
proposition, like all the propositions in the poem and like all
of Crispin's phases of thought, introduced in order to be
tested, modified, and rejected by Crispin's experience, as the
poem proceeds from formulation to reformulation like a
Platonic dialogue, to its resolution. The proposition is stated
and elaborated, but on a level of metaphor so sustained that
it is necessary to concentrate the attention on the connection
between the abstractions of metaphor and the thematic progress of the subject. Man is "the sovereign ghost" because with
his intelligence he rules over "his soil," the physical world,
but also because as an intelligence merely, he is cut off from
the physical world, disembodied. He is its Socrates and musician, inquiring into and expressing its nature, "principium
and lex," its first cause and its law. The figures describing
man so conceived are comic, undercutting, belittling, from
the greater to the lesser: "Socrates of snails," "lutanist of
fleas," "wig," for head of things, "nincompated pedagogue."
Crispin, the example of the proposition, is by the manner of
his description made ridiculous. As example, he is put to the

test of experience in a setting calculated to reduce him still further.

The eye of Crispin, accustomed to homely objects and a landscape ordered by man (I, ll. 8–15) cannot fathom the sea, "inscrutable world," and is overwhelmed. Setting out to inquire after answers, he discovers that there are even fewer at sea than on land ("One eats one paté" no matter where; it is no different even at sea: "even of salt"). His identity as one who assertively and swaggeringly inquires into the nature of reality and pronounces its meanings (I, ll. 20–28) is dissolved in the sea (I, l. 52). He had been verbose: "lutanist" of silent fleas, "bellowing," the noisy "haw" of the quiet hum of things, "lexicographer" of "mute" nature (since he is a botanist, "greenhorns" is a generalized image for plants, here especially young plants, "maidenly" neophytes). Now he has no words to describe either himself or the reality that surrounds him,

> Ubiquitous concussion, slap and sigh,
> Polyphony beyond his baton's thrust.

because its meaning is beyond him, its music (as opposed to that of pears and fleas) no longer follows the direction of his intelligence (I, ll. 29–36). The sea outspeaks him, but whether whispering (I, l. 41), or bellowing (I, ll. 66, 70–71), it is speech he cannot understand. His "verboseness" is stemmed in the sea. "On the clopping foot-ways of the moon/ Lay grovelling," refers to moonlight shining on the waves and is in description of the intangible Triton, who as an exhausted personification of the sea is a character without tangible identity, as the sea is without meaning. Crispin is confronted with "the veritable ding an sich," a reality about which he cannot generalize, which is impervious to abstract thought, and onto which he can neither impose meanings nor project his own identity. It is that alien reality, utterly nonhuman, that is represented by the star in "Nuances of a Theme by Williams," which Stevens adjures,

. . . shine like bronze,
that reflects neither my face nor any inner part
of my being, shine like fire, that mirrors nothing.
  (CP, p. 18)

And it is that reality of "Metaphors of a Magnifico," which
keeps resisting abstract thought and finally resolves itself in
its particular details:

The first white wall of the village . . .
The fruit trees. . . . (CP, 19)

This is the world, as the title of the section puts it, without
imagination, and reality so seen has for Crispin the nature
and impact of revelation: "Crispin beheld and Crispin was
made new" (I, l. 80). The sea salt paralyzed his spirit as if by
frost, and the dead encrustation of the ideas he held melted
coldly as if in winter, dissolving his older self (I, ll. 58–61.
"Beetled," I, 65, suggests, perhaps, the sun casting highlights
on the "bouquets.") The sea has destroyed an evasive and
egocentric distortion of reality by the imagination:

The imagination, here, could not evade,
In poems of plums, the strict austerity
Of one vast, subjugating, final tone. (I, ll. 81–83)

The imagination must not evade, but direct itself to reality
so that it may be perceived without "stale" preconceptions
about it. It is because Crispin's revelation enables him to do
this that the sea's destruction also brings "something given
to make whole among/ The ruses that were shattered by the
large." (I, ll. 88–89).

  In section II through part of III Crispin tests and rejects
various modes of expression to accommodate his revelation.
He rejects the commonplace sentimental and its imagery:
sonnets addressed to the nightingale, the couplet written
yearly to the spring, "The stride of vanishing autumn in a

park/ By way of decorous melancholy" (II, ll. 1–20). Simons correctly describes this as "a period in which Crispin regarded himself an intellectual and aesthetic *avant-gardiste*, rebelling against conventions, experimenting with poetic forms, and testing, elaborating, and beginning to exploit a new conception of the relation of art to life."[8] Now a freeman without preconceptions, empty ("sonorous nutshell"), destitute of abstract ideas about reality, his enlarged apprehension requires an expression more inclusive of the particulars of reality. Crispin has passed from the civilized park to the savage jungle: Yucatan represents a new subject matter with which he is confronted, a barbaric nature untamed by the civilized mind, that demands articulation. He responds by writing fables of an aesthetic quality that is "tough," of "the mint of dirt" (II, l. 35), so that he can get down to the reality of earth, that "soil" of which, at the outset, he seemed the intelligence (II, ll. 21–43). But the jungles of Yucatan lead Crispin to a realism effective only because its subject matter is by nature exotic. So "the fabulous and its intrinsic verse" (II, l. 44), are rejected with a down to earth "So much for that" (II, l. 58). Next, in the thunderstorm, as once in the sea, Crispin has a second germinal insight. In face of the storm, instead of "making notes" (II, l. 63) on the cathedral, Crispin the "annotator" (II, l. 75) takes shelter in it; but his experience there is not a religious one. If in the "shifting diaphanes" of the sea, "Triton incomplicate with that/ Which made him Triton," he perceived a reality whose matter is in flux and whose form is inconceivable, so in the thunderstorm he perceives the magnitude of an ultimate energy, "the span of force," which is the quintessential fact of reality in his new vision of it (II, ll. 83–84). It is this fact he now desires to express in speech (II, ll. 85–86).

> . . . the thunder, lapsing in its clap,
> Let down gigantic quavers of its voice,
> For Crispin to vociferate again. (II, ll. 94–96)

In section III Crispin rejects what the moonlight represents. What it represents can best be known by understanding how the image is used rather than by ascribing to it an *a priori* and rigid significance.[9] Stevens' poems do not employ symbols in this way. As in "Thirteen Ways of Looking at a Blackbird," the image acquires meaning only as it functions in specific contexts. The image becomes a symbol by the accretion of its contexts, either in a single poem or, occasionally, in the body of Stevens' work, and this determines where its meaning may be sought by the reader. It is not only pointless but wrong to try to assign constant meanings to many of the recurrent images in his poetry. In his use of colors, for example, with the usual exception of blue, meaning is peculiar to each evocation.[10] It requires only common sense to understand the quality indicated by "Catches tigers/ In red weather" in "Disillusionment of Ten O'Clock" (*CP*, p. 66). Moonlight, then, represents a kind of vision of reality—in this case Carolina—that is imaginative (III, ll. 6–8), but sparsely productive, almost sterile (III, ll. 19–27), attractive (III, 30–39), but unclear (III, ll. 18 and 40), and if not an evasion of reality, then "A minor meeting, facile, delicate" (III, ll. 45–46). This is that fanciful view of reality described in parts of "Thirteen Ways of Looking at a Blackbird." The moonlight thoughts, "Like jades affecting the sequestered bride" (III, l. 33), are like the "bawds of euphony" of that poem, and their fellow illegitimates of the imagination, the "pimps of pomp" (*OP* p. 19) and the "fops of fancy" (*CP*, p. 16)—illegitimate because they evade, rather than direct themselves to, reality. Crispin oscillates between this state and that of his Yucatan experience in which he seeks a vision which includes a reality that is coarse but productive and energetic, not tuned to a limited and over-refined sensibility. The fancy here is not swept aside but put in its place in a hierarchy of the imagination. Crispin is like those philosophers in "Homunculus et la Belle Etoile" who allow themselves to be charmed by the star of ideal and unattainable beauty until they bathe their hearts in moonlight, knowing they can bring back hard thought later. Crispin then confronts the real Carolina, not the legendary Carolina of his mind. This Carolina represents prosaic reality, as opposed to the exotica of Yucatan. Seeking the "relentless contact" (III, l. 30) he desires with reality, he tries to get down to the "soil" in order to grasp the "essential prose" (III, l. 89) of the commonplace (III, ll. 67–94).

Section IV, following from Crispin's experience in the preceding section, reformulates the poem's initial proposition to read: "his soil is man's intelligence." "The essential prose," the commonplace particulars of a world formerly falsified (III, l. 90) by sentimental, fanciful, and stale impositions of the intelligence, now becomes the determining factor in Crispin's vision of reality. The esthetic expression of this vision, the music of this reality, celebrates the "rankest trivia" (IV, l. 18), the more unaccommodating to esthetic expression, the better a test for both his vision and his esthetic (IV, ll. 16–24). Instead of man determining the nature of reality as in section I, the particulars of his world determine man's nature: "The natives of the rain are rainy men" (IV, l. 32). Man, in turn, becomes the voice and expression of his environment: "The man in Georgia waking among pines/ Should be pine-spokesman" (IV, ll. 52–53). Like the dress of the woman of Lhassa in "Anecdote of Men by the Thousand," his words are "an invisible element of that place/ Made visible" (CP, p. 52). The inhabitants of Crispin's colony are to compose poems that are accurate expressions of their environment and so live in harmony with it. Secular clerics ("Shrewd novitiates") would mediate—as clerics do—between experience and the understanding and expression of it, ensuring in the harmony of such compositions a harmonious relation between man and his physical environment. This is the "application" (IV, l. 45) for which Crispin strives in his projected colony. Lines 46–47 mean that Crispin now prefers the practical to the far-fetched and to that which is beautiful but useless. Crispin seeks to fix revelation in law, to ritualize it, to socialize it (IV, ll. 68–75).

But Crispin finds that the formularization and institutionalization of his perception of reality promotes the falsification of it that started him on his voyage (IV, ll. 76–88; 76–80 may be paraphrased, "These utopian prophecies, related in their romanticism to regressions to his original sentimentality, contained in their spirit the same falsification which prompted Crispin to undertake his voyage.") Thus he forgoes ritual for "chance event" (IV, l. 90). For the secular man there is no final revelation which fixes the order of reality and predetermines his response to it through law and ritual. There may be a series of revelations, but their structure can only be the structure of his experience, not of an idea that orders it. What is revealed is that the last revelation is no longer sufficient. "The poet must get rid of the hieratic in everything that concerns him and must move constantly in the direction of the credible" (NA, p. 58). Rather than fitting the flow of reality into a predetermined order, the idea of that order must be reconstructed to accommodate "chance event." Reality must be progressively reapprehended, always with the awareness that reality exists beyond one's perception of it. There is the implication here that all ideas about reality are illusory, and interfere with direct, intuitive apprehension of it. The dreams we would impose on reality are monotonous because they depend on our insistent desires ("dreamers buried in our sleep"); they are not imaginings which might be realized, to our advantage, in reality (IV, ll. 92–95). Crispin therefore directs his attention to the particulars of reality exclusive of any theories about them:

All dreams are vexing. Let them be expunged.
But let the rabbit run, the cock declaim. (IV, ll. 98–99)

Here Stevens writes of Crispin that he preferred "text to gloss" (IV, l. 89). Elsewhere he wrote, "What the eye beholds may be the text of life. It is, nevertheless, a text that we do not write" (NA, p. 76). Between these two statements Crispin fluctuates. Each idea he hits upon to account for his experience turns out, upon being tested by his experience, to falsify it, to change it into something it was not. But Crispin does not want to fob off a bungled token of a work ("Trinket pasticcio;" the latter word means a bungled work in Italian), fanciful and insignificant.[11] He keeps returning to the text of his experience for an accurate account of it: "veracious page on page, exact" (IV, l. 102). But he is to discover that experience is a text that cannot be reproduced but only glossed, not recaptured but only reinterpreted.

> Can one man think one thing and think it long?
> Can one man be one thing and be it long? (V, ll. 53–54)

With these rhetorical questions, Crispin (section V), rationalizes the "haphazard denouement" of his quest. It is haphazard because the soil—now "suzerain" (V, l. 20)—which he had once believed he dominated, later sought to interpret, and to whose commonplace reality he now wishes to direct his thought, itself deflects his thought and saps his will to make formulations about it (V, ll. 10–22). The purple of his imaginative speculations is taken care of by the requirements of the immediate quotidian (V, ll. 16–17). The pleasure ("carouse") his "soil" now gives him shames him into forming an attachment for it even as he domesticates it (V, ll. 20–23). As realist Crispin settles for the text of experience rather than the gloss:

> The words of things entangle and confuse.
> The plum survives its poems. It may hang
> In the sunshine placidly, colored by ground
> Obliquities of those who pass beneath,
> Harlequined and mazily dewed and mauved
> In bloom. Yet it survives in its own form,
> Beyond these changes, good, fat, guzzly fruit. (V, ll. 27–33)

Words are only an approximation of the object seen from one point of view or another, as the plum is seen obliquely from changing points of view on the ground. They do not capture the full sensuous reality of the object which, like the plum, survives in its own form its metamorphoses in poetry. Thus it is direct experience that is reliable, and words about it "entangle and confuse." This passage (ll. 22–33, to be exact), in which Yvor Winters sees the substitution of experience for poetry,[12] is rather a declaration of respect for the integrity of sensory apprehension. It is not that poems are pointless in face of plums, but that plums have their own existential integrity beyond language about them. The passage Winters calls a farewell to poetry (V, ll. 36–47) is rather Crispin's abnegation of tragic bombast over abandonment of his grandiose pretensions to founding a colony ("loquacious columns") that would institutionalize his esthetic and epistemological discoveries. The waning of Crispin's colonizing impulse is due to the exhaustion of his will by the quotidian (V, ll. 1–22):

> . . . the quotidian saps philosophers
> And men like Crispin like them in intent,
> If not in will, to track the knaves of thought. (V, ll. 79–81)

Crispin is no philosopher. He concludes that if ideas about experience are confusing, then he will surrender to experience itself, satisfying himself in its daily flow (V, ll. 70–74). It does not follow that Crispin renounces poetry for experience as Winters says; that is not the subject here. Crispin renounces his overly ambitious speculation and his grandiose esthetic stratagems in favor of the commonplace of the quotidian. He can therefore forget about what "shall or ought to be" and settle for what is; if he were to write poetry it would not be about the former but the latter, about his experience of the quotidian.

Crispin submits to a quotidian that is benign, offering as it does the normal domestic fulfillments (V, ll. 58–77), and it normalizes Crispin's defeat with the implication that man struggles unwittingly to be so defeated. This is the note of "Last Looks at the Lilacs" (CP, p. 48), in which the young man is derided for his carping suppression of desire:

> . . . say how it comes that you see
> Nothing but trash and that you no longer feel
> Her body quivering in the Floréal
>
> Toward the cool night and its fantastic star,
> Prime paramour and belted paragon,

Well-booted, rugged, arrogantly male,
Patron and imager of the gold Don John,
Who will embrace her before summer comes.

"Poor buffo," doomed victim of the intrigue of flesh and
spring contrived for his own hapless but happy denouement.
He is in the same way as Crispin a comic character. This is
the doom, to paraphrase a much later poem of Stevens', of
intelligent men in an unintelligible world (*CP*, p. 495). If
reality is always beyond the intelligence, then formulations
based on experience of it which is always in the past can
never remain adequate, must constantly be reformulated.
One's experience of reality is limited ("What is one man
among so many men?" V, l. 51), and always changing ("Can
one man be one thing and be it long?" V, l. 54). A man
cannot, therefore, "think one thing and think it long."
   Crispin, then, submits to reality, no longer choosing "from
droll confect/ Of was and is and shall or ought to be" (V, ll.
4–5). (V, ll. 55–56 should be read: "The man who despised
homely quilts now, despite himself, lies covered in quilts up
to his head," reading "head" for "poll." Compare I, l. 11.) His
final formulation is, "what is is what should be" (V, l. 57).
That "is" is benign, since Crispin's poem, as Crispin's world,
is comic, but also because it is given as the normal condition
of an unextraordinary man, "yeoman and grub" (V, l. 74),
with the normal satisfactions, domestic, personal, unpresum-
ing. The "blonde" of V, line 60, is "prismy" because she will
break up the "one, vast, subjugating, final tone" (I, l. 83) of
reality into the many meanings of domestic felicity—the one
"tone" becomes a variety of sounds and colors in the description of Crispin's daughters. (I suppose "rumpling bottomness" is a pun referring to the newlyweds as they rumple their
sheets with their bottoms; the shutters are cracked because
the interior scene is not disconnected from the mood of the
summer evening outside from which the crickets of V, ll. 68–
69 watch as "custodians" in V, l. 89.) Crispin's quotidian
"saps" as life saps, giving in return. While what it gives may
of course be more or less, the indication here is that in normal

conditions it pays out ("exchequering") more ("a humped return," with a sly sexual reference to "rumpling bottomness") from its treasuries than it takes (V, ll. 93-95).

The grandiose announcement and description of Crispin's "last deduction," his daughters (section VI), is humorous in tone partly because of the joke played on Crispin by the quotidian and his own nature. Defeat is turned into rout, and Crispin, the voyager, the seeker, is stopped by that which is of his own creation. He is stopped finally by his own fertility, parallel to that of the quotidian described in the preceding section. His cabin was "phylactery" because it contained the text of his experience, now displacing his projected poetic texts (a phylactery contains texts from the Torah).[13] A "palankeen" is a litter for carrying someone; the "vexing palankeens" of VI, l. 17 are probably cribs. A "halidom" (VI, l. 20) is, in an archaic usage, a sanctuary. These lines are humorous in the high spirits of a happy hymn "bubbling felicity in cantilene" (melody, VI, l. 3), in celebration of Crispin's fertility. The defeat is a fulfillment. Crispin sought to discover a way of regarding reality without falsification, and on that epistemology to base an esthetic by which he might accurately sing of man's relation to reality. He found that reality impossible to apprehend except as it was immediately experienced, and so was forced to surrender to immediate experience: the quotidian, the family and return to social nature (VI, l. 13), and his daughters. Now, that harmonious relation with reality that he hoped to discover and to express in poetry is created beyond and despite Crispin's will and within his immediate experience through his daughters, "his grand pronunciamento and devise" (VI, l. 8). I see nothing to indicate that Crispin's daughters are "without doubt the seasons" (Kermode, p. 48): they are merely daughters, "four mirrors blue/ That should be silver" (VI, ll. 59-60), four mirrors of Crispin's self that stir his imagination instead of merely reflecting it. Nassar (p. 170) contends that the daughters are poems; rather, they are taking the place of poems. They have "stopped" (VI, l. 25) Crispin's ambitions, but with a greater complexity (VI, ll. 29-31) of imaginatively

stimulating experience than he would have expected. Riddel
(p. 101) pertinently observes that "chits" can mean both
sprouts and "vouchers for debts incurred"; thus, "the cost of
living an every day life" (p. 100). The daughters represent, as
consummation of his experience with reality, the harmony
with it that he sought. They are the answers to his questions.
Thus his tale of quest comes to its end,

> . . . muted, mused, and perfectly revolved
> In those portentous accents, syllables,
> And sounds of music coming to accord
> Upon his lap. . . . (VI, ll. 77–80)

The end of his journey finds Crispin back in the same domestic scene where he began, and he is left confronting the
world, the same "insoluble lump" (VI, l. 70), admitting as
fatalist that the course of his experience, since it is beyond
his intelligence, is beyond his control. He sought to see the
world beyond imagination ("purple"), and finishes by confronting the world in terms of the consequences of the domestic imagination—his daughters. He has been a comic
character, struggling clownishly to come to terms with a
world which is as indifferent to his struggle as it is unchange-
ably benign. Since this is a comic poem, it must, for one
thing, have a happy ending. Even "if the anecdote/ Is false"
and its reasoning fruitless (VI, ll. 83–85), though Crispin
only proves "what he proves/ Is nothing" (VI, ll. 94–95),
"what can all this matter since / The relation comes, benignly, to its end?" (VI, ll. 95–96). Happiness is more
important than the formulations by which we try to achieve
it. (VI, l. 93 should be read: "making quick cures out of the
unruliness of life." In the preceding line, "sequestering the
fluster" means trying to remove the confusion.) The journey,
nevertheless, has not been pointless. He has come to accord
with that same world with which he had been in discord at
the outset. It is not the world that has changed, it is Crispin
who has become adjusted to it. But it is a new adjustment
based on a reapprehension of his reality. Thus happily may
each man's story end.

"On the Manner of Addressing Clouds" (CP, p. 55)

The clouds are "grammarians" because they elicit speech from men as a grammarian, or philologist, might elicit meaning from a text. They submit meekly to their transitory nature, to their gloomy rendezvous with death ("mortal rendezvous"), and in so doing elicit from men that splendor of speech ("pomps"), that poetry whose power to exalt (a power which, like music, seems to affect the spirit rather than the ear), continues to sustain us. The clouds are "Gloomy" (l. 1): the utterances of the most pessimistic ("Funest," portending death or evil) thinkers and the feelings they evoke are elicited by the clouds, are "the speech of clouds." This speech of their march through the sky recurs as the random ("casual") recurrence of the clouds (keeping "the mortal rendezvous," l. 2) evokes such thought and feeling in their progress throughout the seasons, which are "stale" because they are repetitive, and "mysterious," ultimately, as part of our problematic universe. Such pessimistic utterances as that of the "Funest philosophers" are the poetry of appropriate ("meet") resignation to the nature of the world; this kind of poetry is "responsive" to that nature of which the clouds are part, it is this kind of poetry that provides us spiritual sustenance in face of that nature. This, therefore, is the kind of poetry the clouds should encourage and augment if, in the random, meaningless heavens ("drifting waste"), there is going to be any meaning, which is to say any human meaning, along with the meaningless ("mute bare") magnificence of the sun and moon.

"Of Heaven Considered as a Tomb" (CP, p. 56)

How are we to interpret the dead: men who, since god himself is dead, walk in "the tomb of heaven"—the night sky which is merely sky—with the stars as their lanterns,[14] the ghosts of our human comedy of life? Do they, within the cold of death, believe that they wander around and around the sky, freed from death, looking for the kind of heaven they had expected? Or does their death ("That burial"), confirmed by our experience ("pillared up each day") as being no more than the door and passage of the spirit to mere nonexistence, foretell to us at night, when we are inclined to worry about the nature of death, our own death: "the one abysmal night," when, with the extinction of our consciousness, we will no longer see the stars in the night sky? Make an outcry among these "dark comedians," who mimic, in death, the human comedy of life, call them for an answer from their cold heaven (Élysée) of the night sky, of the tomb. That they will not answer is our answer.

"The Emperor of Ice-Cream" (CP, p. 64)[15]

The muscular figure with whom the poem opens is a kind of pleasure master: he produces "big cigars"; he makes tempting food (whipping "concupiscent curds"—this is close enough poetic approximation of ice-cream churning to lead us to conclude that this is the "Emperor" himself); he is powerful ("muscular"); even the verse here, especially in line three, is given over to the pleasure of sound, to the fun of the alliteration which is, then, not merely gratuitous word play. The poem, in other words, begins by summoning up the king of pleasure. Moreover, the description of the women to be present suggests that they are ladies of pleasure—"the wenches dawdle." Here, however, a new note is introduced, that of the impoverished commonplace, even common: the women are not to dress up as for any special occasion; flowers are to be brought, but, with insistent casualness, they are to be wrapped in "last month's newspapers." (Stevens says of the words "concupiscent curds" that "they express the concupiscence of life, but, by contrast with the things in relation to them in the poem, they express or accentuate life's destitution"—LWS, p. 500.) Let us not try to make a special occasion, let us not try to veil the ordinary quality of this event: let the seeming quality of things yield to the way they actually are ("Let be be finale of seem"). The only extraordinary thing in this occasion is to be pleasure, for pleasure is the only power we will recognize to govern us: "The only emperor is the emperor of ice-cream." Pleasure is the only force that has dominion over the commonplace.

In the second stanza pleasure is again juxtaposed with the common. From the cheap dresser ("deal" is a cheap kind of wood), in depressingly ill repair, take the sheet embroidered with fantail pigeons (LWS, p. 340) and cover her with that which she had once enjoyed decorating. Here we recognize that the occasion is a kind of wake, at which death, too, is treated as something commonplace, and at which only pleasure can give relief from that fatal commonplace to which we are all reduced. Thus the corpse is covered with the decorative sheet. If the feet stick out they only serve to affirm the common fact of physical death. There is no more to death than this, no separation of the soul, no supernatural myth. The lamp, with its ordinary light, confirms as with the seal of the commonplace this common fact. Our only resort from it is to pleasure.

"Sunday Morning" (CP, p. 66)

In "Sunday Morning" the poet conducts a meditation through the woman whose mind is the scene, so to speak, of the meditation, resolving the questions that she raises. Unlike Stevens' later meditative poems, however, this one presents a cohesive argument rather than a series of reflections. The blank verse and the diction have little of the extravagant virtuosity of "The Comedian as the Letter C" and "Le Monocle de Mon Oncle" and, as a result, the poem is itself less idiosyncratic. The occasion of the poem is the hour for church. But the setting is one of sensual comfort, "complacencies of the peignoir," which dispels the holiness of the hour that ordinarily reminds of Christ's sacrifice. From the outset, then, a conflict is presented between the secular and the religious which provides the subject of the poem. The woman, despite the secular setting and because of the religious hour, feels the encroachment of the religious sensibility. In revery she returns across the "wide water" of time and space to the crucifixion in ancient Palestine, and the memory of it gives rise to a nostalgia for the balm of religion. The rest of the poem is concerned with the catharsis of this nostalgia through reconciliation to existence in a secular world.

The poem has the movement of a dialogue, from idea to idea modified. Here the dialogue is between the author and his persona, the former resolving the questions that arise in the thought of the latter. Thus the train of thought returns (II) from the memory of the crucifixion to the initial sense of sensual well being: the oranges and the bright rug, or, possibly, a real cockatoo on the rug. Cannot such satisfactions replace the idea of heaven in a secular world? Divinity, with the power to mediate between man and heaven, can now lie only in her responses to the physical world, which is the only kind of heaven she will know. In support of this point a history of divinity is traced (III), from the nonhuman Jove, through the partly human Christ in whose divinity man partook, to the possibility of the idea of god being wholly humanized if the idea of heaven were merged in the reality of earth:

Shall our blood fail? Or shall it come to be
The blood of paradise? And shall the earth
Seem all of paradise that we shall know?

The sky would not then seem a barrier between earth and heaven but part of the physical world which is the source of all evil as of all good. With such a recognition of the nature of the physical world, living in harmonious well being with that world would take its place as a kind of felicity second only to that possible in the relations among men, or "enduring love."

The woman then raises the question of the transitory character of such an earthly paradise (IV). The answer is returned that there is no eternal realm of the supernatural ever imagined that has endured as transitory nature endures in its seasonal repetitions. More permanent than the nostalgia for the supernatural is the remembrance of the satisfactions of nature and the desire that may be consummated in nature itself:

> . . . her remembrance of awakened birds,
> Or her desire for June and evening, tipped
> By the consummation of the swallow's wings.

She grants that nature offers such fulfillment to mortality, but insists on the need of a fulfillment that will not pass away, that is immortal; in contentment with life she is troubled by the obliteration of death (V). The reply, that carries through section VI, is a description of the conditions of mortality that is the crisis of the poem. "Death is the mother of beauty" because implicit in it is the principle of change, and in change alone can come fulfillment of desire. Thus fulfillment, here expressed in terms of the fulfillment of beauty, is dependent on its transitory nature, and "imperishable bliss," the deathless fulfillment of paradise, is therefore impossible. Although death means the certain obliteration of experience, it also ensures continuation of the transitory process of desire and satisfaction of desire. Death as the principle of change, and therefore as mother of the processes of life, ensures their continuation which is mortality's only memorial. Thus death "makes the willow shiver in the sun" in living memorial of dead maidens who used to sit gazing on the grass which they used to tread, and which is now withdrawn from their feet. Death causes the repetition of desire after desire has been satisfied and the salvers on which the feast was served have been cast away; a new generation of boys will inherit the plate of the old and make use of it to tempt a new generation of maidens (compare Stevens, *LWS*, p. 183):

> She causes boys to pile new plums and pears
> On disregarded plate. The maidens taste
> And stray impassioned in the littering leaves.

The living maidens in their turn taste the fruit and, touched by desire, "stray impassioned in the littering leaves" which are the "leaves of sure obliteration" and in which they, nevertheless, go seeking satisfaction of desire.

By way of illustrating change as the condition of fulfillment, transitory mortality is compared with hypothetical paradise (VI). If there were a state of existence like that of earth, but without the change that death brings, there could be no cycle of desire and fulfillment, no consummation, and such an existence would be one of eternal ennui. Its characteristic would be stasis rather than change. Death is the mother of beauty then, because in the fire of her bosom which consumes, is contained the principle of change which creates, as earthly mothers create life. In death, therefore, we may figure ("devise") a return to the creative principle in life ("earthly mothers").

The argument, having established that earth is "all of paradise that we shall know," returns to the supposition raised in section III (ll. 12–15) as to the consequence if this were true. Granted that earth is the only possible equivalent of paradise, the source of happiness for men would be the sense of sharing a common fate of "men that perish," but who live in that fellowship in harmony with the physical world as a substitute for heaven. Section VII is a celebration of that condition, in which a ring of men chant to the sun of the particulars of the physical world, in an expression of their harmony with it. Again in answer to section III, "Shall our blood fail? Or shall it come to be/ The blood of paradise?" their chant is a "chant of paradise,/ Out of their blood, returning to the sky," signifying harmonious union with the physical world as if it were divine, just as "our blood, commingling, virginal,/ With heaven," once united with divinity in Christ. In the same way they chant to the sun, "Not as a god, but as a god might be," the idea of divinity merged in the reality of the physical world as a source of creation. The men celebrate a transitory world, and know their kinship with the "summer morn" that will pass away; and their destiny is signified by the ephemeral dew on their feet: "Men do not either come from any direction or disappear in any direction. Life is as meaningless as dew" (Stevens, *LWS*, p. 250).

The woman hears, in that revery or suspension of time and space which began with the pacification and stillness of the "wide water" in section I, the cry that Christ did not rise as god, but was mortal and is dead (VIII). The poem concludes therefore with a description of a secular world, a "chaos" beyond rational order, "unsponsored, free" of the supernatural dominion of Jesus, an island inescapably separated by the "wide water" of time and space from the crucifixion. As in section II, the only possible felicity lies in response to the physical world. The poem ends with a notation of the sensuous detail of that physical world which must take the place of paradise. The last of these notations, the pigeons, suggests a state of existence which, like that described in the poem, is isolated from the supernatural ("isolation of the sky"), and ambiguous in the meaning of its destiny as are the undulations in the course of the pigeons as they sink to darkness, but with wings extended, as if in knowing acquiescence to that destiny.

"Bantams in Pine-Woods" (*CP*, p. 75)

This poem concerns a challenge flung from the personal imagination to the world of reality. The imaginative world of the individual is placed in opposition to the overbearing reality of the universe. The universal reality is metaphorically described as a "ten-foot poet," a universal imagination as against the imagination of individuals ("inchlings"). Stevens sometimes figures nature as a cosmic imagination within which the individual imagination operates (for example, "The World as Meditation," *CP*, p. 521, ll. 10–11). In this particular case the individual imagination triumphs in imposing its personal vision of the landscape, in giving point to the pines and their smell ("tangs"; but "tangs" also itself means points—thus also: "give point to their points"). But there is a double pun in the name of "Iffucan of Azcan": give me the lie if-you-can and, in fact, as you can.

"To the One of Fictive Music" (*CP*, p. 87)

The poem is addressed to the muse of poetry—she is of that "sisterhood" of the muses who, though not alive, are alive to the poet and to the imagination, hence "the living dead." (Stevens, however, after glossing the One and the sisterhood as the muses, makes it clear that he prefers not to specify them except as they are specified in the poem—see *LWS*, pp. 297, 298.) It is she among the muses with whom the poet feels most intimate, whose works seem most tangible ("clearest bloom"). Considered as source of the creative spirit ("mother") rather than companion ("sister," l. 1) she is chief among the other muses; and she is the object of his warmest transcendental love. But she is not distant, exotic ("cloudy silver"), not a femme fatale ("venom of renown"), but simple, as she is close and clear.

The "birth" in stanza two is that of our human consciousness, which separates us from nature while leaving us in it,[16] so that, seeing so much of ourselves in nature, it comes to seem to us a large and coarse image of ourselves ("Gross effigy and simulacrum"). The "music summoned" (stanza 2, l. 1) by this birth is art, which attempts to bridge the separation between man and nature (compare, "From this the poem springs: that we live in a place/ That is not our own and, much more, not ourselves," "Notes toward a Supreme Fiction," *It Must Be Abstract*, IV). Coming thus out of our "imperfections," no art renders more perfection than poetry. The muse is referred to as "rare" because of the rarity (fine, unusual) of such perfection, but "kindred" because the more perfect the poem laboriously wrought, the more of ourselves, of the "near," the familiar, will be in it. The more the poem, as our bridge to nature, retains of ourselves, the closer it brings our selves to nature.

For in this effort to bridge the gap between the self and nature (stanza 3), men so desire to retain as much of their selves as possible that that art is most intense for them which makes a point of the familiar, what they know (l. 3), that meditation on the obscure (Riddel, p. 68, notes the pun on "musing" here) most acute which grasps, through poetry ("As in your name"), what is familiar and certain ("sure") in that unmitigated ("arrant") nature we live in. Thus here the muse is referred to in terms of the familiar detail of nature which yields a poetry that most resembles our own lives.

Yet, though poetry can proclaim the familiar, we would not like it to be too literal. In our art ("feigning") reality should be endowed with the interest that the imagination can give it ("the strange unlike"), which provides it with the saving difference from reality without the imagination. (As in Wordsworth, the imagination is to be cast over the ordinary, in order to present it to the mind in an unusual way.) To this end the muse must also be the exotic femme fatale, as well as familiar and simple. She must give us that element of unreality, the imagination, which makes reality so alluring.

"Peter Quince at the Clavier" (CP, p. 89)

Peter Quince is the stage manager of the rustic actors in A *Midsummer-Night's Dream*. He is perhaps à propos as the speaker of the poem in that, as he day dreams at the key board, he is in a sense the stage manager of the imagination. The poem is a flight of imagination that takes place as Peter Quince plays, and one should note the high frequency of musical terms used. It is like a key board impromptu in which each of the four sections resembles a "movement" whose metrical tempo helps set its mood.

As the player strikes the keys of the clavier (I), so the

sounds produced strike a music from his spirit. By logical extension, then, the music is essentially the feeling it produces; since music is feeling, the desire he feels for the woman of whom he is thinking is a kind of music. There follows a projection of this feeling into the story of Susanna, the story serving as an extended simile for the feeling. (The poem is in this respect a compliment to the woman, referred to in the second and third stanzas, desire for whom provokes the reflective revery that follows.) This projection becomes a speculation on the nature of desire and the bodily beauty that is its object. Susanna awakened a similar music, or "strain" (tune, tension: desire) in the elders. Since their lust is, in terms of the poem, a kind of music, it is appropriately described in musical terms (note especially the triple meaning of "The basses of their beings"—"bass" as musical term or instrument, as depth, and as evil.)

The poem then gives a description of the music of Susanna's feelings (II). The warmth of the water, its sensuous "touch," brings forth in her the "melody" of sensual day dreams or fantasies ("concealed imaginings"). The cooler air as she stands on the bank is echoed by her "spent emotions." She feels, "among the leaves," a gentle residue, or nostalgia ("dew") for her amorous attachments of the past ("old devotions"). As she walks away she still trembles ("quaver," a trill or tremolo in music) with the emotions she has just felt. Then the breath of the elders suddenly deadens ("muted") the feelings which the night had evoked in her, and their intrusion is put in terms of the brash, brassy interruption of the cymbal and horns.

The "attendant Byzantines" (III) serve as a choral expression of feeling about the elders' accusation. They are silly ("simpering"), frightened. Their "refrain" (or possibly Susanna's) is weeping, like a willow in windy rain.

The mind's response to beauty comes and goes (IV); it is spasmodic, changeable, giving only the vaguest suggestion of access to beauty as it exists in the flesh ("The fitful tracing of a portal"). But "in the flesh" beauty never dies. The apparent paradox is immediately qualified and then resolved in three metaphors. Though the body itself dies, bodily beauty lives on in new embodiments. In the same way evenings die: the "green" of their "going" is descriptively apt, but also indicates that it is a "going" that is perpetually renewed, just as a wave flowing through the sea at the same time both passes and continues. Gardens die under the "cowl of winter" (winter covering the landscape, and also, a monk's cowl, winter itself like a monk now finished with its seasonal repentance), but they die to be reborn in the spring. Maidens die in marriage, to be replaced by other maidens who will, in their turn, die a similar death (compare the maidens in "Sunday Morning," V, CP, p. 69). The lust that Susanna's beauty aroused in the elders' minds was momentary and left only the prospect of their mortality (the "white" elders; "Death's ironic scraping"—in the *Apocrypha*, after falsely accusing Susanna, they are put to death). But Susanna's beauty has become immortal. Her beauty, her "music," is reborn in memory of her, and serves to consecrate that memory in praise.

"Thirteen Ways of Looking at a Blackbird" (*CP*, p. 92)

"Thirteen Ways of Looking at a Blackbird" is written in that kind of free verse whose line is defined by a natural pause in the speaking voice and a break in the sense. It consists of a series of statements in no particular order, each of which involves the figure of a blackbird or blackbirds.[17] But the difficulty of the poem is not diminished from section to section by the figure of the blackbird itself, for it does not have any constant meaning. In this respect the title is possibly a little misleading. "Sea Surface Full of Clouds" (*CP*, p. 98) is in fact five ways of looking at a seascape, an exercise in impressionism, in which the sea, though changing, is a constant in the poem, the thing being described. The blackbird, on the contrary, acts in each section to bring out the meaning of the context in which it is involved. Its meaning depends on each context, just as the meaning of that context depends on it. It does not have a constant signification but it has a constant function: to act as a focus that brings out qualities in what is put in relation with it. Beyond this, the poem is unified only by what the figure of the blackbird has suggested to the proliferating imagination.

The sections of the poem are not easy to understand, because the discrete descriptions and statements of which they consist are abstracted from any larger context. It is therefore difficult to tell what they refer to beyond themselves; they have, to generalize, an unusually limited amount of defined reference, and an unusually wide range of suggestive reference. The greatest danger in explicating them is perhaps that of rigid over-interpretation. Beyond repeating what a section says in what is often, here, unnecessary prose paraphrase, one can for the most part tell of it what kind of imaginative statement it is, in what way it appeals to the imagination. There may be no specific meaning beyond this, or, to put it another way, there may be an indefinite range of meanings suggested.

The poem, then, can be considered a series of examples of how the imagination works, and although some sections are also figurative statements about the working of the imagination, others are merely instances of it. In the latter case one must be content to accept the image or comparison presented, for to seek more would be to baffle oneself and defeat the intention of the poem. If the poem can be considered a series of instances of how the imagination works, the fact that the sections are insistently cryptic implies the assumption of a certain relation between the rational mind and the imagination which, as it happens, is stated in the last section of "Six Significant Landscapes":

Rationalists, wearing square hats,
Think, in square rooms,
Looking at the floor,
Looking at the ceiling.
They confine themselves
To right-angled triangles.
If they tried rhomboids,

Cones, waving lines, ellipses—
As, for example, the ellipse of the half-moon—
Rationalists would wear sombreros. (CP, p. 75)

Rationalists confine themselves to one kind of perception.
There is a more extensive kind of perception available through
the imagination. It follows that, as in "Thirteen Ways of
Looking at a Blackbird," specific rational communication may
be limited for the sake of imaginative statement, which may
be rational but is also more than rational, and may, in Stevens' view, be non-rational (see below, pp. 76–77). One finds
in this poem that there are degrees in kind of imaginative
statement, from those which are figurative, but whose meaning may be specified, to those whose meaning is ultimately
ambiguous, but which for that reason are highly suggestive.

Considering the poem as a series of instances of imaginative statement, I will discuss the sections in groups that cor-
respond roughly to the ways they appeal to the imagination.
This seems more convenient for purposes of discussion than
adhering to a numerical order (which appears, in any case, to
be arbitrary). Section I is a description in which the eye of
the blackbird provides a focal point for a landscape which it
composes, in the sense that a compositional center composes
a landscape painting. The effect of the blackbird among the
twenty snowy mountains is similar to that of the jar in "The
Anecdote of the Jar":

It made the slovenly wilderness
Surround that hill.

The wilderness rose up to it,
And sprawled around, no longer wild. (CP, p. 76)

The jar, the blackbird, serve as points that order what surrounds them. So, in Stevens' belief, may metaphor order
reality in poetry. Speaking of "resemblances," the name he
gives to the basis of metaphor, comparison, he says: "The
eye does not beget in resemblance. It sees. But the mind begets in resemblance as the painter begets in representation;

that is to say, as the painter makes his world within a world"
(*NA*, p. 76). The mind orders reality by perceiving significant
relations within it, as the artist abstracts and composes the
elements of reality in significant integrations that are works of
art. The blackbird serves the same purpose in IX:

> When the blackbird flew out of sight,
> It marked the edge
> Of one of many circles.

The blackbird, seen as a point of reference, defines an intelligible area among many possible but undefined intelligible
areas.

In II the blackbird is used as the comparative term in a
simile. Given that one blackbird is like another, the blackbirds sit in the tree like three equal possibilities. The blackbird in V is used in an ornamental and illustrative comparison. It adds nothing to the sense, which is that esthetic
satisfaction may be found equally in statement and implication. The blackbird in III is used as a specific image that
represents a general phenomenon, a synechdoche for autumn.
The blackbird is one part of the entire process of autumn. But
it is part of a pantomime in that autumn is a performance in
which many elements, like the blackbird, mimic its general
qualities, among which that of whirling is given here. In
XII, the flight of the blackbird is juxtaposed with the movement of a river, as if there were some causal connection between the two kinds of motion: if "x" is happening, in other
words, "y" also has to happen. Stevens comments sparingly
on the section that its point is "the compulsion frequently
back of the things that we do" (*LWS*, p. 340). But the imagery further suggests that both river and blackbird must be
parts of a whole of which motion is an essential attribute.
The blackbird must be flying if the river is moving, but a
river is always moving. The blackbird is chosen from an almost unlimited range of natural objects that might have
equally served as an image and term of comparison, and
therefore implies them. Thus, the figure suggests a physical
world that is constantly in flux.

It is possible that IV is merely an assertion that all things are one, but this interpretation seems inadequate, because it fails to account for the particularity of the examples involved. Something other seems implied by the use of the man and woman than could be if two randomly dissimilar objects had been chosen. The blackbird here is without significance in itself, but brings out meaning in that with which it is put in relation, just as, in Stevens' analogy, the imagination, like light, adds nothing, but illuminates (NA, p. 61). A man and a woman are one, perhaps in love, perhaps in that they are complementary opposites; the blackbird adds an unknown which denotes an element of mystery that they should be so. The figure of the blackbird is meaningless except as it is in the given context, like the "x" in an equation. The blackbird in VII has a similar function. Exclusively because it is placed in juxtaposition with golden birds, it comes to suggest the mundane, as contrasted with the exotic. But that the black-bird walks around the feet of the women adds a sense of mystery to them, "the strange unlike" that imagination brings in "To the One of Fictive Music" (CP, p. 88). Hence the passage reads, "why imagine the exotic, when the ordinary is exotic." The extravagance of the first verse of the section, "O thin men of Haddam," attempts to show this through rhetoric. Haddam is a town in Connecticut (Poggioli, pp. 184–85). In VIII the blackbird again works as an unknown which gives and gains significance in the particular context. The sense of the section is that there is something else in-volved in poetry besides the beauty of which language is capable. That something else is represented by the blackbird, but not specified by the context in which it is placed. The blackbird here has a suggestive value, especially in connection with the other sections of the poem: it suggests mundane reality, and it also suggests the imagination itself as it is used in this poem. It is not more specific than that, and does not need to be.

In X the blackbirds represent an image from reality strik-ing enough to impress even those who evade reality in order to indulge the beauties of language alone. The "bawds of euphony" are like the "pimps of pomp" in "Stanzas for 'Le Monocle de Mon Oncle'" (OP, p. 19). The "fops of fancy" of "Le Monocle de Mon Oncle," X (CP, p. 16) are closely related. They all evade reality in poetry, rather than address it. The blackbirds would suddenly cause the bawds to "express themselves sharply: naturally, with pleasure, etc." (LWS, p. 340). In XI the blackbirds are juxtaposed with a "glass coach." Whatever the nature of the coach, its only specified quality seems to place it, as something artificial, in contrast with the blackbirds, which are natural. Thus, he who rides in the artificial equipage feels afraid of what he thinks is the intrusion of real birds into his fanciful scene. The implication would be that reality threatens fancy, which is an evasion of it.

In VI the blackbird serves to construct a word picture whose literal sense creates an effect without specifying a meaning. The mood, presumably created in the room by the barbaric glass in the long window, makes of the shadow in the window a mysterious phenomenon, something with an occult cause. The cause is the mundane blackbird. An ordinary object, because of the circumstances in which it appears, comes to have an extraordinary effect. This is as far as the sense can be pushed. In the final section the blackbird is again used to create a word picture which in this case has only a literal sense. It is not "about" anything else. There is only the picture to accept on its surface, as one accepts the surface of a painted canvas. There is no implication: it suggests nothing beyond itself, or it suggests what you want to make it suggest. It has the autonomy of a chance scene in reality, or of a piece of music, or of a painting, which catches and absorbs the attention, and composes the feelings in its own composition. It represents another use of the imagination in poetry, otherwise put in the "Adagia": "A poem need not have a meaning and like most things in nature often does not have" (OP, p. 177).

In terms of this analysis, the poem may be considered in the light of the tradition that descends from Baudelaire and particularly Mallarmé, in which there is a conscious division between the creative and communicative functions of language,[18] and in which, therefore, the creative value of words depends on their suggestiveness, rather than on their strict sense, so that lack of specificity and the presence of obscurity become virtues. Stevens wrote in *The Explicator*:[19]

> [Poems] have imaginative or emotional meanings, not rational meanings. . . . They may communicate nothing at all to people who are open only to rational meanings. In short, things that have their origin in the imagination or in the emotions very often take on a form that is ambiguous or uncertain.

In this tradition, the poem, increasingly independent of definite subject matter, tends to be reduced to a purely esthetic effect, as in Mallarmé, or may, as in Valéry, turn in upon itself to find a subject matter in its own genesis and nature.[20] But Valéry does not, like Baudelaire and Mallarmé, try to arrive at an ideal or an absolute through the creative function of language; rather, he tries to order the world through the use of analogy (the faculty of combining images), and metaphor.[21] Here there is a point of contact between this poem and the French Symbolist tradition, for in manner it is limited to the figurative aspect of language; it concerns itself with the uses of the imagination, and it does so by demonstrating how the poetic figure can order and illuminate reality by discovering significant relations within it.

This says something about the poem's obscurity. It is an insistent obscurity because it intends to appeal as exclusively as possible to the imaginative, as opposed to the reasoning faculty. The less specific the language of a poem is for the reason, presumably, the more suggestive power will it have for the imagination. "The poem," says Stevens, "must resist the intelligence/Almost successfully" (*CP*, p. 350). That is why it is less a matter of penetrating the meaning of the poem than of knowing how to read it. It must be explained not by being reduced to prose statement, but by being described as a poem. I take it as part of the intention of the poem to baffle prose statement in order to defy such a reduction.

"Anatomy of Monotony" (*CP*, p. 107)

We are derived from the earth (I), which brought us forth as part of that nature which it breeds. The earth was "lewder" when it bred us, in that it was less chaste, therefore, more fecund. (Also, perhaps, "lewd" in the obsolete sense of secular, as opposed to clerical: our origin was natural, not divine as in the religious myth which later grew up about it.) We are of the same nature as the earth. Therefore, since we age toward death, so must the earth. As we have an aging autumn in our life, so she has the autumn of her planetary life, an old age larger than that earthly one which chills our spirits; and beyond our skies, bare of the promise of heaven after death, the earth lives and dies in terms of the still barer, bleaker expanse of the cosmos ("sky that does not bend").

The body exists in terms of its physical life in nature (II); it is in our naked bodies that we live. Nature, out of affection for us, or sadness for our fate, comforts us with companions who complement our desire and pleasure ("phantasy" and "device," archaic usages, also, our illusions and contrivances), who, through their finesse in gesture, touch, and sound, arouse in us desire for the still finer, more urgent pleasures ("implacable chords") of sexual love. But this nature in which the body exists and which seems so benevolent is a deception, for its light and space have as their source that bleaker cosmic sky in which the earth, and all that exists on it, lives and must die (therefore, "fatal"). The spirit senses this, and is oppressed. It is this oppression of cosmic bleakness, this "monotony" or ennui, that the title speaks of analysing.

"The Idea of Order at Key West" (*CP*, p. 128)

The woman that the poet heard beside the sea sang a song that was beyond the ability, intelligence, of the presiding spirit of the sea ("beyond the genius of the sea"). The sea never completely crystallized into an intelligence, never became completely articulate: it was like "a body wholly body" and nothing more, without head, or even the expressive hands and arms, its sleeves empty. And yet its "mimic motion," mimic because it seemed that of an intelligence, but was only an imitation, created an intelligible articulation, not our articulation, though we understood it, but an inhuman cry, that of the ocean itself ("the veritable ocean"). The sea was not a disguise for our intelligence ("a mask"), nor was the woman. The song was not a mixture of the woman's utterance with the sound of the water ("medleyed sound"), even though it may have been an expression of the sea sound, because the song could be distinguished "word by word," unlike the sea, completely articulate. It may be that her song was of the sea, but it was her distinct articulation we heard, and not the sea. For she created the song, and the mysterious ("everhooded") tragic-seeming sea was merely a place where she chose to sing. But it was not she in herself, but the spirit embodied in her that we sought. If her song were simply the sounds of the seascape, it would merely be their low pitched ("deep") reverberations in the air, the sounds of a summer sea in the semitropical climate of Key West ("a summer without end"). But the song was more than meaningless sound; it was more than her voice alone, and more than ours adding meanings to the meaninglessness of the waves, wind, and clouds ("bronze shadows"). It was an imaginative version of the world that the spirit, through her, created. Thus it was her voice that gave point to the sky ("made/ The sky acutest"), made the sky most meaningful, most poignant at sunset ("its vanishing"). She gave to that time its feeling of loneliness. She made, through her art, the world in which she exists ("maker," a few lines below, has the obsolete meaning of poet). When she sang, the sea took on the identity that her song gave it. When we recognized this we realized that her world was the one she made up in her song, that of the imagined. Thus the spirit is the imagination, mediating between the self and reality, neither one nor the other. The poet then apostrophizes "Ramon Fernandez," a French critic with whose critical theory Stevens may have been familiar, though Stevens has insistently denied that he had the critic in mind.[22] It is, in any case, a name appropriate to a Caribbean scene. After the singing stopped and they turned from the sea toward the town, the lights in the harbor, tilting on the masts of the fishing boats, seemed to order the sea and the night as it fell, giving them, as the song had given the seascape before, a particular emotional tone. The imagination, through the song the woman sang, has cast its spell on the scene ("enchanting"), "Arranging" it, making it responsive to the feelings ("deepening"). It is our "rage for order" ("Blessed" because it makes the world meaningful) which thus, through the imagination, enchants reality; it is that which impels the poet ("maker") to compose poems of reality ("of the sea"), of the evanescent ("dimly starred") entries into the kind of desirable experience of reality just described ("fragrant portals"), and of ourselves and our "origins" (in terms, probably, of tracing our human identity), in more spiritual definitions ("ghostlier demarcations") and in more acute poetry ("keener sounds").

"Evening without Angels" (CP, p. 136)[23]

There is no reason for a picture of the world with the supernatural addition of angels hovering miraculously in midair, playing their heavenly music. Nor should the poet, who helps to create our picture of the world, conduct, help to create, this music of the eternal. "Air is air," it has no reality beyond itself. It is empty, but filled with light ("glitters"); it is a desirable emptiness, the element in which we live. The music that we find there is not that of the angels, but our own: the poetry in which we attempt to define ourselves, a means to realize more acutely our own poorly realized ("unfashioned") human spirit. Further, that light of reality which sustains the angels ("fosters," also in the sense of sustaining something not of its own nature, fostering offspring not its own), and which creates their adornments as "coiffeur" and "jeweller" —was it not made for men, rather than angels? The supernatural is an imaginative projection of the human. Men who were sad about their own mortality created angels from the light which illumines reality, and from their imagination (the "moon," often, but not always, associated with the imagination in Stevens) made up the idea of the soul ("attendant ghosts"), which would continue living after death and lead them "back to angels" in heaven (in a kind of substitute return to that reality of the sunlight from which the angels were made.) But we are of the nature of the sun, of the real, and not of night, of the moon and the imagined meanings of night ("pointed" probably in the sense that night makes its own peculiar points, meanings). We make poetry that expresses our harmony ("an accord") with the enduring manifestations of that reality ("antiquest sounds of air") by repeating, in our poems, what we find in it. Yet, though we repeat those manifestations of reality in our poems, they are to begin with native to us, in our own language, are natural expressions of our selves. We are of the nature of the reality we imitate, and it is of ours. Its light, which encases us, crystallizes and forms our thoughts and desires which are then satisfied by reality itself: thus, "desire for day" is satisfied by dawn, for rest, by nightfall. The peace of evening ("rest and silence") is a transition to the slower tempo of night and its emotion-filled ("seething") minor key. This is the best time to confront reality, at night when there is little interference or distraction. The night, the earth are best bare of the supernatural, bare of everything but ourselves and what is familiar to us under the "arches" of the sky and its stars ("spangled air"). The stars ("fire and fire") then seem to be making a rhapsodic music to which we respond aptly ("a true response") with our own voice, our own emotion-filled music demanding expression ("great within us"). This is the appropriate moment for us to use our imagination, represented by the moon, as we compose our poems of bare reality rather than of the supernatural reality of angels.

"The Man with the Blue Guitar"
(CP, p. 165)

"The Man with the Blue Guitar" is a set of thirty-three variations as if played on the guitar as a symbol of the imagination, by a figure presumably suggested by a Picasso painting. The guitar player in the poem represents the poet, "meaning by the poet," in Stevens' words, "any man of imagination."[24] With regard to Picasso, Stevens has written that he "had no particular painting of Picasso in mind" (LWS, p. 786). The identity of the Picasso is, of course, incidental; the relevance of the painting is that through it are combined in their exercise of the imagination, painting, music, and poetry. The implication is that the guitar symbolizes not merely an art, or art in general, but is what Stevens in fact has called it, "a symbol of the imagination."[25]

Stevens thought of the arts as deriving commonly from the imagination (see NA, pp. 160, 170–71). This helps to account for the extent to which music and painting play a part in his poetry. The high incidence of metaphors from music, painting, and sculpture is obvious in even casual reading. The various manifestations of the imagination are often used interchangeably; music frequently stands for poetry and the figure of the statue is frequently a synecdoche for the inventions of the imagination. Items from the history of art as seen in a museum are used as illustrations in his poetic meditations. The succession of sections of fast and slow rhythms in "Peter Quince at the Clavier" (CP, p. 89), and the variations on a theme of "The Man with the Blue Guitar" and other poems, resemble forms of musical composition. That the titles of the poems are often like titles of paintings is a common and correct observation. One critic has found in the impressionism especially of a poem like "Sea Surface Full of Clouds," and in Stevens' sensitiveness to the changes of weather and to change, in general, a resemblance to the arch-Impressionist Monet.[26] Stevens' conception of reality as a series of changes, not the least important of which are those that occur in the mind of the observer (OP, p. 214), leads him to the relative value of the object described, and the final importance of the time, the climate, and the point of view. These points, along with the pervasive references in the poems and essays to modern French painting, indicate at least a considerable rapport with that school especially, and with painting generally. In the degree to which the arts represent for Stevens a common exercise of the imagination they may also be commonly ad- dressed to the problem of belief: "in an age in which disbe- lief is so profoundly prevalent or, if not disbelief, indifference to questions of belief, poetry and painting, and the arts in general, are, in their measure, a compensation for what has been lost. Men feel that the imagination is the next greatest power to faith: the reigning prince" (NA, p. 171). So it is that in "The Man with the Blue Guitar" a reference to one of the arts is a reference to the others and to the imagination itself.

Stevens comments as follows on the intention of "The Man with the Blue Guitar": "The general intention of the *Blue Guitar* was to say a few things that I felt impelled to say 1. about reality; 2. about the imagination; 3. their inter- relations; and 4. principally, my attitude toward each of these things. This is the general scope of the poem, which is con- fined to the area of poetry and makes no pretense of going beyond that area" (LWS, p. 788). The "area of poetry" should be read in view of what has been said above.

With regard to the first two lines of section I, Stevens writes: "This refers to the posture of the speaker, squatting like a tailor (a shearsman) as he works on his cloth" (LWS, p. 783). The day is described as green, possibly with refer- ence to the fertility of vegetation to indicate that it will be fruitful. In any case the green of the day contrasts with the blue of the guitar. Blue, in its contexts in this poem, usually represents the imagination. Thus the shearsman does not play " 'things as they are' " (couplet 2); rather, as he points out, " 'things as they are' " are changed by the imagination (cou- plet 3). The audience then demands that the player include this imaginative element in his tune, in order to express peo- ple as they are. Stevens writes of this section that the poet is "required to express people beyond themselves, because that is exactly the way they are. Their feelings demonstrate the subtlety of people" (*LWS*, p. 359). The way people feel prompts their imagination, and this too is part of what they are. The poem returns to this idea in section IV, according to Stevens. The player continues, in section II, by explaining (couplet 1) that he cannot re-create " 'things exactly as they are' " (I, l. 10); consequently, with regard to a conception of man, he can only produce a version of man's reality through imaginative constructions such as the statue he describes. In interpretation of this section Stevens writes: "It is never possible for the artist to do more than approach 'almost to man' " (*LWS*, p. 789). Such a version of man as is comprised by the "hero's head" (II, l. 3) must answer the request of his listeners in section I for, " 'A tune beyond us yet ourselves' "; that is, a credible representation of themselves. Section III asserts the value of a dissection, or analysis, of such an abstraction, "man number one," an idea of man, which Stevens also characterizes as "Man without variation," "Man in C Major," and "Man at his happier normal" (Poggioli, p. 174).[27] The source of the image in the third couplet, according to Stevens, is a custom in his native Pennsylvania of nailing up a hawk to frighten off other hawks (*LWS*, p. 359). Stevens explains the fourth couplet as follows: "This means to express man in the liveliness of lively experience, without pose; and to tick it, tock it etc. means to make an exact record of the liveliness of the occasion" (*LWS*, p. 783).

In IV "things as they are" changes from one meaning at the beginning of the section to another at the end. In the first line it is asked whether life may be equated with "things as they are" as it represents reality. The next two couplets question whether everyone can be confined to reality. Stevens comments on these lines, "It is not possible to confine all the world (everybody) to reality. They will pick beyond that one string merely by picking it into something different" (Poggioli, p. 175). Thus life as "It picks its way on the blue guitar" of the imagination (l. 2) is transformed by the feelings (l. 7), which will not allow of one static interpretation of reality. "In this poem," Stevens comments on the section, "reality changes into the imagination (under one's very eyes) as one experiences it, by reason of one's feelings about it" (*LWS*, p. 793). The last couplet answers the first by asserting that the idea of "things as they are" as shown in the intermediate couplets, cannot be confined to reality, but will be metamorphosed by the imagination, "This buzzing of the blue guitar."

Section V speaks directly of poetry and belief. The great poems are no longer meaningful to us except as poems. The poetry of old mythologies such as that of the Classical era, and, perhaps, of the medieval heaven of the *Paradiso*, like the noble horses of Plato (*NA*, pp. 3–5), move us as imaginative constructs but do not move us to faith (ll. 1–3). We live in a secular world (ll. 4–5) and we face reality without the mediation of a faith; hence, "The earth, for us, is flat and bare." We are in need of a poetry that moves us beyond the esthetic pleasure of its music to a point where it can take the place of faith. Poetry,

> Exceeding music must take the place
> Of empty heaven and its hymns.

We need a fiction credible to the present as is prescribed in "Owl's Clover" and the poems of *Ideas of Order*. Such a fiction will be based on a secular conception of man—"Ourselves in poetry"—instead of on a conception of god. Poems about ourselves must replace hymns to god. (See Stevens' comments on the section, *LWS*, p. 360.)

An adequate fiction will not distort the nature of reality (VI, ll. 1–2). Stevens' idea of the imagination is that like light, it adds nothing but only allows us to see more (*NA*, p. 61). Again, in the same essay, he notes that, "the imagination never brings anything into the world but that, on the contrary, like the personality of the poet in the act of creating, it is no more than a process" (*NA*, p. 59). The idea or version of man, first mentioned in I and developed in II and III, is conceived in the imagination as if it were in reality ("as if in space"); the imaginative version is based on the perception of reality, but is drawn from reality into the imagination: "Yet nothing changed, except the place." Since the conception is withdrawn from reality by the imagination, it is "beyond the compass of change" to which reality is subject. As such the fiction is "For a moment final," in the sense that poetic, or imaginative truth is final: it brings about that agreement with reality believed, for a time, to be true (NA, p. 54)—believed, that is, until the constant change of reality demands a new imaginative adjustment. This is the compensation of the imagination in an age—in Stevens' terms—of disbelief (NA, p. 171), when theology is "smoky dew," or inane. When this finality in the conjunction of the imagination and reality is brought about, a transformation takes place. It is no longer "as if" the imaginative construction were in "space," or reality, while it exists in the imagination. The distinction between the two terms disappears. Stevens summarizes by saying that "things imagined . . . become things as they are" (LWS, p. 360). The metamorphosis of the imagination becomes reality ("The tune is space") and the realm of the imagined and that of the real are identical (ll. 12–13). Thus the imagination brings about a transformation of reality in which the "senses"—by which Stevens means "an assembly of all possible senses: the totality of understanding" (Poggioli, p. 175)—are composed. The process described is like one of contemplation at the end of which reality is brought into intense rapport with the mind, in a state which bridges what Stevens has elsewhere described as "the dumbfoundering abyss/ Between us and the object" (CP, p. 437).

Human activities have to do with the sun, or reality (VII). The moon, or the imagination, is meaningless to that working world of reality, a sea, as in "The Comedian as the Letter C." If one were to exclude reality from one's work, the work would be abstracted from the life lived in reality, so that men would seem "Mechanical beetles never quite warm." One would not then, as one could when a sharer in reality, be able to call on the imagination, the moon, as a "merciful good" for relief from reality. (Literally, ll. 8–10 read: "could I then call on the sun, reality, the way I now call on the moon, the imagination, as an escape?") Such a state of mind, withdrawn from life, leaves the imagination cold; the speaker cannot approve of it and hopes not to fall into it. (See Stevens, *LWS*, p. 362.)

The first two couplets of VIII describe, according to Stevens, the morning after a storm (*LWS*, p. 783). The poet is "struggling" to express himself with regard to the scene he observes (ll. 5–8). Although he knows "that this poem . . . does little more than suggest the tumultuous brightness, the impassioned choirs, the gold shafts of the sun as the weather clears" (*LWS*, p. 791), it is "like the reason in a storm" (l. 10) in that it brings the chaos of the storm into significant rapport—"brings the storm to bear"—as distinguished from understanding it. His words "control" the storm "and bring it to bear: make use of it" (*LWS*, p. 783); the poem "puts it in the confines of focus" (*LWS*, p. 791).

Stevens begins his comment on IX by stating: "The imagination is not a free agent. It is not a faculty that functions spontaneously without references. In IX the reference is to environment" (*LWS*, p. 789). He goes on to explain that the overcast blue of the air here represents the environment, and the weather—of which, presumably, the air is to be considered an element—is "the stage on which, in this instance, the imagination plays." The guitar, then, is "described but difficult," the man "a shadow," and the tune as yet unmade, because the imaginative creation is here not clearly distinguished from the environment on which it depends. Thus the figure blends in with the background, and emerges from it like a thought from a mood, colored by that from which it emerges; "the color of the weather is the robe of the actor" (Poggioli, p. 176);[28] and the color of his background, as his environment, determines "half his gesture, half/ His speech," and the manner of his expression ("the dress of his meaning") which in this case is tragic. Stevens considered VIII and IX companion pieces in the first of which the imagination is comparatively passive in relation to the environment and, in the second, more dominating (*LWS*, pp. 362–63).

Section X begins with the raising of "reddest columns" and the tolling of bells because the occasion is a red letter day, the occasion of a parade, but the tone toward it seems to be derisive, as indicated, among other things, by the noise of tin in the second line, which Stevens paraphrases, "Fill the air with the banging of tin cans. Hollows = spaces" (*LWS*, p. 793). The papers thrown in the streets are "the wills/ Of the dead" possibly because the celebration of the hero betrays the dead and makes their wills worthless. For the rest of the poem, Stevens' explanation is adequate:

> If we are to think of a supreme fiction, instead of creating it, as the Greeks did, for example, in the form of a mythology, we might choose to create it in the image of a man: an agreed-on superman. He would not be the typical hero taking part in parades (columns red with red-fire, bells tolling, tin cans, confetti), in whom actually no one believes as a truly great man, but in whom everybody pretends to believe, someone completely outside of the intimacies of profound faith, a politician, a soldier, Harry Truman as god. *This second-rate creature is the adversary.* I address him but with hostility, hoo-ing the slick trombones. I deride & challenge him and the words hoo-ing the slick trombones express the derision & challenge. The pejorative sense of slick is obvious. I *imagine* that when I used the word hoo-ing I intended some similar pejorative connotation as, for example, booing or hooting. . . . The word back of it in my mind may have been hooting. Yet it may have been *hurrooing*, because the words that follow:
>
> Yet with a petty misery
> At heart, a petty misery
>
> mean that the cheap glory of the false hero, not a true man of the imagination, made me sick at heart. It is just that petty misery, repeated in the hearts of other men, that topples the worthless. I may have cried out Here am I and yet have stood by, unheard, hoo-ing the slick trombones, without worrying about my English. (*LWS*, p. 789.)

Section XI initially presents two versions of the effect of environment on life, neither of which is correct. The propositions may be stated as follows: "One becomes his environment—but the statement (chord) is wrong, for the environment becomes the person and overwhelms him." The first of these propositions is false in that it is too complacent, and the second is no better because it is excessively negative: "The discord merely magnifies." In both versions it is the consuming effect of the environment on life in the course of time that is being emphasized. ("Slowly the ivy on the stones/ Becomes the stones"). But more remote ("Deeper") in the gestating process ("the belly's dark") of time[29] may lie an era when life is nourished by reality rather than consumed by it ("time grows upon the rock"; Stevens glosses "time" to mean life, and "rock" to mean the world in this phrase, which he says looks forward "to an era when there will exist the supreme balance" between reality and the imagination—LWS, p. 363).

In section XII the poet begins by identifying himself with the blue guitar, by which we may take him to be at one with his imagination. He thus interprets the music of the orchestra in an imaginative way so that, as Stevens puts it, "The orchestra by the music it makes also makes one think of a multitude of shuffling men who are, in height, as high as the hall and who fill the hall with their forms" (LWS, p. 790). The sanction for such an imaginative conception of a multitude lies in the individual's resolution of the distinction between his ego and objective reality or, as the question is specifically put, "Where do I begin and end?" To what extent may the ego project itself upon reality? The answer to the problem is that in fact as the imagination operates ("As I strum the thing,") he perceives that which seems to be apart from the ego ("That which momentously declares// Itself not to be I") but which, like the tall men, is not part of reality and thus must be the product of the ego. That is, there is a realm which is neither that of the ego nor of reality, but in which the demarcation between ego and reality breaks down: the realm of the imagination. This section, in which the poet states at the outset that he is wholly identified with the imagination, is a demonstration of that realm. The tall men are purely products of the imagination, and what follows is a justification of such a projection. In "The Man with the Blue Guitar," as throughout Stevens, the relation between reality and imagination fluctuates; here the relation is entirely in favor of the imagination. "We live in the mind," as Stevens puts it in one of his essays (NA, p. 140); the mind is more or less in contact with reality, and it is not always bad for it to be less so.

Like the preceding poem, and in contrast to IX, section XIII presents the relation between imagination and reality as wholly favorable to the imagination. Stevens says of it that it "is a poem that deals with the intensity of the imagination unmodified by contacts with reality, if such a thing is possible" (LWS, p. 785). The "pale intrusions" into the blue of the imagination represent the invasion of the imagination by something of an alien nature, perhaps thought, perhaps experience. They may prove fruitful to the imagination as "blue buds" or, possibly, they may not as "pitchy blooms"; they may prove expansions of the imagination, or diffusions of it.[30] Whatever the nature of these intrusions, they are "corrupting" to the imagination. The artist is adequate as a pure, thoughtless ("unspotted imbecile"), focus of the imagination, and as such is a symbol of the imagination ("heraldic center of the world// Of blue"), which, as Mac Hammond has put it, is "enormously fat with potential"[31] ("sleek with a hundred chins"). Imaginative contemplation is a "revery" because it is in this case divorced from reality, like a dream. The "amorist Adjective" means blue, according to Stevens (LWS, p. 783). It is "aflame" because the blue of the imagination is here intensified until, as Stevens says, "intensity becomes something incandescent" (LWS, p. 785). The "Adjective" is qualified as "amorist" because at this intensity the imagination would be in sympathetic rapport with everything, and because, as Hi Simons says, the impulses of the imagination and love are loosely associated for Stevens.[32]

Stevens has glossed the first half of section XIV as the

coming of scientific enlightenment (*LWS*, p. 363), though the imagery seems derived from a seascape on a misty dawn. "One after another," he comments, the discoveries of the sciences "irradiate us and create the view of life that we are now taking." Each of these discoveries is both a star that shines with its own light and, possibly, a world in itself ("orb"). The abundance or "riches" of their luminous atmosphere is day, or enlightenment. The profusion of beams and of light is compared to a German chandelier which, in Stevens' words, is "oversized, overelaborate" (*LWS*, p. 783). It may be that this scientific enlightenment is "just a bit of German laboriousness. It may be that the little candle of the imagination is all we need" (*LWS*, p. 363). The imagination is sufficient to order the world and bring things into meaningful relation. Lines nine and ten indicate that the candle is not a real, physical light, but the light of the imagination. The candle, as opposed to the elaborate chandelier, brings imaginative order to the ordinary things it lights, as the light effects of chiaroscuro compose a painting (compare "Final Soliloquy of the Interior Paramour," *CP*, p. 524).

The first three lines of XV ask whether our society is in the state of dissolution reflected in the intentional deformation of reality in a Picasso painting. (The quoted phrase, "hoard/ Of destructions," is from a comment by Picasso in "Conversation with Picasso," published by Christian Zervos in *Cahiers d'Art*, VII–XX, 1935, 173: "Chez moi, un tableau est une somme de destructions.") The poet continues by asking whether he, as a member of his society, is deformed like the reality in the painting. "A naked egg" refers, perhaps, to a condition of pure potentiality, unformed by the forms of society which the poet here questions. Stevens writes of lines five and six, "the words Catching at Good-bye refer to a popular song entitled Good-bye, Good-bye Harvest Moon. I suppose I had in mind the way that particular line kept coming back to mind. . . . In line 5, harvest moon is, as I have just said, a part of the title of the song. But in line 6 the words harvest and moon refer to the actual harvest and the actual moon" (*LWS*, p. 783). Thus lines five and six may be taken to ask whether the poet as an individual in his society has been so deformed by the dissolution of the forms of the society that he can mechanically repeat the cheap lyrics about the harvest moon without being aware of the real harvest or the real moon. The formerly acceptable vision of social reality has been destroyed (l. 7); the poet asks if he has been destroyed in a corresponding way (l. 8). Has his sensibility been killed with regard to the food before him as it has been in the case of the harvest and the moon (ll. 9–10)? And does he sit at a feast which, like the former vision of social reality, is already stale? Is his thought merely the mechanical memory of stale perception, as in his recollection of the popular lyrics? Is the spot on the floor the spilt wine that is thus wasted or the spilt blood that drained his life? If either are his, the implication is that he is past revival.

Stevens says of the repetition of "but" in the first two couplets of XVI that "it implies a stubborn and constantly repeated rejection of the image of the earth as a mother" (Poggioli, p. 178). In the first three couplets, then, earth is seen as alien and oppressive to life. "To chop the sullen psaltery" means, according to Stevens, "to write poetry with difficulty, because of excess realism in life" (LWS, p. 360). To live on these terms is to live joylessly at odds with earth, or one's environment (ll. 7–8), in "war" that at best might accomplish material amelioration ("sewers," "electrify") of a difficulty that is spiritual ("Jerusalem," "nimbuses"). One disenchanted by these considerations ("You lovers that are bitter at heart"), might as well sacrifice any hoped for sweetness in life ("Place honey on the altars") and give up the "war" ("die") which on these terms is not worth fighting.

Stevens comments on the first two lines of XVII as follows: "Anima = animal = soul. The body has a shape, the soul does not" (Poggioli, p. 179). The soul is not such as "The angelic ones," the religious or spiritual ones, conceive it but, as Stevens goes on to say, "The soul is the animal of the body." That is to say, the conception of the soul is secular and based on the sensual nature of man. Through the imagination, or blue guitar, the animal tries to give a definite mould to itself; its claws propound on the guitar and it tries to articulate its situation on a desert that is secular and arid of religious myth. But, as Stevens' comment concludes, "Art deceives itself in thinking that it can give a final shape to the soul." Hence, "The blue guitar a mould? That shell?" The tune of the guitar can give a version of the soul only as the sound of the north wind manages to express the wind in the image of the worm, whose soundless composition is the final decomposition of all composers. (Compare Stevens, *LWS*, p. 360). That is, the tune of the guitar, the particular articulation of the soul, is transitory, not final.

Section XVIII is an important statement of the operation of the imaginative construction, here called a dream, elsewhere, a fiction. A fiction which is credible in face of reality and through which reality is interpreted, is no longer a fiction. That is to say, a myth which is believed in is not a myth; a myth is an archaic belief. Such a fiction becomes the version of reality as perceived—"things as they are." As a belief it is not held as an intellectual construction, but has a reality like that of the wind whose sensory presence is its only meaning ("wind-gloss"); or like dawn, whose light makes the cliffs rising from the sea seem without reality (*LWS*, p. 360), and the sea itself seem unreal ("a purely negative sea," a "realm of has-been without interest or provocativeness," as Stevens defines "a sea of ex"—*LWS*, p. 783), while one knows at the same time that they are in fact real.

The monster of section XIX represents nature, according to Stevens (*LWS*, p. 790), which he further defines as "the chaos and barbarism of reality" (Poggioli, p. 179), and which he wishes to "master, subjugate, acquire complete control over and use freely for my own purpose, as poet" (*LWS*, p. 790; there is a less careful, but parallel reading in a letter to Hi Simons, *LWS*, p. 360, in which the monster is identified as "life"). The poet desires to be more than a part of nature; he wants to be of the essence of nature "in the form of a man, with all the resources of nature" (*LWS*, p. 790; ll. 3-5). When he thus acquires control over nature so that all its resources are available to him, he wants to face nature as a poet and be its interpreter, or "its intelligence" (ll. 5–10). As such he will be the "equal in strength" (*LWS*, p. 790) of the monster he seeks to interpret, facing nature "the way two lions face one another" (*LWS*, p. 790): the lion of poetic interpretation ("of the lute"), and the lion of that which it interprets, and which is otherwise imprisoned in its own element, uninterpreted ("locked in stone"). Stevens sums up his comment by saying, "I want man's imagination to be completely adequate in the face of reality."

Section XX parallels to some extent section XVIII. Stevens says of it, "This stands for the search for a belief" (*LWS*, p. 793). Belief would not be a matter of holding an idea but would be a matter of more sympathetic rapport than the rapport with sensory life itself ("Friendlier than my only friend,/ Good air"), as it brings that sensory life into a sympathetic agreement with the ego. Belief, in fact, would be that agreement with life rather than an idea, would be "the mere joie de vivre" (*LWS*, p. 793). Since the passage is in the conditional, the guitar as the imagination is here in a condition of no belief and is therefore addressed as forlorn: "Poor pale, poor pale guitar . . ."

"The shadow of Chocorua" of section XXI, as in the poem "Chocorua to its Neighbor" (*CP*, p. 296), is one of those representative abstractions by which men conceive themselves and which take the place of the religious myth. Since it is a secular fiction it is not anthropomorphically supernatural ("not that gold self aloft"), but is a magnification of "One's self and the mountains of one's land." Stevens gives the information that Chocorua is a mountain in New Hampshire (*LWS*, p. 783), and comments on the passage, "The anthropomorphic can only yield in the end to anthropos: God must in the end, in the life of the mind, yield to man" (Poggioli, p. 180).

In section XXII the statement, "Poetry is the subject of the poem," derives from Stevens' conception of the poem as an esthetic abstraction with a reality of its own. Its subject matter is not reality or an imitation of it but an esthetic integration of "things as they are." The end of the poem is not imitation but poetry. Its perception of reality, or "absence in reality" ("absence" from its esthetic essence), provides the version of "things as they are" embodied in the esthetic integration. (Stevens says of this section that "I have in mind pure poetry," then goes on to add that "imagination has no source except in reality"—LWS, p. 364.) But immediately following this argument is the suggestion that the argument is sophistic (ll. 6–7). The poem's "absence," or perception of reality, is always an imaginative version of reality: perhaps it should not be considered separate from the poem's esthetic character. The poem's perception of reality, from which it gains its "true appearances," is at the same time the projection of an imaginative version of reality which amounts to metamorphosis; thus, "Perhaps it gives,/ In the universal intercourse," and thus the projective distortions of the fifth couplet. Section XXIII follows from this one. It consists of a series of contrasted terms, all of which parallel the basic opposition of "The imagined and the real," as it is put in the fifth couplet: "thought// And the truth," or "Dichtung und Wahrheit," poetry and the truth, the mortal ("the undertaker"), and the transcendent ("the voice/ In the clouds"). These terms are resolved because they are complementary and participate in a continual interchange, coming to progressively new adjustments to each other. This is "the universal intercourse" referred to in the preceding section.

The "poem like a missal found/ In the mud" (XXIV), specifies a poem that recites credible belief about reality ("the mud") as the prayers of the mass recite religious belief, that gives knowledgeably (in "latined," or learned phrase) a sharp vision of reality, and which may therefore be called a "hawk of life," a "hawk's eye" (compare LWS, pp. 783–84, 790). Stevens comments on lines 7–9: "The sort of scholar to whom one addresses oneself for all his latined learning finds in 'brooding-sight' a knowledge that seizes life, with joy in his eyes." The last line is explained as deriving from the poet's (player's) reticence to give any indication of meaning beyond what is expressed in the poem itself: he limits himself to playing his tune, to writing his poem for such a hawk-eyed scholar (*LWS*, pp. 360–61).

The personage of XXV is, according to Stevens, any observer (*LWS*, p. 790), but Stevens also says that his robes and symbols show that he is a great personage (*LWS*, p. 793); in an earlier gloss (*LWS*, p. 361) he identifies him as "the man of imagination" who moves the world though people do not realize this, and as the poet, who is "a comedian." Stevens further says of the passage: "A man who is master of the world balances it on his nose this way and that way and the spectators cry ai-yi-yi" (*LWS*, p. 784); he "revolves it to see it this way and that" (*LWS*, p. 793). What he finds in this examination is that the world is subject to change, evident in the metamorphoses of the seasons, of life, and of the cosmos (the "grass," the "cats," and the "worlds"); that, in short, "Everything revolves, goes through transformations. The grass revolves (the first meaning) and changes through the seasons (the second meaning)" (Poggioli, p. 181). Only the poet, who stands for the imagination, the master of transformation, the nose on which the world is flung, is eternal. The world "is fluid, its changes are like generations, but there is an eternal observer—man" (*LWS*, p. 793). The "fat thumb" of the last line represents, according to Stevens (*LWS*, p. 361), "stupid people at the spectacle of life, which they enjoy but do not understand."

Section XXVI deals with the changes wrought on reality by the imagination, in contrast with the preceding section, which deals with the changes of reality itself. Reality is here treated from the point of view of perception, so that it is seen as an abstraction in the mind: "The world washed in his imagination." It was "a bar in space," or "a sand-bar in a sea of space" (*LWS*, p. 784) on which his imagination washes and ebbs. Reality is the point of departure for the flights of the imagination, its "swarm of thoughts, the swarm of dreams/ Of inaccessible Utopia." Stevens comments: "Our imagination of or concerning the world so completely transformed it that, looking back at it, it was a true land's end, a relic of farewells" (*LWS*, p. 364). But reality is also the point

to which the imagination must return, and so it is described
as the "giant that fought/ Against the murderous alphabet";
that is, against words as a medium of the imagination. One of
the "adagia" is apposite: "The real is only the base. But it is
the base" (OP, p. 160). The "mountainous music" is a music
that accompanies these transformations of reality ("mountainous") as, perhaps, they are expressed in poetry which, like
the changes of the imagination, is not static, but seems always "To be falling and to be passing away." (Compare
LWS, p. 364.) Section XXVII shifts the balance in the
interchange between the imagination and reality in favor of
reality, and the juxtaposition of the two sections indicates
that the relation between the two may first be dominated by
one and then by the other (compare section XXIII, ll. 5–10).
Thus, for example, Stevens speaks in one of his essays of a
picture that is "wholly favorable to what is real" (NA, p. 12).
This section is like the first section of "The Comedian as the
Letter C" in its use of the sea to represent reality as it overwhelms the imagination. The sea here is not a real sea but
"the sea that the north wind makes," suggested by its sound
in the wintery scene: "The noise creates the image of the
sea" (Poggioli, p. 181). If the sea were not incomprehensible
the geographers and philosophers would be able to discover
definitions of it. But as it is, "The sea is a form of ridicule"
that satirizes the observer (or "demon"; see LWS, p. 790)
who does not accept the changes of reality as they occur, but
goes in search of them, goes on a quest for metamorphoses of
reality or tries to create them himself ("tours to shift"), when
all the while reality is itself changing ("the shifting scene";
compare LWS, p. 790). Thus the sea mocks the imagination
when the latter tries to project its metamorphoses onto it. It
eludes the formulations of the imagination and must be perceived in its reality: "Why traverse land and sea, when, if you
remain fixed, stay put, land and sea will come to you" (LWS,
p. 790). The "tours" or flights of the imagination are in this
case useless.

Section XVIII is the end point of all the formulations of
the poem, and is one of the major statements in Stevens'

work of his central concern: the discovery of a favorable adjustment to secular reality.

> I am a native in this world
> And think in it as a native thinks.

His thought drives constantly from the position described in the preceding section in which reality is a chaos inconceivable to man who is an alien in it, to a position in which man is brought into an agreement with reality through the imagination by means of a credible description of his relation with it. This section itself comprises such a description and is one of those imaginative constructions that mediate between man and reality which Stevens' theoretical formulations, as in this poem, attempt to define. The credible relation to reality, although it is created by the imagination, is not solipsistic, because the imagination must always adhere to reality (ll. 3–4; compare section XXVI). Reality, furthermore, provides in its cyclical changes constant points of reference, landmarks for the mind of the native: the mind may change, but the pattern of changes in reality are "fixed as a photograph" (ll. 7–10). In agreement with reality, one draws strength from it as a native from his soil (ll. 11–12). "Things are as I think they are" because they are things as perceived in, though not divorced from, reality, and expressed in the imaginative construction created by the blue guitar. "Gesu," in the second couplet, is not intended to be blasphemous; it perhaps is meant to lend the fervent tone of faith to the secular belief that is to replace religion. Stevens says of it, "it was just a word with that particular spelling that I wanted" (LWS, p. 784), possibly to ensure the soft "g" in its pronunciation as opposed to the possible "y" sound of "Jusu."

The subject of section XXIX is a speculation like one that might appear in "a lean Review." The speculation includes the second through the sixth couplets. In paraphrase it says that the delights of religious experience, or the " 'degustation,' " presumably of wine, in the vaults of the cathedral which opposes the past for the sake of present pleasure, balances the pleasure of the festival outside, with its " 'nuptial song,' " which is "a wedding with reality" (Poggioli, p. 182). The point of resolution in the search for the credible is a point of balance between possible attitudes, the spiritual and the earthy, each of which has its merits (ll. 7–8). Now one version of reality may seem credible, now another, in an "ancient argument" between reality and the evasions of it, between "external life" and "religious ceremonies and delights" (Poggioli, p. 182). The point of balance, the particular resolution, is never the same as reality itself (" 'the mask is strange' "), and is always changing (ll. 10–12). This argument is "like a comparison of masks" (Poggioli, p. 182) to choose the most appropriate (ll. 9–10). The comment on this speculation is that though the version of reality implied by the shapes and bells of the cathedral is wrong (ll. 13–14) for one who would read a Review in it ("I" of l. 1), the speculation ("fertile glass," or mirror of reality) it gives rise to is as fruitful as any that one of the faithful ("Franciscan don") might have there (ll. 15–16).

Stevens says about the first line of XXX that "The necessity is to evolve a man from modern life—from Oxidia, not Olympia, since Oxidia is our only Olympia" (Poggioli, p. 182). For the rest of the section his explanation is both full and adequate.

> Man, when regarded for a sufficient length of time, as an object of study, assumes the appearance of a property, as that word is used in the theatre or in a studio. He becomes, in short, one of the fantoccini of meditation or, as I have called him, "the old fantoche." . . . As we think about him, he tends to become abstract. We cannot think of him as originating in Oxidia. We go back to an ancestor who is abstract and being abstract, that is to say, unreal, finds it a simple matter to hang his coat upon the wind, like an actor who has been strutting and seeking to increase his importance through centuries, whom we find, suddenly and at last, actually and presently, to be an employe of the Oxidia Electric Light & Power Company. (*LWS*, p. 791.)

Of the line, "his eye// A-cock at the cross-piece on a pole," Stevens says: "man facing his particular job: in this case, an electric lineman" (Poggioli, p. 183). But in an earlier gloss (*LWS*, p. 362), Stevens identified "the old fantoche" as "a fantastic actor, poet, who seizes on the realism of a cross-piece on a pole (the way the nightingale, I suppose, pressed its breast against the cruel thorn)"—as the poet, in other words, deriving poetry from the banal. This would make the "fantoche" the poetic exponent—in both senses of the word—of common man. Stevens here includes a drawing of a smoke-stack with a lid on top (Poggioli, p. 183); it is this lid on which he comments:

> This is a dew-dapper clapper-trap. It goes up and down or is fixed at an angle. Dew-dapper is merely an adjective. Clapper refers to the noise as this opens and shuts. Obviously, not a modern piece of equipment. When flame pours out at white heat it looks dew-dapper [in the earlier gloss Stevens defined "dew-dapper" as "bright"].

> . . . if I am to 'evolve a man' in Oxidia and if Oxidia is the only possible Olympia, in any real sense, then Oxidia is that from which Olympia must come. Oxidia is both the seed and the amber-ember pod from which the seed of Olympia drops. The dingier the life the more lustrous the paradise. [This probably refers to the penultimate line: Oxidia is to Olympia as soot to fire; and the line probably is meant to indicate in addition that Oxidia is the grimy product of its industrial fires.] But, if the only paradise must be here and now, Oxidia is Olympia. (*LWS*, pp. 788–89).

With regard to the last line Stevens further says:

> These are opposites. Oxidia is the antipodes of Olympia. Oxidia (from Oxide) is the typical industrial suburb, stained and grim. (*LWS*, p. 790.)

This poem may be said to answer to the demand of section I for "A tune beyond us, yet ourselves/ . . . / Of things exactly as **they are**."

Section XXXI speaks of the reality of nature as opposed to that of modern civilization, the former represented by the sleeping pheasant and the latter by the employer and employee who contend while the pheasant sleeps, spring sparkles, and the cock-bird shrieks. The pheasant can sleep because he doesn't have to get up and go to work, but there is no place with the employer and employee for an absolute and idyllic conception of nature (ll. 8–10); the cock will serve only to awaken them for work. Neither is there place for a morning of sun; morning is a posture of the nerves in which a poet blunted by business civilization desperately grasps, or tries to grasp (*LWS*, p. 362), the nuances of poetry. His poetry must be of things as they are in this description of them: "this rhapsody or none."[33]

Section XXXII means that it is necessary to break through preconception in order to perceive the unpredictable variety of reality, "the madness of space." The use of the phrase "jocular procreations" for this variety indicates that it is the joyful fruit of life. One must throw away all preconceptions to gain progressively fresh perceptions of reality. To do this one must accept the direct response of the senses to the stimuli of the environment without the intervention of old definitions or, in fact, of any definitions (ll. 8–10). Thus the conception of the self to be taken in face of reality ("You as you are"), is that dictated by the direct response of perception: "You are yourself." To be oneself in this way, to allow oneself to be defined by one's spontaneous response to the "jocular procreations" of space is, Stevens observes (*LWS*, p. 364), to be such a "jocular procreation" oneself. This would be, Stevens continues, "the key to poetry, to the closed garden, if I may become rhapsodic about it, of the fountain of youth and life and renewal."

"That generation's dream" (XXXIII), probably the dream of the creative generation of 1910–1920, was "aviled" (degraded, violated) in the light of Monday's work-a-day world. The trouble with that generation's dream was that it was the only dream they knew: it was static and final. One must conceive the future not as the domination of one dream, which has proved unfeasible, but as the "wrangling" of two: one concerning the imagination, and one Monday's world. This will be the reality ("its actual stone") of time to come, and our portion ("bread") in it. We will accept that hard reality, and take in it what comfort we can. We will forget other concerns in our daily life, except on occasion, when we choose to indulge in the exercise of the imagination. So may this dream evade the "dirty light" of the work-a-day world, and still coexist with it.

"The Man on the Dump" (CP, p. 201)

The scene is that of nightfall. The setting sun with its colors, is like a basket of flowers, "a bouquet" placed on the horizon by the moon, which is "Blanche," white. The poet gloats ("Ho-ho") over the images to be found on the "dump" (such as the moon as "Blanche" and the sunset as "a bouquet"). The days themselves are like daily papers which bring their contents to the dump, including their daily sunset ("The bouquets"). The daily advent of the moon, as well as that of the sun, comes to the dump, along with the most ordinary things ("the janitor's poems/ Of every day"). These things come to the dump as our stale descriptions of them. Thus, the days come like old newspapers, and the rejected trash of the quotidian comes in terms of "the janitor's poems." The real, beyond stale descriptions of it, endures in its freshness. But even as one describes that reality it turns stale and literary. The "blowing of day," like a wind blowing, ever fresh as it passes (and perhaps also "blowing" in the sense of the blooming of day at dawn) may be described as comparable to a reading of Cornelius Nepos (a Roman historian of the first century B.C.) insofar as his style, presumably, conduces to a fresh and breezy reading. One may compose this or that metaphor in description of the day. The fact is that one's experience of the day is immediate and sensuous, not descriptive and literary. The images used to express this are concrete and sensuous, especially in comparison with the literary metaphor about Cornelius Nepos. How many men and women have copied the ephemeral freshness ("dew") of reality in order to make of it something decorative, merely pretty, something with which to adorn themselves? One grows tired of such artificiality except as it is rejected on the dump. Now, in the freshness of spring, with the flowers blooming, one feels, in that moment of the present between the stale past and our descriptions of the immediate moment which will soon become stale, the freshness of reality itself. As one feels "the purifying change" of season from the staleness of the old to the freshness of the new, so one feels the change from our stale images of reality to immediate perception of reality in the present moment, before one has a chance to make new images of that reality which will themselves become stale. One rejects "the trash" for reality itself. It is in that moment of the immediate present that one sees reality afresh. It is a quietly dramatic moment, as if accompanied by the music of bassoons, when one sees things as they actually are, and the music and moon rise also indicate a readiness for a new release of the imagination in description of a bare reality ("the elephant-colorings of tires"). One's images for things have been stripped away, and one sees the moon as the moon itself rather than in terms of metaphor like that of line two (the moon as the woman Blanche placing a basket of flowers); one sees things as a man rather than as a literary conception of a man ("an image of a man"), and the sky is empty of all descriptions of the sky. One keeps stubbornly making a point of the ordinary ("lard pail"), calling attention to it. It is that which one believes to be real, which one desires to approach. Could one, on the contrary, be trapped in solipsism? Could the real "Be merely oneself?" could the mind be projecting itself onto reality, making meanings of it as the ear makes meaning of a meaningless crow's call? Would the song of the nightingale have such an unpleasant effect on us as that of the crow (packing the heart, probably, with unpleasant feelings, and grating on the mind)? Would the ear choose such an ill-tempered bird as the crow, if it were in fact creating what it heard? Does one find peace and perfection ("philosopher's honeymoon") on the dump, and, since one does not, would the mind create such an imperfect reality for itself? One does not, conscious of all the trash rejected by reality, utter more sentimental trash that will in turn be rejected (*"aptest eve"*). One does not try to project mysterious and euphonious nonsense (*"invisible priest"*) onto reality in face of the unpleasant cries of the blackbirds ("blatter of grackles"). One does not "eject" the trash of stale images and "pull the day to pieces" to get at its reality while maintaining a precious estheticism (*"stanza my stone"*). How does one find one's way back to the place where one first heard about "the truth," here apposite with "The the," the predication of that which is, the particulars of reality itself.

"Connoisseur of Chaos" (*CP*, p. 215)

This poem makes use of a mock pedanticism which Stevens sometimes employs as a stratagem in his most logically discursive poems (compare, for example, "Extracts from Addresses to the Academy of Fine Ideas," *CP*, p. 252).

The poem begins with two paradoxical propositions. An order imposed on reality distorts it and thus is a "disorder" in that it denies the order of reality as it exists; on the other hand, "A great disorder" like the great disorder of reality, has an order inherent in itself, the order, simply, of that which is. The poem provides illustrations to the effect that the two initial propositions are actually different statements of the same idea.

The second section presents three seemingly paradoxical illustrations. The greenness of spring is blue, the color usually associated in Stevens with the imagination, because the burgeoning of spring stimulates the imagination, and it is also like a burgeoning of the imagination. This is followed by two apparent matters of fact which, in a parallel way, seem paradoxical. Since such paradoxes are merely verbal and in reality resolve into simple matters of fact—since, despite their seeming self contradiction, or disorderliness, in life such things go on as a matter of routine, there must be, in reality, as opposed to the mind's impositions on it, a law by which opposites are dialectical and resolve into "essential unity." Such a law is pleasant to contemplate, esthetically pleasant in the same way as is a particular in a painting. (Jean Hippolyte Marchand, 1883–1941, was a painter, lithographer, and illustrator who did illustrations for books by Valéry, Claudel, and Jammes.)

The third section begins with the old religious rationale for such unity, but considered only as a dead option. Life and death were a "pretty contrast," esthetically pleasant, when they could be resolved in the idea of god and its corollary idea of immortality. But the facts of contemporary life are too difficult to be handled by a closed, rigid mentality ("squamous," covered with scales, sometimes with reference to a kind of armor and, also, part of the bone structure of the temple), especially such a rigid religious mentality as the "bishops" might exemplify. And yet, beyond the comprehending mind, relation between such opposites as life and death—that is, order—does make itself felt, ephemerally, ambiguously, but with expanding relevance.

Section four works variations on the initial propositions. An old order, like that of the "bishops' books," is an imposition on reality that distorts it. However, this, though true, is trivial, since it is just one fact among all the unrelated facts of which reality consists. B also returns to the initial proposition B. The facts of the weather, the seasons, comprise a great disorder. Should this disorder of the weather, the seasonal cycle, this natural disorder ever become fixed in a stable, powerful, old order ("Plantagenet"), it would be a violent order, and thus would be a disorder of reality as it is. This leads back to the initial statement of B: reality as it is in itself comprises an order; which in turn is to say that any imposition on that order of things as they are would be a violent order and therefore disorder, part of the great disorder which is an order. Thus A and B, as was stated at the outset, are one. These ideas are not meant for academic consideration, like objects in a museum. They are meant for the thoughtful man in his everyday life ("chalked/ On the sidewalk") to help him resolve the problems of that life, such as the opposites, life and death, considered in nonreligious terms. The man who takes thought (section V) can see unity in the complexities of reality.

"The Sense of the Sleight-of-hand Man" (CP, p. 222)

The felicitous spiritual events in one's life occur fortuitously ("Occur as they occur"). Felicitous events also occur fortuitously in nature, such as the chance composition of clouds, houses, and rhododendrons, or as the way the clouds change, shape and color as the wind contorts them in the sky. Nature is in this sense a sleight-of-hand man, bringing things about that one least expects. Who could have predicted the movement of the bluejay? In a parallel manner, the poet here improvises metaphors to describe nature: sun rays become spokes of a wheel. The reality of the sun, here captured in the improvised metaphor of the wheel, outlives man's myths about it—the myths die, but the sun keeps rolling around again; and, in another improvised metaphor for the sun, the "fire eye" outlives the gods men derive from it. The poet shifts by association with the word "eye" to another improvised metaphor. As with nature, so with the mind; the operation of the imagination is fortuitous and unpredictable —its metaphors, for the pink-eyed dove and pines that make wind sounds like cornets, the imaginary island, occur as they occur. It may be, therefore, that only "the ignorant man," whose mind works without preconception and without premeditation, thus in a way parallel to nature's operation, in a natural way—it may be that only a man with such a mind can apprehend nature in such a way as to become one with it, "to mate his life with life," that life of nature which is "sensual" and beyond the mind, therefore unavailable to systematic thought or intellectual preconception. (The realm of nature is to be joined as a "pearly spouse," in a sensual marriage, not in theory.) The "life" of nature is, even in winter when most barren and static, "fluent" like the mind of the poet in this poem which flows from one improvised and unexpected image to another in order to capture it.

"Of Modern Poetry" (*CP*, p. 239)

Modern poetry concerns itself with the mind as the mind tries to discover belief that will enable it to confront the contemporary world.[34] Playing on the word "act" in the first line, the poem goes on to develop the metaphor of a play. When the world we know was based on stable tradition, the mind did not have to search for belief: since the culture was stable, one merely had to repeat what was known. But then the whole situation changed and the traditional past became nothing more than a memory, a memento of a time gone by ("souvenir"). Modern poetry cannot be of that dead past, but rather must be of the present, "living." It has to speak to the people of the present in their own language; it has to meet their needs; it has to consider such things as war, and discover how the mind can confront them. Since the historical environment, the "theatre," has changed, the imagination must find a new artistic vehicle to contain our modern experience, poetry must "construct a new stage" within the "theatre" of our environment. On that stage, in that art, poetry must be like an actor whose impulse to act can never be satisfied; here, however, the act is that of the mind as it continually meditates the words which are an exact expression of the mind, words which have the right sound to the "ear of the mind," and which compose, therefore, apt modern poetry. The "invisible audience" of contemporaries should, in fact, find such poetry so apt that it will seem, in listening to it, that it is listening to itself. In creating through his expression the perfect expression of his audience, the poet unites their feeling with his and the feelings of both become identical. The "actor" is the imagination, thinking like a "metaphysician" in "the dark" of the mind, a metaphysician who transforms the content of his mind into the imaginative expression of poetry; he gives this content the "sudden rightness" of art which is a perfect expression of his mind, "wholly/ Containing" it at a level of aptness beneath which poetry cannot afford to sink and above which it has no need to rise. Poetry must in this way satisfy the mind in the poem, and in doing this the subject is a secondary consideration: it may be of any ordinary, everyday activity; essentially it will not be a poem about a given subject, but one that is concerned with the operation of the mind as it seeks to confront the circumstances of contemporary reality.

"Asides on the Oboe" (CP, p. 250)

"The prologues are over," states the prologue to this poem. There must be an end to tentative formulations of belief; one must choose "final belief." This being so, the poet proposes "that final belief/ Must be in a fiction."

The first section begins by elaborating on why there is a need to choose "final belief." The old beliefs are dead: the ancient myth of the underworld is "obsolete" ("the wide river," Styx, separating life from death in the "empty land" populated only by shades); Boucher de Perthes, the nineteenth century archeologist, in investigating the prehistoric origins of man, killed the gods of our myths of genesis; our past beliefs, embodied in graven images, have been destroyed by time. We are left with the idea of the "philosophers' man," the ideal of the philosophers as one who understands everything, and understands in human rather than in religious terms. This mythic figure alone is still fresh and real to us ("walks in dew"); he meditates pure thoughts which are nourishment to us ("mutters milky lines"), the "imagery" of a myth pure of time's corruption ("immaculate") in which we can still believe. If one's image of man, as expressed in art (as in music on the oboe), describes man as inadequate, as unable to replace the dead gods, as imperfect however god-like ("naked, tall"), there still remains the tantalizing possibility ("impossible possible") of an ideal projection of man, "who has had the time to think enough" to understand and explain the human condition. He would be the man who would stand as the central ideal for all men, self-contained like a globe, in whom all men would be reflected and who, in the reflections he gave back would answer our questions about ourselves. Thus he is "the man of glass," who in his complex reflections, as "in a million diamonds," explains us to ourselves ("sums us up").

The philosophers' man (section II) is described as a "transparence" because, though not real, invisible, he makes things clear; that clarity, in which our questions are answered, pacifies us. He is the spirit of a place, its image, its imaginary projection ("the transparence of the place in which/ He is") and as such, he is that imaginative element of a thing which allows us to fully realize its nature. Thus the philosophers' man takes the season of later summer, nondescript, unspecific, like, presumably, a "peddler's pie," and gives it an imaginative identity, that of August. He specifies it with a particular image of August. He is "cold and numbered" because he is an abstraction, an imaginative projection, unreal, though with an effect on reality ("numbered," as if he were composed of numbers, like an abstract formula). Thus we are provoked to imagine romantic rendezvous, because August suggests itself to us as a season for love ("his cuckoos call").

The catastrophe of war (section III) prevented us from regarding the world as an essentially pleasant and peaceful place (jasmine scented; the poem was first published in 1940 —jasmine is a tropical and semi-tropical plant, but "jasmine islands" probably do not refer to any particular battle grounds of World War II). If we did not then find peace through the philosophers' man, we found a true understanding of man, "the sum of men." If we saw life stripped of our illusions about it ("the central evil"), we at the same time saw life as it really is ("the central good"). Thus we accepted death without our old illusions ("without jasmine crowns") that made it seem consolingly less evil than it actually is. Our image of man as seen through "the central man," the philosophers' man, was stripped of all illusions; therefore there was nothing that the philosophers' man "did not suffer"—and since he is nothing more than our imaginative projection of ourselves, his suffering is our suffering.

Our old illusions never returned, but instead we now accepted an image of man that mirrored the human, that was totally a reflection of man himself rather than an image partly derived from some myth of the super human. Thus as we united with an image that derived wholly from ourselves, we became "wholly one." It was in this image of man that we mourned for the dead, "those buried in their blood," those buried in the sole reality of their flesh and blood rather than in terms of a myth which makes a distinction between the body and a soul that outlives the body: this despite the fact that we were still haunted by nostalgia for our old illusions ("jasmine haunted"). We finally came to know the "glass man," the image of ourselves which is totally a reflection of ourselves rather than an image of ourselves derived from reference to something beyond the human. Thus the "glass man" is sufficient in himself as a reflection of humanity and needs no "external reference."

"Extracts from Addresses to the Academy of Fine Ideas" (CP, p. 252)

Part I begins by making a comparison between the artificial and the natural, between the paper rose and the real rose. "That states the point"; that is, that establishes the subject at hand: the distinction between the artificial world of the mind and the real world of nature. As if in a lecture at an academy, the poet goes on to state that the world we know is an artificial one. Since what we know of the world we can know only through the mind, the rose we know is of the nature of the mind, or artificial. The sea to us is simply the words through which we conceive it, the sky is just a list of words we use to describe it, the mountains are like paintings or descriptions of mountains. The real rose, natural reality, belongs, on the other hand, to those who do not perceive the world through the mind, who are naked to reality, innocent of any intervention of the intellect. (Compare "The Sense of the Sleight-of-hand Man," CP, p. 222: "It may be that the ignorant man, alone,/ Has any chance to mate his life with life.") Such people would resemble Adam and Eve in their agreeable climate, naked in their "covert," in their sheltered refuge, innocent of their nakedness (clean of "the lascivious poisons"). In such a state of innocence we would not have knowledge of nakedness "as part/ Of reality," nor would we have knowledge of reality itself; rather, we would be beyond such knowledge—we would be united with reality, in fact part of it, "part of a land beyond the mind." But this is put as a mere rhetorical question. For the mind to bypass itself and accept reality beyond the mind, the "Rain," as such, would be "unbearable tyranny." Thus, in practice, we live in an artificial world. The "eye" of the sun reveals to us only imaginary things ("a monster-maker"), shapes that have merely visual reality as in a painting, "paper things." In our experience, the distinction between the artificial and the real, the "false and true," collapses: they "are one."

Part II takes up the argument of the last part of I, and elaborates on it. The eye believes that what it sees is real, and in that belief seems to unite with reality, participate in "communion" with it. But the mind (here the "spirit," probably from the French "esprit," which means both) knows that visual reality is artificial, and therefore "The spirit laughs." The speaker elaborates on this proposition in the mock pedantic tone Stevens sometimes uses for the discursive arguments in his poems (see, for example, "Connoisseur of Chaos," CP, p. 215), addressing "the Secretary for Porcelain" as one concerned with the artificial. Evil considered imaginatively ("made magic"), as for example in tragedy, an imaginary construct in which evil culminates in the "catastrophe," if the catastrophe is well made ("neatly glazed"), becomes elegant, esthetically pleasing (as the fruit presented to royalty would have to be), a good. Evil, from an esthetic point of view, becomes good; and since good, in this sense, is created by evil, it is "evil's last invention," last because furthest removed from its own nature. The tragic poet (the "maker of catastrophe") invents the point of view, "the eye," through which evil events are made to seem good. The thing seen depends on the way it is seen.

Evil laughs cynically at its illusory inventions of good ("ricanery," from the French "ricaner," to snicker). Generalizations about death ("ten thousand deaths"; compare II, l. 10) that allow one to give it such an esthetic veneer, are evil, the invention of evil. One must accept the evil that comes to one ("Be tranquil in your wounds"); that death is good which is accepted and therefore does away with illusory rationalizations about death ("evil death"). One will be more reconciled to death ("The placating star/ Shall be the gentler") if one accepts its fact, and the philosophers, though helpless to do anything about death, say things that are still consoling—such as, perhaps, the idea that life has its times of ripeness and fulfillment ("the reddened flower, the erotic bird").

"The lean cats of the arches of the churches" are priests, (part III), "lean" because ascetic, other-worldly. The "old world" (European, Catholic, pre-modern) was the priests' domain, but in the new world (American, Protestant, modern) all men have a direct relation to whatever divinity may exist; all are priests. They preach a gospel not yet formulated because a description of the time and place to which it must pertain is not yet formulated. If only they could formulate their different ideas into one representative idea, symbolized by one religious figure: a "queen" who, like the Virgin, would be an "intercessor" for man with the divine by virtue of her innate relation ("rapport") with both man and god; or a "king," a deity ("*roi tonnerre*," king of thunder) whose existence would be intensely real to the imagination ("dark blue," intensely imagined, in terms of Stevens' characteristic association of blue with imagination), whose worthiness, like a god's, would be in his mere existence. But such a being cannot be successfully formulated—thus he is referred to as

"Panjandrum," which is a mock title for an exalted personage. Perhaps the very fact that there are many such ideas held together in the relativist consciousness destroys the possibility for one to exist in sovereign exclusion of the others. Perhaps the sovereign idea of the single divinity, "the single man," is killed because he is not sufficient for the multitudes; perhaps he represents spiritual starvation ("starvation's head") because the old bread and wine of one belief in Christian communion is not adequate to the demands of modern relativism. The priests of the old world are thus "lean cats" also because they hunger for an inadequate god. They fit into a picture of the world supposedly designed by god ("X") in which they feel comfortable ("Bask") and which gives them a sense of clarity, understanding ("feel transparent"). They know where they fit into the picture and this security allows them to bear cheerfully what little they do not understand ("beyond/ Themselves"), and which they fit into the picture in any case, through theological rationalization, "the slightly unjust drawing that is/ Their genius": imperfection is merely an error in the constitution of the temporal world, "exquisite" because it fits into their divine picture of things. This is another example, then, of the process described in part II, by which evil is transformed into illusory good.

At first the lake seems to the subject of part IV something general, indefinite. But while the scene in winter had seemed thus vague ("an empty place"), in early spring, it seems more particularized ("the empty place"). The "difference between the and an" is the difference between the particular and the general and, since no man's experience is general, the "difference between himself and no man." Since in winter he had experienced the scene as something unspecific, it was as if in winter he had suffered a loss of his particular self (IV, l. 12). Because of his curiosity to see the specific place again, it is time to regain that self, to make his experience particular. He wants to see whether the scene, despite its barrenness, is nevertheless particular enough to differentiate his experience of it from experience in general, enough to make the difference between himself and no man. If, when he looks at the lake, he can see the water spray into the air ("ran up the air") or break against the broken ice, it will mean that the snow and ice which had blanketed everything with the generality of winter has broken up into the particulars of spring. His experience of the scene would no longer be general, or abstract, but particular, specific, and he would become his particular self again. He would have broken through from the abstract to the real and, in so doing, have realized himself. This confrontation with reality as an actual good is in contrast with that transformation of reality into an illusory good described in II and III.

The process in which ideas are accepted and rejected (part V) is not orderly but chaotic, involving improvisation and change. "Ideas are men" in that they have existence only in the minds of men. Therefore the totality ("mass") of meaning is equivalent to the totality of men. But chaos is not the totality of meaning; rather it is the competition of ideas held by whatever number of men. These ideas fight for general acceptance until one gains such acceptance. Then the ideological chaos which had obtained gives way to order. The accepted idea orders or harmonizes, through art, the meaning of reality (an "agreement between himself and night") and men's belief in relation to itself, having effect far beyond that of reputed art dealing with sentimental trivia. The agreement with reality expressed in such art reconciles us with reality —it is the expression, through art ("music") of what men believe ("the mass of meaning"). It is "singular" because it is apparently paradoxical that, though our life is of the body, we should desire so warmly an abstract idea, that we should constantly search for that idea expressed in art ("that right sound"), the imaginative expression of what we believe. Thus the poem moves from confrontation with a particular good in reality in IV, to the possibility of general belief which will reconcile us with reality as a whole.

Part VI begins by considering the possibility of systematic thought that might arrive at such general belief. "Ercole" is Italian for Hercules. Systematic thought is represented here as a kind of misguided Hercules, wasting a powerful physical being ("skin and spine and hair"), thinking in a "cavern," isolated from life, oriented to death. Another kind of thought, however, is oriented to life. This is a kind of thought which, rather than trying to establish an abstract system, aims at satisfying the needs of the mind as it confronts life. The mind is like a poem, requiring affective resolutions rather than resolutions in abstract, systematic thought. It is the "ultimate poem" because it contains that which all the resolutions of poetry are directed toward resolving, our experience of life itself. This statement is tentatively qualified so that the "ultimate poem" concerns not merely the mind in isolation, but the mind in relation to reality ("half earth"), our daily experience, which comprises the only Elysia we will ever know; it is reality ("Half sun"), and our thought about reality ("half thinking of the sun"); it is half "sky" (another synecdoche for the real,) and half our desire to retreat into the mind.

This other mode of thinking, in contrast with systematic thinking, has happiness as its end and is necessary for happiness ("They had to think it to be"). This kind of thought is not concerned with distinguishing the real from the imagined, as systematic thought might be; on the contrary, it wants to unite the two, the mind with reality. For the additions which the imagination makes to reality, "the images we make of it," are the means by which we "think" our way to happiness, knowing that to attain happiness the mind must be satisfied by such images. In other words, it is not the philosophical nature of reality that is important, but the psychological question of a happy relation of the mind to reality which must be achieved through the imagination, rather than through systematic thought. The analytic distinction between mind and reality is secondary to this, must wait until the "mind is satisfied." From time to time "the redeeming thought" that satisfies the mind comes to us; it is not thought out but comes in the course of time when we are least capable of systematic thought ("sleepy mid-days"), and it is too indefinite for intellectual expression. It is not a "thought" in the ordinary sense at all, but a felt relation of the ego with reality.

Part VII pursues the argument. To satisfy the ego in such a relation with reality as is sketched in VI, is "as much belief as we may have." Such belief will resist our relativistic knowledge of the failure of past belief ("each past apocalypse"), will allow us to reject yearnings for more remote, exotic belief ("Ceylon"); it will satisfy the mind with its description of reality so that belief will require nothing further from reality, "the sea," which then becomes like a beauty to be enjoyed ("*la belle/ Aux crinolines*"); and thus there will be no "mad mountains" that do not seem to fit into the picture of the world that our belief gives us. It is not the nature of reality that matters, but what one believes about it. Stevens seems to speak of belief here in the sense that a fish believes in water; that is, as an ideal adjustment of the self to its environment, "one's element," in exhilarated unions, fortuitous "reunions," meditated "surrenders" of the self to the real. Belief through which we may in this way relate to reality, feeling oneself a part of that reality, is all the belief we need. If one were then suddenly transferred to another reality to which one were totally unadjusted, one would be overwhelmed by it, "Incapable of belief." And, on the contrary, the slightest perception of the reality to which one was adjusted would be sufficient, without any need of illusion, to orient the world around one's belief.

"We live in a camp" (part VIII), in that our life is an impermanent abode, and is like a concentration camp in which we are destined to die. Within this fact of impermanence the only "final peace" lies in what the feelings can make of our condition, in what remains to the heart, "the heart's residuum." So be it. But if the opposite were true, could we thus ratify the situation with an "amen"? If we lived in permanence, as in the permanence of life after death, the evil we experience would never die; we would be fated to outlive every mortal wound since we would be unable to die "a second death." The only ultimate end to evil, which is part of life, is death. Yet if there is no resolution to evil but only the escape of death, if "evil never ends," if after death we lie "in evil earth," then death is really not an escape from evil—death, as a permanence, simply emphasizes the permanence of evil, for after death, we cannot die again. Neither immortality nor mortality, then, gives "final peace." Imaginative expressions ("chants," "stanzas") of belief are our resort, expressions that grow out of our feelings ("the heart's residuum") about our life. But how can we create such expressions ("How can/ We chant") in face of unending evil? Earth is not "evil earth"; rather, in the dissolution that occurs after death it "dissolves/ Its evil." If earth dissolves evil after death, it must dissolve it while we are alive. It is that dissolution of evil in life that is the motive for poetry; this is the "acutest end" of poetry. We must find in our feeling the poetry for a statement which can confront our experience, all we know ("Equal to memory"), a statement which, as in poetry, is "vital" because it is dictated by feeling. The final couplet is an example, giving the doomed soldiers as a metaphor for our fate, yet making the fate seem noble.

"Dutch Graves in Bucks County" (CP, p. 290)

This poem resembles a march of time in the on-going present of the living, counterpointed by the static past of the dead from which time continually breaks.

The horde of the living swarms through the poet's imagination, figured in the metaphor of an army in the sky. The wheels of their machines are unreal, therefore silent, too large for sound, since the army represents the imagined totality of the living. As the poet imagines them, he also imagines the dead in the grave yard, his "semblables" (fellow, counterpart, reminiscent of Baudelaire's "Au Lecteur"—Stevens' father was born in Bucks County, Pennsylvania, and was of Dutch descent; Stevens was German, or "Pennsylvania Dutch" on the maternal, Zeller, side. Stevens himself was a native not of Bucks, but of nearby Berks County. See Stevens' account of a visit to the old Zeller home and to a similar, but Pennsylvania Dutch, grave yard, NA, p. 99–102, apparently made considerably after the poem's composition). They, skeletons residing in the darkness ("sooty") of the grave, tap out the beat of death which is the ultimate measure of life. The living are at large, "marching" through the on-going present of time, while the dead Dutch have as dominion only the "tiny darkness" of the grave. From the living's preparation for the conflict of life there is a sense of an expected pronouncement, one that will come out of the conflict itself, some rumor that will be expressive of the living ("expressive on-dit"), a "profession" of belief, a statement of self-definition. In contrast with this activity, the dead seem doubly dead, to have been buried in so unproductive a place.

The flags of the living, in contrast with "the old flag of Holland" in the grave (refrain 2), are symbols of new self-discovery. The living grow more acute in their aims as they live ("Rifles grow sharper on the sight"; less likely, the rifles become more sharply visible). Their marching is "autumnal" because like an army they march toward death, as autumn moves toward the seasonal death of winter. There is no comfort and no relief from this fate, since the latter, as a "desperado," one without hope, leaves no escape from death for those alive in the present. The dead, however, exist only as remains in the dead past of which they were part.

Though the call to the life struggle (drums and bugles) is strong, there is a force that is even stronger and that will make its claim with the power of an instinct. The dead know nothing of our instincts, since the total of their memory includes nothing which happened after their death. This instinct tells us that all life ends in death ("a merciless triumph"), that in death the evil of life ends (which is its "profounder logic") in peace that is more than temporary "refuge" because it is absolute and permanent; because death ends evil it is an instinctual end ("will") of all men when life, in its progress toward death, is exhausted. The dead, who know nothing of the present, know therefore that the past is not part of it: their end has been absolute ("Gaffer" is an old term of respect like "goodman"; "green" because of the grass which now, in a sense, clothes the venerable dead.) Others, from earliest history ("early children," with the suggestion, also, of primitive innocence), and those who have come more lately and who have no sense of their destiny ("wanderers"), have struggled into existence like the sun slipping under the barbed fence of night at dawn, and year after year have always been defeated by death and lost in oblivion. While this has always been so, the dead know, since they know the finality of death, that the present is not continuous with the past of those others who came earlier, that their death cuts us off from their experience. The present does not consist of these old, "rusted armies"; the present is immediate and vital, composed of the struggle of the living to win their heritage in defiance of the past, in defiance of the wishes of the dead who have come before ("torn-up testaments"). The dead know that those who inherit them are not their children, have no connection with their selves, because they have been absolutely cut off from them by their death.

Who are these old "cronies" (derived from the Greek *chronios*, contemporary) who mutter to one another, unnatural people grown old and gaunt, wild ("haggard") in their fervor for past thought? Why are they so concerned with this dry, arid ("crackling") dialogue that is of the mind merely, academic, unconnected with our lives? The voices in such a dialogue speak timidly, inconsequentially ("pitter-patter") of old freedom, of every kind of freedom except freedom in the vital present, our own freedom. The old Dutch of Pennsylvania, by contrast, were not emotionless and timid, nor disconnected from their own lives. Freedom does not lie in concerning oneself with the past but in cutting oneself off from it, "Each night," incessantly, by destroying freedom which is no longer appropriate to the present, and which therefore can only be a kind of bondage. It is in its exercise of liberation from the past that freedom grows acute ("whose knife/ Grows sharp in blood"). The armies of the living, in freeing the present from the past, must in effect free it from themselves, must "kill themselves," but in so doing release the present from a past no longer appropriate ("an ancient evil dies"). This is the "incorrigible tragedy" of the present, that in order to remain present, it must destroy itself. The dead of the Dutch grave yard, whose "glory" when they were alive was that of "heaven in the wilderness" of Pennsylvania, are now insensate witnesses to the fact that the present brings a new ideal, "a new glory of new men."

One may not even die peacefully in the knowledge of having perfected an ideal that will endure; on the contrary, one is tormented by the idea that those living in a new present will "Avoid our stale perfections," using what is left of ours for their own ends, seeking their own perfections. For the stars of the present are not relevant to the dead imaginary beings ("chimeres"), but to the living present "of those alive." The living who people the present ("Under the arches, over the arches" of the sky), on the edge of future death ("autumnal horizon"), march through segments of a chaos which, since it is reality itself, is "more than an order"—toward an ideal that will be an expression of their particular generation, "a generation's centre." The fact that the dead can so subtly bear witness to the effects of time in sustaining a living present shows both that time was not wasted on the dead, and that the differences that time has wrought were not made too difficult for them to track down.

"No Possum, No Sop, No Taters" (CP, p. 293)

As the title indicates, the poem presents a barren landscape. The sun is not only absent but seems as if it belonged to another realm all together. The scene is frozen, dead; "Bad" seems final because the scene is static, frozen, as if it will never change. Appropriately, therefore, the remnants of dead vegetation suggest images of impotence, incapability: "arms without hands," "trunks// Without legs," "without heads," heads whose tongues are incapable of expressing their anguish. As the stalks suggest the failure of speech, the snow suggests the failure of sight (in language that calls up the pertinent feeling of Nashe's "Brightness falls from the air").

Even the dead leaves "hop," as though lame or crippled. The
sky, hard as if frozen, the stalks rooted in ice, emphasize the
fixity of the scene. One single sound, composed of the stupid
("gawky"), inconsequential sounds in the landscape—the
"savagest hollow" of the wind as it sweeps across the scene
—expresses its monolithic barrenness. It is in a "bad" so
extreme that we can know the "good" at its most absolute,
stripped of all inessentials ("last purity"): that all things are
destroyed, as in the cyclic death of the seasons in the present
scene, that even the "bad" of this season will be destroyed
by that cyclic change. In tone with the rest of the scene, the
crow seems accustomed to stasis, he "looks rusty as he rises
up." But the "malice in his eye" seems vivid, alive. He seems
to represent the necessary destructive principle that motivates
seasonal change, and therefore, in sympathy, "One joins
him," but only "at a distance," out of caution and distaste.

"So-And-So Reclining on Her Couch" (CP, p. 295)

This is one of Stevens' funnier poems. The poet describes
himself in process of painting a figure with words, as though
on canvas, to illustrate his idea. Thus the figure is both a
functional "mechanism," and an "apparition," something
that has suddenly materialized. It is a hypothesis: "Projection
A." The figure is without context ("floats in air"), on a canvas, "at the level of/ The eye," without name, and without
meaning except for the sensuous one expressed by "the curv-
ing of her hip." She is so freshly imagined that the paint is
still wet, indicating her total innocence ("Eyes dripping
blue"). If one placed above her head an old crown artfully
painted into the picture ("practic," in an obsolete usage,
means artful, a usage here suggested by the archaicized spelling), suspended as if in three dimensions by the artist, that
suspension, apparently indicating a magical or miraculous
phenomenon, would represent on the part of the artist a
"gesture," an expression of meaning regarding the figure, "in-

visible" because the hand that made the gesture, painted it in, is now removed. This gesture is the second hypothesis, B. If one could get at one's meaning without such "gestures" to represent it, as philosophy might, one could get at it as pure idea. This figure, incomplete as a work of art, half conception, half execution, fluctuates in the contention between seeing meaning in the object or in an idea of the object, between "idea as thing," or "thing as idea," in the dispute between philosophical realism and nominalism. The figure, only half executed, is still tangibly half the idea of the artist: this is the final hypothesis concerning the figure. It represents "the desire of/ The artist." However one does not place confidence in the obviously artificial but in the real, "what has no/ Concealed creator." One does not accept the world as the representation of an idea, but as the thing in itself, the "unpainted shore" rather than the artificially created sculpture. It is the thing itself rather than the idea of the thing that has reality. In a final stroke the poet, by naming the figure, makes of it such a real thing, a real woman in our ordinary world rather than an artificial entity, a mysterious gesture. He makes of the painting (and the poem) a completed work, by dismissing her, the demonstration being over, as one might dismiss a real model into the world of the nonphilosophical real.

"Esthétique du Mal" (CP, p. 313)

"Esthétique du Mal" is written, for the most part, in loose blank verse whose chief irregularities are a high degree of anapestic substitution and the inclusion of extra unaccented syllables before the caesura and line end. It includes fifteen sections of more than twenty lines each, in some of which the pentameter is arranged in various stanza forms. It is Stevens' major attempt to discover a tenable attitude in face of the evils inherent in life without the consolations of supernatural belief.

The poem begins with a description of an attempt to achieve what is the poem's general intention; that is, as the title implies, to come to terms with evil through the imagination. (Stevens says that he was thinking of esthetics in connection with the poem "as the equivalent of aperçus [sic], which seems to have been the original meaning," LWS, p. 469, so that the title might also be interpreted to mean a view of evil.) Thus the personage in Naples tries to make use of a treatise on the sublime (whether Longinus or not seems irrelevant) in order to describe the eruptions of Vesuvius as a metaphor for pain. But his description falsifies. The rhetoric he applies does not come out of his own experience, and his description of the volcano as an epitome of pain is a mere trick of fancy that does not adhere to reality. He can describe the sound because it is old and descriptive phrases for it have already been invented. Pain is real only as it is registered on the nerves, but his own nerves are attuned to the comforts amidst which he speculates: "It was almost time for lunch. Pain is human./ There were roses in the cool café." He is not willing to face the reality of pain: "His book/ Made sure of the most correct catastrophe." This is a falsification of rhetoric, the same esthetic veneer that glazes catastrophe in "Extracts from Addresses to the Academy of Fine Ideas" and makes of it an illusory good:

> Let the Secretary for Porcelain observe
> That evil made magic, as in catastrophe,
> If neatly glazed, becomes the same as the fruit
> Of an emperor, the egg-plant of a prince.
> The good is evil's last invention. (CP, p. 253)

In fact, Vesuvius does not know our pain, and would be ignorant of the advent of our death ('the cocks that crow us up/ To die"). Pain is not to be confounded with the metaphor of Vesuvius, or any metaphor, but is an exclusively human experience. It is this fact that is difficult to face, and that the imagination must account for in "the sublime," in the lofty but credible agreement with reality that will enable us to come to terms with evil. This defines the subject of the poem.

In the second section the same problem is addressed more successfully. At first the sounds of night that surround the man on the balcony are too much things in the mind, too much merely the objects of perception that can achieve, but have not yet achieved the resolution of his despair. They are "syllables" in his meditation without reality of their own, just as the metaphor for pain was a trope that did not adhere to reality. But resolution cannot come in the mind alone; it can only come as the mind discovers new aspects of a reality free from the mind in which resolution can be achieved. The rising moon is a revelation of such an independent reality. It escapes his meditation and evades his mind.[35] The shadow of night "merely seemed to touch him" because it is actually distinct from him. In this revelation there is a new knowledge that comes from the reality outside himself, "in space," and that brings about the resolution of his despair. Pain is not concerned with ("is indifferent to") reality ("the sky"), despite the sensuous scent and color of the acacias; if it were, it might see ("regard") in reality the latter's independence from the ego, instead of hallucinating an anthropomorphic reality which seems dependent on the ego. Reality is free from the mind that registers pain, as Vesuvius is free from the projections of rhetoric. Thus, the mind can always find relief in a new relation to reality, the final among which would be, by extension, death. The final section of "Extracts from Addresses to the Academy of Fine Ideas" is apposite:

> But would it be amen, in choirs, if once
> In total war we died and after death
> Returned, unable to die again, fated
> To endure thereafter every mortal wound,
> Beyond a second death, as evil's end?
> It is only that we are able to die, to escape
> The wounds. (CP, pp. 258–59)

But it is also true that if death can dissolve evil, so can less drastic changes in the relation to reality give relief:

> If earth dissolves
> Its evil after death, it dissolves it while
> We live. (*CP*, p. 259)

It is only because reality is "wholly other," and therefore does not share human pain, and rejects it, that makes it possible for a new relation with reality to be formed in which pain is dissolved. Pain, in not heeding "This freedom, this supremacy"—the terms are repeated from the preceding stanza where they refer to what is outside the mind—of reality in its separation from the ego, persists in its illusion that reality is part of the mind, and so it fails to see how the independence of reality is its salvation. Here may be seen the importance of a sense of reality beyond the mind in Stevens' work. If in Wordsworth it is necessary to sustain a duality between mind and nature in order to perceive their unity in the divine, so in Stevens the same duality must be sustained for a salvation of a different kind.

Section III concerns the possibility of good, as well as evil, within the limits of a secular world. The poetry of the person referred to is like a good ("honey") in hell. (It is possible that the person referred to is Dante, the "firm stanzas" those of the *Inferno*, and that the form of the section is in loose imitation of its stanza form. Kermode, p. 104, makes a similar guess.) But there is no hell, and the modern problem of evil exists within secular limits, because the physical world does not give grounds for faith ("O terra infidel"). In a Nietzschean passage it is averred that the projection of an anthropomorphic god to account for the evil in reality has caused us to misunderstand reality's otherness (compare discussion of preceding section). This "too, too human god" prevents us from accepting the independence of reality from the mind which is our only salvation, and the result, in the face of evil, is self-pity. The section ends with the suggestion that it should be possible to be content with the common good of earth, and that "hell," or evil so changed as to be part of the conditions of life on that earth rather than the manifestation of a supernatural force, "Could be borne." It should be possible to live, not on the supernatural garner of "hives in hell" but, since earth and hell are one and here, on the "golden combs" of earth.

Section IV begins with an illustration of the sentimentalist as general or abstract and imitative ("Livre de Toutes Sortes de Fleurs d'après Nature"). This is opposed to the specific and creative, illustrated by two examples of imaginative activity: the first, by the musician, "B." (the archtypical musician—Bach, Beethoven, et cetera), and the second, by the "Spaniard of the rose" who does not merely see and imitate, but metamorphoses the rose, or rescues it from nature. (Of the latter, Samuel French Morse writes: "Knowing that he is Pedro Dot, the rose hybridizer of Barcelona, is of no importance poetically speaking," but on what authority the identification is made it not mentioned.)[36] We may therefore take the "genius of misfortune" to be imaginative, as opposed to sentimental. The Spaniard sees the rose as something specific and ever new—not, as the sentimentalist sees things, as something vague, and of a general class ("her several maids"). The "genius of misfortune" too is specific, not vague and general like the sentimentalist. He is that evil in the self who, like B. and the Spaniard, imagines specific things, desperate consecrations of the world in the self's image, crude gestures —projections that make everything the cause of misfortune (at fault). He represents our ability to imagine away or rationalize misfortune so as not to accept it. The genius of misfortune is the perverse genius of the mind in its ability to metamorphose nature (like the Spaniard) through the imagination, and in this error we waste our lives trying to find satisfaction in an imaginary reality, rather than in the physical "world" that is our true reality.

Section V is based on the acceptance of the physical world implicitly recommended in the preceding section. In this section, as in "Sunday Morning," the discussion is more oriented toward the discovery of good than the rationalization of evil within secular limits. The general import of the two stanzas is clear: the only faith can be in the good of physical reality, as opposed to the supernatural of archaic belief, the only good life a life in fraternity ("This brother") with the living and familiar. As in "Sunday Morning" the good of earth, of what is real and present, which is "within what we permit," in "in-bar," incorporates the good of paradise and its corollaries and our nostalgia, or "damasked memory," of paradise. The latter is now "ex-bar," or excluded from belief.

In section VI, the sun, which "dwells/ In a consummate prime," shares its perfection momentarily at the prime of day which then passes: thus he keeps seeking "A further consummation." He tries to transmute the month into his own state of perfection, and, as with the day, at the very point of success, fails. Day by day and month by month the years fail, and he rejects them year by year. The sun, then, is like a clown, in that it is perpetually frustrating itself in its desire for an impossible consummation, yet is not a clown because it is perpetually fulfilling itself in perfection. The "big bird" represents the mind as it is nourished by reality (the creation of the sun), and is as insatiable as the sun. Fed by the consummations of the sun, "its grossest appetite becomes less gross," but even "when corrected" the appetite for further consummations remains in "divinations of serene/ Indulgence out of all celestial sight," intimations of perfection the sun can never illuminate. The bird has risen "from an imperfection" like those of space, and is seeking perfection. He, like the sun, rejects momentary perfections and perpetually follows the sun, the "yellow grassman," for the promise of further perfection the sun will cast away in the future. The sense of the parable is that driven by imperfection, we constantly seek a promise of absolute perfection that cannot be fulfilled.

Section VII is one of Stevens' attempts to create "the mythology of modern death" (CP, p. 435) as he puts it in "The Owl in the Sarcophagus," a poem devoted to that subject. The passage at hand may represent an attempt to cope with the violence of World War II (the entire poem was published in November, 1945). The "soldier" is an abstraction, an unknown "soldier of time" commemorating all those who have died in war. The only ease he finds in death is indifference to further, or "deeper" death, and, since he cannot die again, he is called "deathless." In death he nevertheless, with the companions he represents, moves on the wind with the general motion of the creation of which he was part, like Lucy in "A slumber did my spirit seal." Since he ceased to exist when he died, "No part of him was ever part of death." His mortal wound was part of life, not death, and, as part of life, "is good because life was." Since the wound was good as a part of life, it may be described as a rose that represents the goodness of life rather than the evil of death. The sense of the two final lines is that since death is mere non-existence, the felicities of life are the only commemoration for the dead, since they show that their mortality is good, because life is good.

Section VIII refers to the crisis of disbelief, and resolves it by recourse to the psychology of belief. "The death of Satan was a tragedy/ For the imagination" because it destroyed the current myth of evil and its imaginative corollaries ("blue phenomena"). Satan's death was the revenge of men whom he made the sons of evil as they were of good; they simply withdrew belief. Lines ten to fourteen, which assume a tone of pathos, may be read to mean that since the Christian mythology of the supernatural is no longer credible, there is no longer any afterlife (compare "Of Heaven Considered as a Tomb," *CP*, p. 56). The sense of the sentence beginning, "What place . . . ," is that since this mythology is no longer credible, to be in its afterlife is not enough to exist. The phantoms are ghosts of ghosts. However, the negation which reveals reality bare of myth leaves a vacuum of belief. We live by "improvisations and seasons of belief" (*CP*, p. 255), which are doomed to become incredible and be replaced by others:

. . . these philosophic assassins pull
Revolvers and shoot each other. One remains.

The mass of meaning becomes composed again.
    (*CP*, p. 256)

This scene never stops being played, because it is sustained by a psychological need to affirm: "After the final no there comes a yes" (CP, p. 247). Thus the tragedy begins again "in the imagination's new beginning" of belief, and will be played through again to the destruction of that belief, "because under every no/ Lay a passion for yes that had never been broken."

Section IX repeats the description of the loss of the imagination in the first section of "The Comedian as the Letter C," but in terms that parallel the same experience described by Wordsworth in The Prelude, Books Twelve and Thirteen. The "panic" is due to the destruction of belief, as described in the preceding section, resulting in a period when all imaginative conceptions of reality—the moon as "round effendi," "the phosphored sleep," and so on—have become incredible: "The moon is no longer these nor anything." He who has lost imaginative perception of reality, or "the folly of the moon," is impoverished as Crispin was impoverished in the sea. The experience is referred to as the loss of sensibility, and its dynamics are the same as in Wordsworth: "to see what one sees." In Stevens, as in Wordsworth, perception with the physical eye or the senses alone signifies loss of sensibility, because imaginative perception is creative, meta-morphosing the object of perception (see The Prelude, Book Twelve, ll. 121–31). The eye sees, but the mind begets in metaphor, or resemblance (NA, p. 76). Thus the sight has "its own miraculous thrift." To limit oneself, on the contrary, to one interpretation of what is seen when reality is fraught with possible interpretations, "a paradise of meaning," is to impose an order on it that does not exist. Such a "violent order is disorder" (CP, p. 215). This would be to divest reality of its imaginative aspect, or its "fountains." Though the present suffers a crisis of disbelief that is chanted by the "indifferent crickets" (or mediocre critics), what we require is an imaginative conception that like the halcyon will charm the wildness or chaos of reality as yet unreclaimed by the imagination; that will beat back ("buffet") this wildness with its manifestations ("shapes"), blow the halcyon against the haggardie. An example follows that resembles the experience of Wordsworth on Snowdon (*The Prelude*, Book Fourteen) that crowns the recovery of his sensibility. Its diction in part ("a loud, large water") echoes Wordsworth, perhaps intentionally, taking him thereby to represent the type of the experience. The fountain of the imagination bubbles up to drown out "the indifferent crickets" with the graces ("favors," also meaning gifts) of truth presented in a favorable light through the rhetoric of poetry ("sonorously exhibited"). The "primitive ecstasy" is that of the affirmation of reality therein implied.

The student of nostalgias in section X is one who has examined the various forms of longing for a congenial conception of reality. Among them he rejects what is perhaps the esthetic, perhaps merely the elegant and delicate ("mauve *maman*"), as opposed to the gross maternal, others that were fantastic, and still others that he profoundly, perhaps subconsciously, yearned for, "things submerged with their englutted sounds,/ That were never wholly still" (below, ll. 12–17). His soul ("anima") wanted reality in its gross substance, at its most primitive and least controlled by the mind (reality as an "animal" that is "unsubjugated"), so that reality, his "home," is a return to his source in nature ("a return to birth"). Nature is a mother, and, since he is part of nature, she is within him, fiercely goading him to recognize the truth of her reality. Understanding reality as the source of life made him proof against the impersonal pain she inflicted, because he understood that the pain was not the result of her malice, but of her gross, but fertile, innocence. Thus, "That he might suffer or that/ He might die was the innocence of living." This idea, however, is only "the last nostalgia" for a human explanation of a reality that is in fact inexplicable: "that he/ Should understand" reality seems to explain pain or evil that is otherwise incomprehensible. To assert this idea, though false, disentangled him from many possible sophistries by way of explanation of reality.

On the contrary, the argument resumes, in section XI, it is not possible to account for evil by any such facile hypothesis. "Life is a bitter aspic"; life with its evil is hard to swallow. "We are not/ At the centre of a diamond"; rather, life is flawed by imperfection. The paratroopers fall to drag the ground ("mow the lawn") in sudden and random death, and the vessel's "waves/ Of people" meet the same fate, despite the knell of faith tolling in the steeple. This indifference of fate is compounded by all the inconsequential dead, the "poor, dishonest people." The only belief available against the poverty of reality beyond and without the imagination, and against the evil which is the condition of life, is the metamorphosis possible through the imagination as it is expressed in language. The imagination discovers in reality a "paradise" of possible meanings, the "jocular procreations" (CP, p. 183) which are the joy of life, and which allow us to come into an agreement with reality. Hence, "Natives of poverty, children of malheur,/ The gaiety of language is our seigneur," our god, or lord. The "man of bitter appetite," that is, the man who has a taste for the "bitter aspic" of life with all its imperfections, despises the confections of the fancy which evade reality, which are like the contrived scenes of a movie in which the paratroopers "Select adieux" and the ship, if it sinks, does so picturesquely. He also rejects a landscape which is dominated by the symbolic steeple of an incredible belief, and the idea of an afterlife which would disinter the "poor, dishonest people" from whom the violets grow: "the violets' exhumo." Instead, the harsh realities ("exacerbations") of these things are cherished, or caressed, for the sense of reality they give, for they are the means of distinguishing the ego from reality, and so enable the ego to form a credible conception of itself in relation to reality. The harsh realities press the sensitive tongue ("epicure") so that their taste is distinguished from the taster, reality from the perceiving ego, in a process in which it is not satisfaction of hunger that is desired, but the hunger for these harsh realities itself. The "bitter appetite" of the beginning of the stanza is itself the thing above all to be desired, in face of the bitter realities.

Section XII is an effort to rationalize pain out of existence through the understanding, which, however, shows its limits. His two categories are the self and the social world. Initially, he hypothesizes that he would be alone in each category. In the first he is isolated within his mind; in the second his mind is isolated among those of others. In the second, however, he is accompanied by his knowledge of others, and in the first by his knowledge of himself. In which case, would his knowledge be more capable of meeting the situation when the will demands that his thinking be to the point ("true")—which will best accommodate him to face pain? It can be neither, since in each case his knowledge amounts to the same thing. His knowledge, which includes knowledge of pain, destroys the categories, unless he escapes the knowledge. In so doing he would be alone as he thought he was when he contrived the categories. This creates a third category without knowledge, in which he is passive. In this state, whatever is registered on the nerves would be accepted as the truth of reality, including pain, which, if not accepted, betrays one, "is false." Since pain is accepted, it no longer exists as pain. The third world, then, seems to be a passive state of sensuous perception in which the thinking self is eclipsed, in which pain would not be known as pain, such a condition as might be induced by liquor, drugs, or mysticism. But this is merely a construction of the intelligence, an ideal: what lover of reality has such a world? What woman could be so perfectly gratifying? In the imperfect world there is no way of escaping pain.

As section VIII concerned the perpetual tragedy of belief, so section XIII addresses the perpetual tragedy of life itself. Ideas of justice, as "the son's life for the father's," are secondary within the universal tragedy of inevitable death which is beyond justice. This is,

> . . . the unalterable necessity
> Of being this unalterable animal.
> This force of nature in action is the major
> Tragedy. . . .

Inevitable death is "The happiest enemy" because it defines the clear limits, the "destiny unperplexed," within which the good may be discovered. The limits are those which death allows life, which evil allows good. Within this absolute condition there are degrees of evil: "Evil in evil is/ Comparative." Thus a man may contemplate a good in reality and call it the ultimate, since it is the maximum, good. This version of reality is the "assassin's scene," since it does not evade death, but discovers the maximum good in death's dominion. The dominion is life itself, whose destruction can only be endured "With the politest helplessness."

Section XIV revolves the formulations of section IX, but more as they concern the restriction of the imagination than the loss of it. (The quote is from Victor Serge, who was a Marxist and anti-Stalinist historian and novelist. Konstantinov was a former member of the Russian secret police, a meeting with whom Serge recounted in his memoirs.)[37] The committed emotions of Konstantinov require a consistent intellectual structure to justify them, regardless of the truth of that structure. His cause therefore creates a logic of lunacy. Konstantinov's lunacy consists in his obsession with one idea "In a world of ideas." Reality here, as in section IX, is considered rife with possible metamorphoses, a "paradise of meaning." Stevens' point of view is always historical and relativistic: "One wants to be able to walk/ By the lake at Geneva and consider logic," that is, the history of logic, "the logicians in their graves," and their systems buried with them. One would "promenade amid the grandeurs of the mind" as through a museum. Nevertheless, despite the element of reason represented by the lake, one would be aware of the chaos of reality (compare "The Doctor of Geneva," CP, p. 24), and thus be apprehensive of meeting the logically unreasonable Konstantinov. One would feel the same "blank uneasiness" before the lake of reason, in the museum of logic, that Victor Serge felt before the logical lunacy of Konstantinov. A restriction of the mind to reason and logic then, is itself logical lunacy. Konstantinov would pay no heed

to the lake of reason or the history of logic, since, obsessed
with one idea, "His extreme of logic would be illogical." He
therefore represents the element of unreason breaking
through the imposed order of reason, and serves as a double
demonstration of the defeat of reason. Reality is not reasonable; reason only makes tentative formulations about it
which, when they become rigid and restrictive, round the
circle to that extreme which is unreason.

Section XV, as the poem's finale, resumes its major theme
of the feasibility of the good life, despite attendant evil, in the
physical world. "The greatest poverty is not to live/ In a
physical world" because there is no other. It is despair of
fulfillment within the physical world that creates the supernatural ideal:

> Sad men made angels of the sun, and of
> The moon they made their own attendant ghosts,
> Which led them back to angels, after death. (CP, p. 137)

On the contrary, the good of earth is that it is perfectly
suited to human desire,

> . . . as, desire for day
> Accomplished in the immensely flashing East,
> Desire for rest, in that descending sea
> Of dark, which in its very darkening
> Is rest and silence spreading into sleep. (CP, p. 137)

The ghostly consummations of the dead are pathetically contrasted with the "rotund emotions" of the living. Like the
shades of the Classical underworld, or like the ghosts of
"Large Red Man Reading," they "would have wept to step
barefoot into reality" (CP, p. 423). The consummation of
reality dissipates the impulse to abstract thought of the
"metaphysicals," who "Lie sprawling in majors of the August
heat." The "metaphysicals"—or those given to the kind of
abstract reasoning that leads to the idea of a supernatural

paradise, as opposed to the "non-physical people" who are in paradise and can feel little or nothing—are so satisfied by the physical world and the "rotund emotions" therein that they know nothing of paradise. This, then, is the affirmation of a belief in a good life within the conditions of a "physical world," "the thesis scrivened in delight." But its discovery did not lie with the physical eye and ear; it was rather the imagination working on the data of the sense and dealing with "all the ill it sees," and "all the evil sound," that brought the mind into accord with the conditions of life in a "physical world." The imaginative metamorphoses through which the accord is brought about, the various versions of the self and the sensuous world, may therefore be described as "metaphysical changes." They are the imagination's revelations of reality and are all the metaphysic necessary "in living as and where we live."

"Man Carrying Thing" (CP, p. 350)

The psychological process illustrated here seems to concern the poet's composition of the poem rather than the reader's apprehension of it, but could conceivably concern both. The poem must not make itself immediately available to the intelligence. Rather, one apprehends the general outline of it first; that of a brown ("brune") figure, for example, whose details and significance ("Identity") we cannot make out. What he carries remains mysterious even to our most urgently needy ("necessitous") attempts to perceive it. These uncertain details are "secondary"—the certain whole being primary—they are the first hints of meaning that must be given time to accumulate, like the first flakes of a snow storm. Such meaning is opposed to meaning that is immediately obvious; the "horror" is a horror of the easily obvious. We must struggle with our thoughts till dawn to arrive at meaning that is difficult to grasp clearly, and which is therefore worth making obvious.

"Notes toward a Supreme Fiction" (*CP*, p. 380)

"Notes toward a Supreme Fiction" is composed of thirty-one poems of seven three-verse stanzas in a loose approximation of iambic pentameter. It does not present a strictly consecutive line of argument but is organized in reflections pertaining to three topics, or "notes" (*LWS*, pp. 406–7, 538), and it has an epilogue. The introductory lines have no direct connection with the rest of the poem, except that their sentiments echo some of those in the body of the poem. Stevens makes it clear that they are not to Henry Church in *LWS*, p. 538. They seem to be addressed to the muse whom the poet cherishes more than the best knowledge to be found in books. The poet clings to his "single, certain" poetic truth, which is "uncertain" in that it is fortuitous, inspired rather than willed. The fitful quality of poetic truth is equal to the uncertain but vital ("living changingness") character of the encounter with the muse which, despite its changeability, brings us moments of composure ("in the central of our being"). Such moments, in which things are seen in the clarity ("vivid transparence") of imaginative truth, bring peace. It is such resolution, in an accord of the feelings and of subject with object, that is the kind of truth with which the poem is concerned (for example, in *It Must Be Abstract*, VII).

IT MUST BE ABSTRACT. The first section of *It Must Be Abstract* is in the didactic tone of a lesson to an "ephebe," a young man of ancient Greece undergoing his education at the hands of the state as his final initiation to citizenship. In the poem he represents the apprentice poet. The world is an invention because it is apprehended through our conceptions of it, our fictions, which are expressions of the "idea of the sun," or reality. Reality, the world, is the "idea of the sun" both because it is, in a sense, of the sun's conception, and because we can perceive it only through an idea. The ephebe is asked to perceive reality beyond our fictions of it. This reality is "inconceivable"; it exists beyond conception. Thus to apprehend the idea of the sun, the ephebe must see it as "an ignorant man," as one who sees it without ideas about it, in order to realize it beyond conception. Reality is not invented, it is the conception of no mind, nor is the ephebe to suppose for it a creator, a "voluminous master" (stanza 3). When the sun is so seen in terms of its inconceivable idea, it is seen as part of a cosmos purged of anthropomorphic inventions, of "us and our images." The purgation of the principle of anthropomorphic invention kills one god as it kills them all (stanza 5). Phoebus, a personification of the sun, is an example: he has died with the vegetation in autumn, and the ephebe is instructed not to attempt to resurrect him ("Let purple Phoebus lie in umber harvest"—"purple" as the color of the setting sun and also as a shade of Stevens' color for imagination, blue.) Phoebus, as a personification of the sun, was an attempt to name the inconceivable, "something that never could be named." The "project" with regard to the sun is to perceive it beyond conception, beyond names for it, as it exists in itself (beyond names such as "gold flourisher," which we nevertheless need as metaphor to capture, for a moment, its reality). The "idea" of the sun, then, is its mere existence ("what it is to be"), and its "difficulty" is that it exists outside the conceptions of the mind.

In section II, "the first idea" is the idea of the sun, reality in itself beyond our conceptions of it.[38] It is the "quick" of this "invention" because it is what gives life to our fictions of reality. It is ennui with the cosmic scheme ("celestial ennui") as seen from a civilized, or humanly conceived point of view (that of "apartments") that sends us back to the idea of reality, the first idea. But since reality is beyond invention and inconceivable (see section I), when we approach it through our conceptions of it, we lose its "truth." As soon as perception becomes conception, the first idea inevitably becomes another metaphor ("hermit" in the sense of separation from the reality of life) which we ravish from the truth, and which is fatal to the truth. We live in the mind, which, as it contemplates reality, transforms it into metaphor in order to capture it and then, in its ennui of that metaphor, desires to contemplate reality again—so that the first idea is also like a hermit in the sense of a mendicant "Who comes and goes" all day. Although there is an ennui of the world as invention of the mind, there is also an ennui of reality itself. The "monastic man," the priest or philosopher, is an artist in that he develops a conception of man's relation to reality ("Appoints man's place") which is imaginative, a metaphor ("in music"). His conception is of a particular time or state of mind, of, for example, today ("say, today"). But the priest and philosopher are also men who desire, and desire can never remain satisfied, because no fulfillment of it can remain adequate ("To have what is not"—what is no longer real and thus no longer fulfillment—"is its ancient cycle.") Desire must be continuously responsive to the changes of reality. The example of a change of season is given. Desire observes the change of spring in weather and vegetation, and rids itself of old fulfillment ("what is not") which was that "of another time." One grows tired of the stale reality of winter, and seeks satisfaction in the on-coming reality of spring. Change is inherent both in reality and in ourselves; thus we grow tired both of reality itself, and of our metaphors for it.

Section III speaks of the moment in which the imaginative conception of reality, our metaphor of reality, is adequate. The poem gets beyond preconception ("refreshes life"), and gives us a sense of the existence of reality, allows us to "share" in reality. The sense that the poem gives of a reality that is "immaculate," or pure of the projections of the ego, satisfies us as belief about reality. This is the "immaculate beginning" of a process in which the particular imaginative conception of reality, at first adequate, ceases to be so, and must make way for the desire ("unconscious will") to perceive reality in its purity again ("an immaculate end"). It is a repetitive process ("We move between these points") that goes from the "candor," or purity (obsolete sense) of its beginning to the duplicate purity, or "plural" of its end.[39] Their purity is the result of our conceptions ("what we think") which exhilarate our feelings, so that thought and feeling are at one ("thought/ Beating in the heart") through satisfaction of the desire to perceive reality afresh in a conception which enables us to do so. The poem, by means of describing reality without preconception, pure of the projections of the ego ("through candor"), brings an exhilaration, or "power," that gives this fresh nature ("candid kind") to everything. "We say," of the fifth stanza, prefaces three examples of how the bare facts of reality may be captured and brought into relation by the imagination. Stevens writes that "the Arabian is the moon; the undecipherable vagueness of the moonlight is the unscrawled fores: the unformed handwriting" (LWS, p. 433). At night we conceive the moon as "an Arabian," one learned, possibly, in astronomy or astrology, who, with his damned nonsense, disturbs one with vague, unformed portents read in the astrological arrangements (his "primitive astronomy" and his "stars" thrown on the floor) suggested by the moonlight ("the unscrawled fores"): we turn nonsense into portent. The meaningless chant of the wood-dove which is given in nonsense syllables had its meaning for us; and the coarsest appearances of the ocean may speak to us, although they say nothing ("howls hoo"). Thus life's meaningless facts, "Life's nonsense," may be brought into unexpected, but significant, relation, "pierces us with strange relation."

Section IV describes the difficulty of life within a reality whose existence is distinct from the ego. Reality was not the invention of man. The Garden of Eden was the primary example of conceiving reality in man's image. Thus Adam is the father of Descartes—"a symbol of the reason," according to Stevens (LWS, p. 433)—since through Adam reality was first conceived on the basis of the reality of the reasoning ego; and through Eve reality was likewise conceived anthropomorphically ("made air the mirror of herself"—Stevens, LWS, p. 444, comments, apropos Adam and Eve, that "it is not the individual alone that indulges himself in the pathetic fallacy. It is the race"). Their "heaven," or Eden, was a reflection of themselves, "as in a glass," that created "a second earth"; and though earth itself was productive ("green") and therefore hospitable, they lived in an earth "varnished" by their own conceptions. But reality was not a matter of the ego shaping the world in imitation of itself. Reality existed prior to man; there was an order, or "myth," of reality before man's conception of it, "before the myth began." It is this condition that generates the poem, the imaginative conception of reality. We are aliens in a place "not our own," and that is apart from the projections of the ego ("not ourselves") in which it is therefore difficult to live despite our imaginative representations of our life in it or, perhaps, our memorable days ("blazoned days"). It is the poem that bridges the gap between the ego and alien reality. We do not shape the clouds in imitation as in stanza three; rather, we mimic what the clouds teach and reality shapes the ego.[40] The air is not a mirror of the ego, as in the first part of the poem, but rather the air, as the environment, is a "bare board" which reflects nothing of the ego, a stage on which our lives occur as before a set scene ("coulisse") which is both bright and dark, happy and not, a theater tragic and comic without regard to the concerns of the ego. It is a scene accompanied by the music of its own unfathomable meaning ("abysmal instruments") which renders insignificant ("make sounds like pips") the grandiose meanings that we try to add to it.

Section V begins with descriptions of three beasts, each of which is adequate to its environment. The quality of the lion's roar is anger, represented by the color red, and his roar fills the desert with his anger in defying it to produce something that can stand up to him. "Glitter-goes" refers to the effect of the blare of the elephant which "Breaches the darkness"; in Ceylon, according to Stevens, "a tank is a reservoir . . . a basin which may have been an ancient bath or the excavation for an ancient building" (LWS, p. 434). The sound glides over the surfaces of pools which, disturbed, refract light. (Stevens reads "glitter-goes" as "vibrancies of light," "velvetest far-away" as "very remote distance"—LWS, p. 434.) The ephebe, in contrast with the beasts, must struggle to produce the conception that will make him master of his environment. Stevens reads "sigil and ward" to mean that "the person referred to looks across the roofs like a part of them: that is to say, like a being of the roofs, a creature of the roofs, an image of them and a keeper of their secrets" (*LWS*, p. 434). In place of the aggressive confidence of the beasts, he faces his environment, towards which his position is one of participation, rather than enmity, and he is cowed by it. But he is the type of those who, in time, are able to master reality for man who is, in consequence, master of the beasts that are part of reality.

Stevens has described section VI as fluctuating between inaccessible, but immanent, fictive abstraction, and concrete, accessible reality (*LWS*, p. 434). The section begins by describing the abstract "giant of the weather" of its final stanza (who in VIII develops into "major man") before he has been imagined; since he is not to be seen he is not to be realized, and since he is not to be realized he is not to be loved or hated. He must be seen in the context of a concrete landscape, but the one described has the unreality of a painting, one by Hals, whose *forte* was not landscape. Major man will have no reality ("Not to/ Be spoken to") unless he is imagined in human interaction with the landscape, providing it, in turn, with a human context as, for example, a roof, the fields bearing produce under cultivation, the birds imagined as a musical instrument ("the virginal") constructed to play for the human ear, the background of the landscape filled in with flowers that seem gay, against a particularized ("Northern") sky. The giant must be made visible by being particularized, but not completely so, since he must remain an abstraction, even though personified ("The dark-blown ceinture loosened, not relinquished"). So imagined in concrete detail, the giant is satisfactorily real ("nothing to be desired") without an abstract name, and he, in turn, makes the landscape seem real, more human, to be loved or hated ("My house has changed a little in the sun"; compare "The Apostrophe to Vincentine," *CP*, p. 52). Thus the abstractions of the imagination transform reality, as magnolias in their season change a house: its bare form is falsified ("False flick, false form"), but it is a falsification like that of reality when it is imagined so that it is brought into close relation, "close to kin." Reality must be visible or invisible, or both: it is both an abstract conception and a concrete presence which the abstraction helps us to perceive. We do not see the abstraction, but the concrete particulars that give it substance. Reality is composed of its concrete presence ("The weather") and the abstract personification through whom it is conceived ("the giant of the weather"), or better, it is the concrete details ("the mere weather, the mere air") that give life to the abstract idea, that make the picture come alive ("An abstraction blooded") as a man may be said to come alive through thought: reality exists in its concrete details, man's mind exists in the conceptual matter which he brings to that reality.

The speculation of section VII grows out of the preceding section. The mere sensuous relation to reality is good ("It feels good") without the "giant," the abstract personification of he who conceives reality.[41] Perhaps the truth about reality depends on that sensuous relation with it, during, for example, "a walk around a lake," when one becomes composed as the body tires, and physical composure comes to be one with mental composure: one stops to "see hepatica" as one stops "to watch/ A definition growing certain," and one waits in that certainty, as one rests among the pines. Perhaps there are moments when one is at the center of an equilibrium composed of "incalculable balances," as when the parts of a mechanism fall into place and produce a music of enthusiastic devotion ("Schwärmerei") representing, possibly, a state similar to religious beatitude. It is an experience which is not willed, but "fortuitous" as is love at first sight. It is "personal," or subjective, in that it has to do with an accord of the feelings; it is "extreme" in that one awakens into a state of clairvoyance ("more than awaken") as if from sleep, in which the abstract thought of "The academies" seems benighted ("structures in a mist"). It is not merely that one is in equilibrium, but that the "incalculable balances" that comprise the equilibrium include both subject and object: "all/ Is well," when "the cock crows" (as it happens, on the left), both within and without. The mechanism is like that of a Swiss clock which sets up its music within only upon the right moment without. This is a state, then, in which subjective and objective composure are parts of a continuum; each is an extension of the other, so that the distinction between ego and reality is reduced to a point at which intellectual abstractions such as "the first idea," intended to harmonize the relation between the two, become superfluous.

In section VIII it is asked whether we can make of reality an appropriate human abode, "compose a castle-fortress-home", even with the help of an architect known for his reconstructions of such noble monuments in Europe (Viollet-le-Duc), in which an ordinary American, "the MacCullough," may be placed as "major man." "The first idea," reality, can only be reached through the imagination, and therefore what is needed is a "major man," an abstraction through which reality can be imagined as suitable to ordinary man. The democratic ideal of man, "the MacCullough," may be as expedient as any other abstraction of man as "the pensive giant" who is "the thinker of the first idea." It is a matter of "major man" and an appropriate reality in which he may be realized: the giant and MacCullough; word and reasoning, clear theory (l. 7), a beginning ("incipit"), completed by a figure to speak the word and its meanings. So realized, "major man" is seen to be an ideal of a philosopher-poet, thinker and "Beau linguist." But "the MacCullough" is the real MacCullough, the ordinary man ("But the MacCullough is MacCullough"); it does not follow that he is identical with his idealization, that the ordinary man is "major man." However, he might become so by contemplating in reality ("reading in the sound") the idea of the giant ("the thinker of the first idea").[42] He might take habit, whether through experience or poetic practice ("wave or phrase"), or through the recognition of "a possibly more than human human, a composite human" (Stevens' gloss of "a leaner being, moving in on him"—LWS, p. 434). He would then, as philosopher-poet, grow in understanding, and speak flowingly ("As if the waves at last were never broken"), and with ease.

The first stanza of section IX says that poetry ("The romantic intoning, the declaimed clairvoyance"), is of the nature of "apotheosis," or beatitude, perhaps like that described in section VII, and is its manner of expression. It is distinct from reason's mechanical precision ("click-clack") and its instrumental, practical illuminations ("applied/ Enflashings"). Major man, the philosopher-poet, is not himself the product of apotheosis or poetry but of reason, study, and random speculation or "revery." He is the object of thoughts difficult to grasp, and his nature is sought through the night of study to be realized at a propitious dawn when the cocks are calling and, perhaps, when the dew falls ("the good of April falls tenderly"). He is described as an infant to be cared for, who is "swaddled," sung to, and who reposes on a breast; he is a "foundling," orphaned from a sick past, but is "bright" in hope, and causes strong emotion. The passage, then, describes the nativity of major man who comes like a saviour from the reason. As a product of the reason he is a hypothesis, and therefore exists as a possibility ("He is and may be"), an ideal abstraction of the philosopher-poet.[43] But since he is an ideal abstraction, one does not regard his physical attributes, name him, or describe him. Major man is, as it were, an enabling idea, vital to hold in the heart, but is not himself matter for concrete description (compare "Examination of the Hero in a Time of War" XII, *CP*, p. 278). He makes the "apotheosis" of poetry possible—so that the muse is precious for his touch—but he is not of its nature. The muse sings "accurate songs" not of him, but for him, in order to approximate in poetry, from the material of reality, the first idea: the idea of reality. The idea of the philosopher-poet, not itself of the nature of apotheosis, is an intellectual construction meant to make possible the kind of secular apotheosis that occurs in section VII fortuitously, and without the direction of the intellect.

Section X states that the most important abstraction is the idea of man. Major man, a representative abstraction of man as he is, articulates the idea of man. He is an abstraction more productive as a principle than he is in any particular manifestation. He is no exception from the "commonal," but part of it, and he is abundantly productive as the one who expounds the representative type of the commonal itself, that "inanimate, difficult visage."[44] The latter has to be made from the representative type that the leaders and thinkers among men conceive out of the attributes of the individuals who comprise the commonal, a figure of a needy man who seeks a reality that no longer exists ("what was, where it used to be") and must therefore be shown the one that does, in which he can find satisfaction. It is from him that one must devise the idea of man, "The final elegance," not by consoling or sanctifying him, but by describing him as he is, in an abstraction that will bring him into accord with the reality of which he is part. It will be for the ephebe, as major man, to derive from him the idea of man.

IT MUST CHANGE. In section I a scene is presented as if in an Italian painting. The seraph, partly gilded ("parcel-gilded" is a variation of "parcel-gilt," a word used to describe partially gilded plate), inhales an "appointed" odor because the scene is set, as that in a painting. He is an artifact left over from an old mythology. The doves are unreal ("phantoms") as if they were illustrations in old manuscripts. The seraph sees the flowers the girls wear as they have always been, as they had been in "the bandeaux" of their mothers, as they will be again in another generation of girls. The bees and the hyacinths of spring seem as if they have always been there, "as if they had never gone." But things change. The components of reality are not static as they are in a painting, but are inconstant and obedient to inconstant causes "In a universe of inconstancy." Therefore the blue of night passes away, and when it returns is subject to variation. The character of the seraph may change completely, "according to his thoughts." We feel a distaste for the scene described, because it has changed so little it causes ennui: it remains the same; it has no variety in its repetitions. The world changes, and we are in need of its change. A repetition of the description of the static scene ("The bees come booming/ As if—") is interrupted with the violence of reality. In reality it is not as if the bees had never gone. Reality is not "as if," is not a metaphor. The doves are not like illustrations, but are pigeons "clattering" inelegantly in the air. There is no delicate "appointed odor" that the seraph inhales "among violets," but the sensual smell of life, of the body, and of an undisguised sexual acid, not for esthetic appreciation, but intent on copulation. And the sound of the bee has the crudeness of reality, not the delicately painted subtleties of a picture.[45]

Section II further distinguishes change from repetition. Stevens writes of it: "We cannot ignore or obliterate death, yet we do not live in memory. Life is always new; it is always beginning" (LWS, p. 434). No power can make the bee immortal. The President may ordain, but the bee does not obey. Why should the bee seek a life, which, as part of the past, is nonsense in the present ("a lost blague"), find "a deep echo" of his former life in a "horn"—probably descriptive of a flower—and persist at it ("buzz") as if it were a memorial of a past that is inexhaustible ("bottomless trophy"), the present bee merely trying to imitate what he once was ("new hornsman after old")? The physical good of the present is the equivalent of metaphysical perfection. What need is there, then, of immortality? Why, in the midst of life, in spring, should there be any question of nostalgia for life that has passed, or of a life after death consisting of a dream of one's remembered life? Spring is not a sleep in which one dreams, but a season in which lovers act to accomplish their love. Spring is not a repetition, as is memory, but a new beginning of life.

The statue of section III is like Verrocchio's statue of Colleoni, as Stevens uses it in one of his essays to demonstrate an expression of an ideal that is no longer appropriate. Stevens asks whether Verrocchio's statue is "no longer quite the appropriate thing outdoors," and answers: "It seems, nowadays, what it may very well not have seemed a few years ago, a little overpowering, a little magnificent" (NA, pp. 8–9). The statue of General Du Puy remains static, although the people who live near it pass away. The rigid posture of the horse suggests a general immobility, as if, at a final funeral of one of the residents, everything stopped, and the neighborhood became static. Bourgeois professional men, preparing themselves with care for their Sunday visit to the museum, go to look at the statue, and find it "a bit absurd." His posture does not represent a middle class ideal that they can understand. Although the statue was once a credible representation of a man in the flesh ("his true flesh"), he does not look like any conception of man that the doctors and lawyers can recognize. As far as they are concerned he is a useless vestige of the past. Nothing had happened to the statue, because nothing about it had changed; for exactly that reason, it "was rubbish in the end." The ideal and its representation, for not changing with the change of reality, have become obsolete.

Section IV describes, in a series of examples, "the origin of change" as the intercourse of dependent opposites that produces a third thing. The language used indicates the passionate nature of such unions. The interaction of winter and spring produces the general birth and growth of the latter season, the "particulars" of the rapture of their embrace; the interaction of music and silence produces its effect in the listener; that of rain and sun produces the vegetation. The inherent interaction of a condition of solitude and its particular expression distinguish it from another condition of solitude, and the interaction of the string of a musical instrument with a crowd produces the expression of the latter. The interacting opposites become one. One must do likewise by participating in change through such interaction. Hence the reader, or the poet himself, or the ephebe (they do not exclude one another), is addressed in a variety of oppositions and unions through which he may participate in change.

The fable of section V follows the formulation of the preceding section, obeying the bidding of its last lines: a man becomes one with his environment, and is changed by it, "The partaker partakes of that which changes him." His memorial after death is the remains of his plantation, which was his planter's reality, his "zero green." (The "patter of the long sea-slushes" in l. 9 is a description of surf.) His ideal of heaven, which grew out of his life, was a planter's paradise on

"An island to the South." His nostalgia for his native land came to be expressed in plantation terms: that land was a melon, not so lush or vivid as plantation country, but which might possibly ripen from pink to red. A man not so affected nor so positively involved in his environment could not have done his work in it, nor left it so regretfully at death as he did. However, in the end, it was not his rather magnificent metaphors about his life that he clung to, but a discrete, still meaningful part of that life itself ("the banjo's twang"; see *LWS*, p. 435).

Stevens writes of section VI: "This is rather an old-fashioned poem of the onomatopoeia of a summer afternoon" (for Stevens' difficult and somewhat contradictory notes on the section, quoted in this reading, see *LWS*, pp. 435 and 438). He identifies "bethou" variously as the call of a catbird and of a sparrow. William Van O'Connor[46] has suggested that the section is a parody of Shelley, presumably of the lines, "Make me thy lyre . . . Be thou, spirit fierce,/ My spirit! Be thou me, impetuous one!" from "Ode to the West Wind." However Stevens apparently considered "bethou" merely as a translation of the French "tutoyez-moi." The sparrow addresses the other birds, and, according to Stevens, mocks them; this is probably why he writes that the sparrow "probably was a catbird" (the latter is, of course, another name for the mockingbird). The sparrow, as he does with the "crackled blade" of grass, invites the other birds' familiar attention. In effect he is saying to them, "Stop your mindless, mechanical songs, and pay attention to me." The wren is "bloody" because "wrens are fighters." The bird sounds had been producing "a wild minstrelsy" (Stevens' reading of "idiot minstrelsy"). Their song was "inarticulate," in Stevens' words, "like clappers without bells"; he further writes of this latter phrase: "drops of rain falling made lines which were clappers without bells." There was so much meaningless music, so many birds singing without saying anything, that the meaningful "bethous" of the sparrow, by comparison, compose a significant articulation, a "heavenly gong." The repetitions of the other birds are, in contrast to the articulations of the sparrow, "a single text" that has a static monotony like granite. Their composite song is like a variety of faces become one face, like fate caught in the immobility of a photograph, like the destiny of a glass-blower repetitively creating the same basic shape, like a priest ("episcopus," bishop, from the Latin) who participates in life, but without vitality ("blood-less"), like an eye without a lid which therefore cannot close to dream, not an imaginative expression ("dream") but a mechanical repetition. This composite song is of singers who sing without imaginative art ("of minstrels lacking min-strelsy"). The repetitious manner in which they sing of earth suggests a world in which the first leaf of spring appears and stays forever, as if that were the only episode in the "tale/ Of leaves"; and in which the sparrow, himself unchanging, sings the one permanent song of earth. The sparrow may be the *soi-disant* center of things ("Bethou him, you") but his voice, his claim, is one among many individual claims for attention, many "bethous" (for Stevens' "bethou" seems to represent the expression of the individual ego, "ké-ké," the "single text" of the collective voice which is inimical to the ego). The sparrow's song, which here seems the dominant one, never-theless, like all the sounds in nature, is subject to change, and will come to an end.

The first stanza of section VII tells us that after a beauti-ful night ("a lustre of the moon") we need neither heaven, nor any hymn seducing us into love for the supernatural. It is an easy passion, and we are always ready, to love what is available within reality. Our love expands in response to the attraction of the lilacs. We smell the lilacs to satisfy no other desire than to smell them; it is an absolute satisfaction that has no meaning beyond itself. We encounter nothing but their odor, which is abundant as it is adequate to satisfy de-sire. The lover of the earth within us sighs his satisfaction with the midnight encounter, in which his bliss is accessible and can be won simply, secretly, and without need of hymns of praise or worship. Such "easy passion" is our birthright as natives of the earth. It is not of paradise, but of the present time and place, and may be found wherever we are: in the afterlight of the sky on a spring evening, in the courage of the ignorant man whose bliss must be in faith in the truth of the book the scholar writes, and in the bliss of the scholar who seeks not a final and absolute truth, but changing degrees of certainty and insight that enlighten his lack of a final truth ("scholar's dark").

In section VIII Nanzia Nunzio represents reality. Her last name is Italian for nuncio, messenger, and she does come with a kind of message. Ozymandias represents a fiction which determines the conception of reality, "an inflexible/ Order." As such he is an appropriate symbol since he does not change ("inflexible") and, like Shelley's figure, will decay with time, to be replaced by another order. On the contrary Nanzia Nunzio, the symbol of reality, who is on a "trip around the world" moves from place to place and changes her aspect, as she does here, by changing her garments in confronting an idea of reality. Reality changes according to our fiction of it. Nanzia Nunzio comes prepared as "the spouse" in order to unite with an idea of reality that will define her aspect. She strips herself of her present "fictive covering" so that she may assume a new one. She reveals herself as the essence of reality, not as reality clothed by an idea of it ("As I am, I am/ The spouse"), nor even as reality in its naked physical appearance ("Beyond the burning body that I bear"). She is reality unconceived by the mind ("stripped more nakedly/ Than nakedness"), and only as such is she prepared to unite with a new conception of reality. She asks to be clothed with a conception of the mind ("the spirit's diamond coronal") that will have the finality of an inflexible order, that she will know as the product of love, and that will render her precious, invest her with value. (Stevens has written that this section "is an illustration of illusion as value"— *LWS*, p. 431). Ozymandias answers that "the bride/ Is never naked": absolute reality is inconceivable. Reality is always seen in some fictive version of it, constructed by the feelings and the reason. As in section II of "It Must Be Abstract," the fiction of reality is cast off in order to return to its source in reality itself, which, since it is inconceivable in an absolute state, can only be seen through another fiction of it.

Section IX asks whether the medium of the poem fluctuates between the nonsense ("gibberish") of poetic language and the nonsense of common speech, or whether it is both at once. Does it flit between two things or is it concentrated in one? Is there an inarticulate language, the gibberish of the vulgate, and a poetic language that is equally gibberish since it "chaffers," or idly talks the time away to no point? Or is the poem both the peculiar speech of the poet and the general speech of the vulgate? The question is not precisely put, or it is put evasively. The poet does not evade us in gibberish, "in a senseless element." Could the poet be evasive, who is the enthusiastic and dependent spokesman of the vulgate at our plainest limits? ("Bluntest barriers" is read by Stevens as "our limitations"—*LWS*, p. 435.) He articulates meaning for us, for the vulgate. He is the exponent of the vulgate by virtue of his peculiar form of speech, a speech that tries to reach meanings beyond speech itself ("only a little of the tongue"). He rather seeks the nonsense of the vulgate and tries to articulate it, to combine—as in the "imagination's Latin" of the last line—the learned language of the imagination with the vulgate, which is both the common language ("lingua franca," a jargon once used among different Mediterranean nationalities; also "franca" as free) and the most pleasant one ("jocundissima").

In section X, "a bench as catalepsy is a place of trance" according to Stevens (*LWS*, p. 435). Since the subject apprehends what he sees imaginatively ("full of artificial things"), the park in which he sits may be described as a "Theatre of Trope," of figurative language. He sits in an imaginative trance in the theater of figuration, and he sees one thing turn into another like a chain of similes. The lake is like a sheet of music, so that the objects on it must be interpreted by the imagination, as musical notes must be imagined as sound. It is like a sky or heaven ("upper air"), like a color which appears for a moment to change the next, in which the swans are essences whose appearance changes from seraphs to saints, from one metaphor to another. The west wind is music, motion, force to which the changing swans move, and represents "a will to change"; the wind is nature's will to transform the blank sheet of the lake with multi-colored patterns.[47] The will to change is not to be denied ("necessitous"), and is inherent in the ever-changing present; it is a "presentation" in the Thaetre of Trope that consists of a world in which one thing changes easily into another as liquid turns into gas ("volatile world"), whose changing presence is constant, a world which exists in casual changes, like a "vagabond in metaphor," the transformations of whose eye compel our attention. But we cannot depend on merely casual change. The freshness of transformation is that of the world, which, since it is the world as we conceive it, is also the freshness of ourselves. We must facilitate the will to change through the transformations of the imagination. The will to change is a necessity through which—since the freshness of the world is that of ourselves —by apprehending the freshness of the world we apprehend ourselves refreshed as if traced in the world's mirror (the "rubbings of a glass in which we peer"). These refreshing ("gay and green") speculations are preliminary encounters with reality which should develop into passionate unions ("amours"). (The relation of the ego to reality is also cast in terms of erotic metaphor in IV, VII, and VIII of *It Must Change*.) Time, which brings about metamorphosis, will record them.

IT MUST GIVE PLEASURE. Section I reads that to sing hymns of joy at conventionalized times as part of the multitude, wearing symbols of its power, to feel thus the common heart that is the most splendid expression of the whole ("fundament," from the musical term, fundamental, the sounds of a whole musical body, as opposed to that of its parts), this is an easy musical exercise. St. Jerome, author of the Vulgate, and known for his scholarly revision of the text of the Psalter (compare Stevens, *LWS*, p. 435), founded the music that could be shared by the multitude. (In this description Stevens may have had in mind a scene from an old stained glass window illuminated by the sun so that the strings of the instruments appear like blowing fire, and the colors of other instruments, having disappeared, make it seem that the golden fingers are picking on sky-colored emptiness). The multitude, by sharing in this music in "companies of voices," possibly in church, finds in sound its essential spiritual source ("bleakest ancestor"), and finds in light—perhaps that coming through the stained glass window—a music which falls in "more than sensual," or in spiritual, "mode" (tune or scale). But there is another kind of exercise, which is personal, and different from the common music of conventionalized spiritual joy. It is to catch our non-rational response to the substance of reality (the first idea), such as to the rising sun, the clearing sea, or the moon in a peaceful sky. These things are not transformed by the mind, the imagination, but they move us deeply as if they were. They do not originate in the mind, since we reason about them only after we perceive them, and they have had their effect on us.

Stevens says of the "blue woman" of section II that she "was probably the weather of a Sunday morning early last April when I wrote this" (*LWS*, p. 444). One projects into this embodiment of the day the feeling that she does not desire that the argentines ("the Cotton Thistle") or clouds be other than what they appear, nor that the blossoms should rest as objects of beauty, rather than participate in a sexual process of fertilization, nor that the fragrant heat of summer night be part of her fantasies ("abortive dreams"). It was enough for her to know, through her memory of other years, that the argentine is a manifestation of spring, the clouds have their own reality, that the blossoms are fertilized and decay ("Waste") without reposing in the virginal beauty of puberty, and that when the heat of summer grows fragrant it does not become part of her dreams, but is the night. These things have always been so, and thus in memory acquire a permanence which gives their present manifestation clarity and intensity (see *LWS*, p. 444). They seem real without the intrusion of the mind, as the whites and pinks of the dog-wood are real, and intruded upon by the mind only insofar as the eye perceives them.[48]

The first five stanzas of section III describe a weather-worn statue, the face of a god (Stevens, *LWS*, p. 438), a single lasting image in an unchanging reality ("A lasting visage in a lasting bush"), but this is an image of a god that no longer completely claims one's faith (Stevens, *LWS*, p. 438). Al-though it endures, it has outlived itself, as it were. The feel-ing has gone out of the frown on its brow, it is weathered, though it has not changed, it cannot escape the crown representing its dominion, and its renown wastes itself on its ear, which is overcome with tedium. The red-within-red lines of its features fade but do not disappear. The tedium of one worn out idea of deity "might have been," but, as one myth goes, another god, Orpheus, came and brought the pleasure of music, the pleasure we find in imaginative con-ceptions. In place of the unfeeling image, this pleasure brings the love of the children, in place of the image's unchanging monotony, the freshness of early flowers and their variety. As one commentator observes, the god destroyed the possibility of endless repetition when, in bringing music from hell, he discovered the beauty inherent in death and change.[49]

The first line of section IV echoes the last line of I. Feel-ing precedes reason. Prior to reason, we make of what we per-ceive through the senses "a place dependent on ourselves," a place that we adopt as ours because we love it. The myth of the "marriage in Catawba" (a river or region in South Caro-lina) illustrates this. First the captain, or hero, and the maiden representative of Catawba fell in love, but refused to marry. Then they agreed to take one another only without ceremony (the sipping of the wine), without rites ("secret cymbals round"), and not in their persons, but as signs of relation with a humanly sympathetic reality ("To stop the whirlwind, balk the elements"). The captain marries the maiden for Catawba (hence her name, Bawda, procuress for Catawba), and the maiden loves the captain as the sun that makes Catawba fertile. The marriage is one of love, and their love is for the place where they marry, which is "neither heaven nor hell," but reality made into "a place dependent on ourselves" because of our love for it, because of the love affair between the ego and reality that the captain and the maiden ("love's characters") represent.

Section V begins with a sumptuous meal that is appropriate since the section is about how to live happily within the limits of reality. The name of the Canon Aspirin identifies him as one who would purge life of pain, rather than the soul of sin. As a Canon he is concerned with the spirit, but as one who enjoys a meal he is concerned with normal, material good. After the meal he praises his sister because she lives sensibly and therefore happily. Stevens says of the Canon: "The sophisticated man: the Canon Aspirin, (the man who has explored all the projections of the mind, his own particularly) comes back, without having acquired a sufficing fiction—to, say, his sister and her children" (*LWS*, p. 445). This sensible sister clothes her children appropriately to their expectations. She paints them with the colors of the imagination, but only within the terms of what is possible. She does not pretend that they are as objectively precious as they are to her, and therefore hides what they mean to her under simple names. She loves them the more for seeing their reality "by rejecting dreams"; she hears and sees them as they are, and as they are her love for them exceeds the bluntest expression of it. The Canon begins to imagine a fugue of praise to his sensible sister. But she herself asks for her children none of the "excitements of silence," among which would be a fugue of praise, but the clear reality of sleep.

Section VI continues with the Canon Aspirin. His "praise of the rejection of dreams" in connection with his sister, "gives him, in the long run, a sense of nothingness, of nakedness, of the finality and limitation of fact; and lying on his bed, he returns once more to night's pale illuminations" (*LWS*, p. 445). When he comes to sleep, and things as they normally are, sensible things, have passed from his mind in a state preceding sleep ("had yawned themselves away"), he is left with a sense of the inadequacy of sensible, factual things

("The nothingness was a nakedness"). Beyond this state, fact can only exist as an element of the imagination, incorporated into fantasy. Thereupon, he incorporates what he knows ("learning") in an imaginative re-creation of the night that exists beneath his eye and in the reality ("mountain") of his ear, which is of the matter of his mind, rather than of reality. He imagines himself as winged and moving among the paths of the farthest stars. He descends to the children's bed and, with the force of his feeling for them ("with huge pathetic force," the force of human pathos), tries to incorporate them into his fantasy in another flight of imagination; thus, in contrast with his sensible sister, he attempts, through thought, to escape the inadequacy of the factual, the normal, even in human relations (compare LWS, p. 445: "If he is to elude human pathos, and fact, he must go straight to the utmost crown of night: find his way through the imagination or perhaps to the imagination"). Here he arrives at the point beyond which thought can no longer be pushed, beyond which, therefore, imagination is of no avail. Having come to an end of thought, he had to decide whether to return to fact. But he had to choose, not between thought and fact, but whether to include both in his concern for the children. He chooses to include both, because thought is based on the fact of reality, and our view of that fact is affected by our thought. The two are interwoven ("complicate") and gather into one harmonious whole.

The subject of section VII[50] thinks of orders and imposes them on reality, as if he had the intelligence of animals in fable rather than real intelligence, and used it, as in a fable, to intrude a moral, an imposition of the intelligence. On the basis of his imposed orders he builds capitols, as parts of a constructed reality and signifying, perhaps, corresponding social orders which, however, exceed in their artificiality the qualities of wax. In their sonorous corridors he commemorates in statues, since this is what fame requires ("fame as it is"), men known for their reasonableness, but who are again denigratingly compared to animals intelligent in fables. But the imposition of an order of the mind is different from the

discovery of order that really exists, such as the order of summer or of winter. It is possible, without reason ("not to have
reasoned at all"), to discover such an order, to find an inclusive or source idea ("major") of the weather where there was
no conception of the weather at all ("Out of nothing"). It
must be that out of the crude compositions of reality will
come some clear idea of it, which will seem at first something
forced out of reality, improbable as a likeness of it, which will
be nurtured only by the desperation of our need for it. To so
find the real would be to cast off every fiction except that one
which comprises a conception of absolute reality. The angel
of a fiction of heaven should therefore be silent to listen to
music accurate with regard to reality. This latter fiction may
or may not be a "supreme fiction," but note that there is a
difference between an absolute fiction and a "fiction of an
absolute." The wording is tricky, but it would appear from
context that Stevens is searching for an idea of reality rather
than an absolute idea. The "absolute" is reality, the "fiction"
our idea of it.[51]

Section VIII hypothesizes an angel to demonstrate an
argument. If one can imagine an angel who gazes at the
chaos of creation ("the violent abyss") and makes of it
glorious music ("pluck abysmal glory"), flies through what
the evening, an ordinary time of day, reveals, and needs
nothing but the chaos of the abyss ("deep space") without
the "gold centre" of god or the "golden destiny" of heaven,
if he is satisfied merely in the equilibrium of his motion
without further destiny or purpose, is it not true that one
imagines this in the angel as a projection of one's own
experience? Is not his satisfaction a fictive version of our
own? If one has felt the satisfaction projected in the angel
for an hour filled with a bliss which, as part of human, not
supernatural experience, can be articulated and understood
through such creations as the angel, in which one is happy
without need of the supernatural ("need's golden hand"),
and is satisfied without its consolations, then there is potentially a lifetime in which the only greatness and glory
("majesty") are not those of god but reflections of the self,

in which one does not have god or heaven but, being satisfied as one is, does not need them. The heavens and their population have no reality but that of our own experience, are only the reflections of ourselves through which we try to escape the condition of death, wish fulfillments that can never be real fulfillment, as Cinderella could never fulfill herself under her roof by dreaming of the Prince's castle.

The subject of section IX grows out of the preceding section. The poet encourages the wren and the other birds in the section because he is in sympathy with them. The wren is described as "too weedy"; "weedy" applies to animals lacking in vigour, here in comparison with the poet. The poet can do "all that angels can" since the angels are fictive projections of himself. He can enjoy the ethereal pleasures of angels and, in addition, the earthy ones of men who, hidden in celestial light, can in the imagination enjoy angels, as gods once in the imagination could enjoy men. The bird is a "forced" bugler because he sings by instinct, not option, and he is encouraged to stop short in his preludes, because the good of his song lies in the mere repetition of the few notes in it. The poet is in sympathy with the birds' songs and their mating calls because their repetitions represent occupations which are ends in themselves, and are therefore good in themselves. The existence of which they are part is composed of such repetitions that are circular processes, participation in which is final and without further end, so that the mere repetition of the process is a final good. The processes are ends in themselves, as opposed to the ultimate ends of religious belief. They are final goods in the way wine at a picnic is a final good, to be enjoyed for itself. We enjoy such processes which have no relation to a fixed center, a *summum bonum*, but which are relative to a series of discrete, final goods; thus we observe with sympathetic pleasure the similar motion of the leaf's eccentric spin. Perhaps, then, it is not the exemplar of men's ideals ("man-hero," one such as major man), but whoever, like the birds, can direct his life most completely to the repetition of self-rewarding processes, that is the exceptional creature, the pattern to imitate. In

contrast to "It Must Change," VI, where the mechanical repetitions of the birds suggests only a "granite monotony,"
repetition here suggests to the poet the type of rewarding
activity in a secular world.

The "fat girl" of section X is a personification of the
earth (Stevens, *LWS*, p. 426), hence the epithets of the
first line. The poet asks why he can find her only in "difference," or in what is never the same, see her in a moving
shape, not fixed, as something in change, not in final form.
She is well known, yet at the same time deviates ("an aberra-
tion") from what she is. In her (earth's) direct presence
("underneath/ A tree"), the feelings she evokes of love and
of her evasiveness require that she be named, held to a single
identity. (Concerning the words "but underneath/ A tree,"
Stevens notes a double meaning: "a. on reflection [a man
stretched out at his ease, underneath a tree, thinking;] b. a
great tree is a symbol of fixity, permanence, completion, the
opposite of 'a moving contour' "—*LWS*, p. 444). But to define her is to characterize her, and to characterize her is to
transform her through the imagination. She becomes again
an elusive unreality ("soft-footed phantom"), the emotional
("irrational") distortion of herself, however one cherishes
her reality. For the ego, that is her only reality: a "more than
rational distortion" that creates a fictive conception of her
dictated by one's feelings about her. The idea can be put in
abstract thought, the province of the Sorbonne, since it is an
irrational process whose laws may be rationally defined. It is
therefore predictable that when touched by emotion in a
propitious scene, with this knowledge in mind, one will
conceive a fiction of her so that she may be called by a name
that describes her; and though the description is of a fertile
and changing ("fluent") world, in the description her constant movement will be captured, fixed and clear as if in
crystal. She will have been given an identity through "The
fiction that results from feeling."

The epilogue points to the relevance of the series of poems
by asserting the general need for the fictions the poet creates.
Thus it is addressed to the soldier who, in war, might be

imagined to represent an extreme test of the beliefs, or fiction, with which the poet is concerned, and in comparison with whom the importance of the poet may be established. There is also a war between the mind and reality in which the poet is engaged, by reason of which he is always at work in reality ("in the sun") and, in his meditations, puts together his imaginative concepts ("Patches the moon together in his room") cast in poetry. The poet's war depends on that of the soldier's, since war brings about changes in the reality to which the poet must address himself. The two are one in that they are part of the same battle to master reality. They meet as parallels, if only in their effects in reality, as the sun shines on parallel lines so that their shadows intersect; or they meet in the written word as the soldier applies it in his own situation. Though the soldier's war ends, and he returns either in triumph or dead ("To walk another room"), the poet's war is constant. The poet provides the soldier with belief he can hold by, through the poems he writes, which bring about conviction ("Inevitably modulating") that is more than rational ("in the blood"). The hero conceived by the poet becomes, if the conception is convincing, the hero in reality. The faith conveyed by the poet, if it is conveyed accurately, and is appropriate ("proper words"), is the spiritual sustenance by which the soldier lives and dies.

Summary

Although "Notes toward a Supreme Fiction" does not develop a strictly consecutive argument, it will be useful to summarize its reflections under the section headings to which, sometimes only loosely, they pertain, as well as to define the more important terms and the relations among them.

It Must Be Abstract. The idea of the sun is the inconceivable existence of reality itself (I), synonymous with the first idea (II). The poem gives us a momentary sense of reality itself, of the first idea (III). The giant is an abstract personification through which the first idea is conceived (VI, VIII). Hence, he is described as "the thinker of the first idea" (VII, VIII). He conceives reality in human terms so that it is relevant to the ego, giving us our particular idea of reality (VI). Major man is a giant who conceives reality, the first idea, but a giant who is of a particular time and place, and has a character appropriate to them. His present avatar is MacCullough, an ordinary man (VIII). He is also the exponent of the idea of man which is part of the reality of a particular time and place (X). As he who both conceives the idea of reality and expounds the idea of man, he is not only the ideal philosopher, but also the master of fictive creation, and so is in addition the abstract ideal of the poet, the idea of the poet that makes poetry possible (IX). The idea of man is the abstract representative of common man as he is, whose character is articulated by major man (X). The idea of man is the major abstraction since it represents the commonal itself from which major man is derived (X), and in terms of which he must conceive the first idea (VIII).

Reality itself exists beyond our conceptions of it (I). This reality beyond the mind may be realized only fleetingly, both because our perception of it quickly becomes stale and inadequate metaphor, and because that reality itself changes. Change is inherent both in reality and in ourselves (II). The poem, at the moment it is adequate as a description of reality, gives us a sense of reality beyond abstraction. It gives us, in other words, an idea of reality (III). The poem is the link between a reality indifferent to the ego, and reality as the ego desires it to be (IV). The poet is thus the type of those who enable us to master reality (V). Reality must be conceived through an abstract personification which allows us to perceive it in human context, thus reconciled with the demands of the ego (VI). The ideal state of harmony between the ego and reality does away with the need for abstract thought, so that the abstractions pertaining to the "supreme fiction" may be taken as merely instrumental to this ideal state (VII). The representative of the ordinary man is capable of becoming the major man who concieves the first idea appropriate to his time and place (VIII). Major man is an intellectual abstraction, the idea of the philosopher-poet that makes possible the apotheosis of which poetry is the idiom (IX). Major man articulates the idea of man, which is a representative abstraction of common man, in such a way as to relate the common man to the reality of his particular environment (X).

It Must Change. Reality is in a state of change beyond any decorum the mind would impose on it, and the feelings require this change (I). Life in change provides good sufficient to render the repetitions of memory and of immortality superfluous (II). An ideal must change with the change of reality, or it becomes obsolete (III). The origin of change is in a passionate union of opposites that produces a third thing (IV). A man is changed by the life he leads, if he embraces it with strong feeling (V). No single expression of reality remains adequate, so that the singer of reality must use his imagination to change his song (VI). The particulars of reality are adequate to satisfy desire; there is no absolute truth to satisfy desire, but only changing degrees of certainty with regard to our relation to the particulars of reality (VII). Reality is always seen through some idea of it which is final for a time, but which changes (VIII). The poem is an articulation of the common speech produced by a combination of the language of the imagination with that of the vulgate (IX). Change in our conceptions of things is a necessity that freshens the world and we who conceive it (X).

It Must Give Pleasure. The pleasure that is referred to is not conventionalized spiritual joy, but that of perceiving the good of reality in its irrational substance, the first idea (I). We must take pleasure in reality as it is, not as we might wish it to be (II). Through the imagination we see reality not in one, unchanging, monotonous image, but in pleasure and variety (III). Our relation to reality is determined through love of it, and is not fixed as if by contract (IV). Our love for reality should operate through the imagination only within the limits of reality (V). Reality and the imagination are mutually inclusive, and the latter goes beyond fact to express our feelings about reality (VI). The order of reality must be found in reality itself, and must not be imposed on it (VII). Satisfaction may be found in the process of life without final ends of supernatural belief, which latter comprise wishes impossible to fulfill (VIII). Enjoyment can be found in the ends in themselves of earthly activities, and fulfillment may best be found in such discrete, final goods (IX). The fiction of reality which describes it is dictated by one's feelings about reality (X). Epilogue: The poet through his fictions provides the faith by which the soldier lives and dies.

A fiction, in this poem, is an idea of reality, a version of the first idea (compare "It Must Give Pleasure," VII and X). It has the function of disclosing the substance of reality in such a way that the feelings of the ego are brought into accord with it. It is neither wholly reality itself, nor merely a projection of the ego, but an abstract construction of the relation between the two, in which the feelings of the ego are adjusted to the fact of reality, in a state like that of the "incalculable balances" of "It Must Be Abstract," VII. Since both terms of the relation change, the fiction must also change; since the relation is one in which the feelings of the ego are to be satisfied, the fiction must give pleasure. The poem does not give a particular fiction but the specifications of a "supreme fiction" which a final idea of reality would have to include.

"Large Red Man Reading" (CP, p. 423)

The personage of the title is "large" in that he is a mythic figure, "red" because he is vividly alive compared to the pale ghosts who listen to him. The ghosts, disappointed in a heaven that has turned out to be merely a "wilderness of stars" (compare "Of Heaven Considered as a Tomb," CP, p. 56), have returned to earth to hear the red man, the mythic figure of the poet, read from "the great blue tabulae," blue as the color of the imagination in Stevens, which contain "the poem of life." The poem of life is of the most commonplace things, and the ghosts, correspondingly, would have been overwhelmed by the simplest sensory contact with reality, would have taken intense pleasure in the most rudimentary sensation of it, as if this sensuous contact were the essence of life. The poet reads from his "purple" books ("purple": a deep blue, therefore deeply imaginative, also, perhaps, a blend of the reader's vivid life with his imagination) a description of existence and its articulations in poetry ("The outlines of being and its expressings"), whose syllables are its "law," in that by giving us the literal content of reality in its inspired ("vatic") lines, poetry enables us to realize reality in terms of feeling, brings us to reality through its feeling for it, as it brings the ghosts to life.

"This Solitude of Cataracts" (CP, p. 424)

His feelings about existence, the "flecked river" (flecked with the details of reality), existed in a continuum of change, as existence itself was a continuum of change (flowing "never the same way twice"). The river, since it is that of existence itself, flows everywhere at once, and therefore seems to stand still (compare "The River of Rivers in Connecticut," CP, p. 533: "The river that flows nowhere, like a sea"; also, "Metaphor as Degeneration," CP, p. 444.) Its surface manifests the details of reality which appear in it randomly, without order or set purpose, like wild ducks "Ruffling" the surface of a lake. These random details of reality disturb our projections of existence which are mirrored in it, our imaginings, our thoughts, and which, therefore, are "its common reflections" (the mirrorings of the New Hampshire mountain, Monadnock, in the lake, are like thoughts, "reflections" —see LWS, p. 823). There seems to be an unspoken apostrophe inherent in the concept of reality represented by this lacustrine scene, and which is articulated by what follows. So much of this already fluid existence consists of our "reflections" on it, so much is imaginary ("not real at all"), that it seems doubly insubstantial. This provokes a desire for the opposite. He wanted the river to flow not in a continuum of change ("never the same way twice," l. 2), but in "the same way," and to keep on flowing in that one way. He wanted the scene to be static, the moon, unchanging, nailed in one place, as he walked under the buttonwoods (one imagines them, in this context, buttoned in place). He wanted to become static himself "In a permanent realization" of himself and of a reality in which there would not be any random detail like that of the wild ducks, in which there would not be any imaginary projections that, though unreal, are part of reality. He wanted to get the sense of a permanent reality, in which one would be released from the continual destruction of impermanence and, by implication, released from death as well. He would then be like a monument, indestructible, in an ambiance of unchanging stone ("lapis"), "archaic" because it has never changed, beyond the fluctuations of the planetary cycles ("pass-pass," also with the implication that such phenomena are illusory, unreal, from the French "passe-passe," prestidigitation—compare *LWS*, p. 823). He would then be non-human, breathing a "bronzen breath" at the "azury"— both heavenly and, by association with Stevens' use of blue as the color of the imagination, imagined—"centre of time," the hub of the wheel, the still point of time where time does not pass.

"Saint John and the Back-Ache" (*CP*, p. 436)

The poem is cast in the form of a dialogue which represents Saint John's reaction to the presence of a pain in his back. The mind is the most potent force in the world, because it alone can defend us against the difficulties of consciousness which it contains. This is suggested to Saint John by the Back-Ache because, in his consciousness of it, his first thought is that its pain is something that can be resolved in the mind. But then it occurs to him that the world does not consist of a force, but of the presence of reality, and that the presence of reality is not of the mind. The Back-Ache replies that presence is trivial, a child's play ("*Kinder-Scenen*," children's scenes). Saint John objects that presence, "The effect of the object," "fills the being" before the mind can grasp it, that this effect is beyond the mind's furthest reach ("Extremest pinch") to achieve, as in the effect of a sudden appearance of color on the sea; yet presence is not that color in itself. Again, presence is beyond the mind as is the somber change of season from summer to autumn, but it is not the undoing of the last yellow leaves of late summer in itself, nor is it the woman in herself who provokes the profoundly moving experience of love at first sight. Presence is not the object but "The effect of the object" (l. 9). He notes that he is not quite articulating his point ("I speak below/ The tension of the lyre"), and goes on to do so. These illustrations of presence are nothing miraculous, but real, even ordinary, phenomena which, because they affect us deeply, because their presence is deeply felt, help us bridge the "dumbfoundering abyss" between ourselves and those objects in external reality which are the cause of such feeling. In bridging this abyss between the self and reality, the mind does not help us, it has no dominion; therefore the abyss is an "ignorance," one which, however small, serves to alienate the self from the world in which it exists. Such examples of presence suggest the hypothetical proposition ("possible," "invisible," "composite") of a time when we will recognize that the venom of reality is also its wisdom, when we will understand that what inflicts pain and kills is also that reality whose presence we most profoundly need to realize. Thus in opening ourselves fully to the presence of reality, the armor of the "stale turtle" against reality will grow useless. Such knowledge would be an insight of great weight. The Back-Ache admits the possibility of this argument, since he cannot know the irrational human reaction to presence, such as that of Saint John's reaction, in its reasoned irrationality, to the pain of his own presence.

"An Ordinary Evening in New Haven" (*CP*, p. 465)

"An Ordinary Evening in New Haven" is written in that kind of free verse approximating a norm of iambic pentameter, which was Stevens' characteristic measure in his later poems. A summary of the poem would be of small help, since there is no argument to the poem, nor progression of any kind. Its form is rather that of a see-saw oscillation between an attitude that everything is "as unreal as real can be" (V), and its counterpart that "We keep coming back and coming back/ To the real" (IX). This oscillation in the attitude of the poem reflects the actual oscillation, as it is described by the poem, of the mind with regard to reality. The poem is a series of qualifications on the "vulgate of experience" (I), the common, received version of experience, as opposed to the fluctuations of experience in the individual and imaginative mind. The fundamental assumption of the poem is that the locus of reality, insofar as it is manifest to the mind, is a realm where it and the mind meet and interfuse one another, with a result that is sometimes in favor of the one, sometimes the other. In this realm the two balance each other, so that sometimes we use the imagination to evade reality (IV), and sometimes we seek "The poem of pure reality" (IX), according to our need. Thus it is not so much the actual nature of reality that is the poet's concern, but the ego's relation to it as it is caught and expressed in description (XXXI).

Section I states the subject of the poem. Sight, or the data of the senses, is unique ("a thing apart") as the usual or received version ("vulgate") of experience. But this statement is to be qualified again and again, as part of the endless meditation on the question, which, since it grows out of the imagination's effect on reality, is itself an imagined thing ("a giant himself"): what is the nature of reality? What does a house consist of, if not the material substance of reality ("the sun")? And yet these houses are "difficult objects"; they appear as decayed versions of appearance, and so seem unreal, things that do not communicate their full reality to the mind, that do not seem to have a corresponding "double" in the mind. They appear unreal unless this imagined version of reality (the first giant) is replaced by another which shows a new likeness ("resemblance") of reality ("the sun"), which comes inevitably and as naturally as the processes of the weather and the seasons ("Down-pouring, up-springing"), and which will provide a more inclusive version of reality, available to more people. Its effect would be to crystallize one's vision of reality, as if the meaningless pieces ("collops") of reality were brought into unity forming a new myth of reality, composing a world as happy as a festival, personified in a god-like figure, a "giant" who is "alive with age" in that he is old as the creation, since he is its creator, and in that we feel creation has always been the way he makes it seem.

Section II supposes the houses to have no reality except as they are conceived in the mind ("composed of ourselves"). Thus they would be without substance ("impalpable"), "transparent" in that they consist of the invisible mental effects in which they are perceived, and seem to exist only in the operations of the mind. Here the objects of sight, the "far-fire flowing" (a phrase employed, perhaps, mostly for phonetic considerations), and those of sound (the bells), would come together in fluid and vague images of themselves ("flowing," "dim-coned"), in a realm of the mind in which we are in equilibrium, regardless of time or place, since it is detached from time or place. It is a realm that is the locus of what we know as reality (thus "perpetual reference"), and is therefore the object of "the perpetual meditation," and the point of love as the mind desires to perceive reality with love ("visionary love"). It is uncertain in its transformations of even the clearest fact, and, since it is the place where reality ("sun") and mind meet, its contents include both the dictates of the spirit, and confused perceptions of the reality beyond the spirit. As such it is a realm of imaginative revery where the ego comes into contact with reality, so suffusing the latter with its own character ("So much ourselves") that we cannot distinguish our idea of reality from the existence beyond the mind which provides the data ("the bearer-being") for the idea.

Since, in section III, "The point of vision and desire are the same," we try to project onto reality what we desire to see. It is to the faculty of meditation ("the hero of midnight") that we address ourselves to make a beautiful world ("beau mont") of the hard one in which we live. If our love of reality, for which we try to make it over in an ideal image, is thwarted, and "beau mont" remains obscured by night unchanged, we resort to the wisdom that, as the will to holiness is next to the fact, so with the desire for love. To love reality requires possession of the object of love. But the desire to love cannot be frustrated, and is secure because by nature desire cannot be in possession of its object. Desire acts in all seeing, desiring to see the objects of sight as better than they are, so they may be worthy of love, and it exists always in unfulfillment, in denial that cannot be content as denial ("cannot contain its blood"). It comprises the potential perfection of a porcelain, as yet unformed in fragments of clay ("bats," fragments of hardened clay). The desire to love reality, in other words, is the unrealized desire to perceive perfection in reality.

The ugliness ("plainness") of ordinary things is cruel (section IV) as, for example, that seen by a man who has fought hard against illusion and what used to be but is no more ("was"), trying to arrive at a final unembellished clarity before his vision is extinguished by the gross relief of sleep. Men in ordinary life are not precise about the mollification they need for their plain lives. For their urgent need a rude kind of relief comes, and is accepted. It changes them, softens their need, and comforts them by bringing them into an unsophisticated but subtle accord of things unlikely ("surprised") to be in accord. It consists of a kind of wishful thinking wherein one is moved by the thought of something opposite to that which needs relief, and which is infinitely preferable to it ("diviner opposite"). So in winter comes the thought of spring, and the approach of winter, like the ghosts of winters passed away, is soothing in the fancy which makes it seem like a fairy tale, a romanticization of summer heat, its "diviner opposite." One thinks of the cold of approaching winter as if it were a story told, assuagingly, in the heat of summer.

Reality is for us what the mind perceives, not "that which is" (section V), and therefore romance is inescapable; even disillusion is another kind of illusion, and we have a choice only among dreams. Reality consists of a series of projections of our own egos, mirrors of ourselves, so that a room contains a lake of reflections and out-of-doors is the larger mirror of a "glassy ocean"; the character of a town depends ("hanging pendent") on the shadow the ego casts on it, a nation is happy in the style we give it, and all of reality is shaped by the unreality of our projections for the eye which does not itself search out such elaborations ("inexquisite eye"). Why then ask who undertook to create the world of the imagination in addition to the common world? The choice is not between the real and the unreal but between a common unreality and a better one. The division is therefore inherent in the pattern of man's nature ("the chrysalis"), and evolves in the self during the day when there is leisure to use the imagination ("blue day"), and especially in the ramifications ("branchings") of the imagination at night after the practical concerns of the common world are past. One part of the ego holds fast to the received version, the vulgate of reality ("common earth"), and the other, in flights of the imagination, tries to find such improvements on it as it can.

Reality is the base on which the imagination elaborates, not the final truth (section VI). Reality is the plain version of things, "Naked Alpha," rather than the one which interprets the plain version, "hierophant Omega," invested with "dense" meanings, and surrounded by the entourage of the imagination. Alpha is the beginning of a process which grows from reality seen in an unsophisticated way ("the infant A") to reality learnedly glossed ("polymathic Z") through contemplation of the possibilities or relations ("distances") within it ("space"). Alpha fears the human interpretation of reality, or imaginative men most given to such interpretations ("Omega's men"), or the imaginative elaborations of the human point of view, since these change the plain Alpha. Both of these viewpoints are present in our lives. For Alpha, the life we lead ("the scene") is adequate, and for Omega it is not, so that he seeks more through imaginative interpretation. For Omega as well as Alpha this scene is not a vacuum, since he, like Alpha, has his way of safeguarding ("custodian") a glory in life that makes it worthwhile; each considers himself the faultless ("immaculate") interpreter of life. The difference between them is that between an end and the way to it. The continual beginning in the plain version of things ends in its continual refreshment in the imaginative.

In the presence of their buildings, the architects, however materially impoverished they may be, seem as fertile and lively in spirit as the chapels and schools they designed (VII). The buildings are lively and move the spectator to feel the same quality. But the spectator is also moved by the lesser productions of "rigid realists," by the exteriorizations of the spirit of practical men, as opposed to the "impoverished" architects. The productions of the realists make it seem as if the men had become the things they created, as if in a play, and stood dressed in the "antic symbols" of themselves. As things they cannot help but reveal their spiritual nature, not merely as to the depth of understanding but as to the height of their fancy as well, and therefore with regard to the "miraculous" or imaginative, as well as to the commonplace. It then appears that realists are also men of imagination, and conceive new worlds besides the common one, in which the mornings, "pinked out pastily," are the artificial mornings of the fancy, but are also dawnings of new possibilities, just as the daytime world becomes credible again at sunrise when it seemed incredible at night. Thus, the imagination of the realists makes possible new conceptions about reality.

The ego is the lover of reality (VIII). Contact with reality ("the street") is like the air itself as we breathe deeply—"a health" that revivifies our "sepulchral hollows." We find love of reality in fragrances that, perhaps, have the pleasant ("soft") quality of waltz time ("three-four cornered") coming from leaves that have the still more exhilarating quality of "five-six" time, as we find it in the earth's green which shows the lover its fertility, and in the blue of the imagination which reclaims points of rendezvous ("a secret place") between the lover and reality from the latter's generally indifferent quality ("anonymous color"). The breath is like an element from which comes a means of communication with reality, and the breath's desperation to communicate must be calmed, so that one can come into rapport with her (reality). It is like a native language found in a foreign land, which we recognize as we breathe like an avowal of rapport that requires no answer ("contains its converse in itself"). It is like a conversation whose participants are mutually modified by their dialogue so that each ceases to be himself ("Two bodies disembodied in their talk") and enters into an understanding with the other so fragile and immediate that speech would only interfere with it.

From the imaginary, which predominates in most of the preceding sections, the poem returns in IX (as it did in VIII) to the imaginary's basis in reality, to our home in reality ("hotel") instead of insubstantial songs about it. We seek to catch reality in the poem unchanged by its language, to find the exact word that reveals the object in its greatest integrity, so that its reality transfixes the mind, as in a view of New Haven that reflects nothing of the ego ("without reflection"). We seek nothing beyond reality, since it includes the spirit's metamorphoses ("alchemicana") and its transcendence of materiàlity, not merely what can be seen and touched, but that which changes ("the movable") with the moment, the holidays we invent and the spirituality of saints, and the pattern we read into the cosmos. Reality includes both the palpable and the mind's interpretations of it, the spiritual, which may also be accurately described.

Everything is both predictable and dead ("fatal") in the moon because nothing happens there, and it is empty (X).

On the earth it is a different story. Here everything is a puzzle that amounts to "a total double-thing" consisting of reality and our perception of it, and in consequence we cannot tell the real from the unreal. The moon is like a statue which does not change ("whose mind was made up") and which, since it became static amidst the change of which it was part, died. Not so with us. While the static moon is imprisoned by the change which surrounds it, our changing spirit is at home in permanent change. The world we live in is faithful to change, as of morning and evening, which come therefore like fulfillments of expectation, of the sun changing from night to dawn to dusk and the festival of heavenly lights that follows. This "faithfulness" is the dependable permanence of change, as opposed to the stasis of the moon. It is the habitual way of the earth estimably sustained through the ages ("venerable holding-in"), and, through the fulfillment of our expectations, it makes gay the different appearances of reality at different times ("hallucinations in surfaces").

Considering the real town in a metaphysical aspect (XI), we remember the symbol of an older civilization of which only the symbol, the "phrase," remains meaningful to us here in a city like New Haven. Each such symbol of the spirit, in the absence of the reality it once represented, is an imaginative light that shines only at night when the rest of reality is not in evidence, and exists only in the mind as an idea, a "transparency" through which we may see reality. The great symbol for us must be potent in the daylight of reality. The potency of the old symbol grows weak since it no longer has the fact to support it, and the fact of our present reality assumes its power. That reality contrives the same kind of articulation of itself, and through it New Haven claims our feelings as Juda claimed those of its citizens, or must come to do so, since man's spiritual needs are constant, though his reality changes. One thinks of such symbols as one walks through New Haven and considers it in a metaphysical way, but one is roused from metaphysics by the reality of New Haven which destroys such creations of the mind. One is thus freed from their majesty, and yet one needs such majesty that is credible in view of the real New Haven, a symbol, a central attraction (the French *clou*, figurative meaning), which that reality will be unable to destroy ("invincible"). It will be only minimally a product of the mind, a true symbol for the belief of the most truthful men that will be an epitome of reality itself, "The propounding of four seasons and twelve months." It will not be a light in the mind, but one at the very center of the earth, the center of meaning in our reality ("central," perhaps as in a telephone system, the point to which everything is referred).

The poem is part of its occasion, not about it (XII). It is the articulation ("cry") of the occasion, an inseparable part of the thing ("res") itself. The poem is an experience of the poet which he sets down as it comes to him, something that is present to him, and not about something else in the past. It is part of an event's effect on him ("reverberation"), his experience of a windy night when the statues seem like papers in the wind. He writes what he sees and thinks as he sees and thinks it. He writes of how things seem at the moment, not of how they will seem in the future. Tomorrow, without the wind, the statues will not be part of his poem, part of his experience which metamorphosed them—not part of the thing itself, but "things about" something else. The fluid and the static things that flicker between immediate experience and past experience are like autumn leaves that are in the process of passing away, which resemble the presence of thought that exists only as it is in process of passing away. The objects of experience exist like thoughts passing through the mind. It seems—in the psychological relation among the ego, its object in reality ("the town"), and the weather (that, like the wind, creates a mood between ego and reality)—as if the dead rubbish which experience becomes when it has passed away indicates that the articulations of experience ("words of the world") are the only things that represent and preserve the momentary life of experience ("the life of the world").

An "ephebe" (XIII) was a young Greek undergoing his final education in initiation to citizenship. Here, as in "Notes

toward a Supreme Fiction," he is an aspiring poet. He is
one who keeps to his own meditations. He does not merely
seek information ("the journalism of subjects"), but rather
the benefits of spiritual perfection ("perquisites of sanctity").
He enjoys a mind superior to his environment ("a weak
neighborhood"): thus, he is a serious man who lacks, and
must seek, the serious. His thoughts are not directed to any
activity, but rather to the meditation for which he is singular.
During his meditative walk at evening he neither prescribes
religion nor keeps order ("priest nor proctor") among those
engaged in learned thought ("perilous owls"; "perilous" is an
archaic form for "parlous," which in Shakespeare meant dan-
gerously cunning) about the mystery ("big X") of divinity in
a return to the supernatural ("the returning primitive"). He
defines a new kind of spirituality, characterized by the cold-
ness of the intelligence rather than the fervor of religion,
found not in heaven, "not deep in a cloud," but in the common objects of reality. It is the assertion not of a faith, but
of a problem: how the visible may be apprehended clearly
by the mind, or, "the nations of the clear invisible," as if
accurate perception of reality (referred to by the synecdoche
of its sounds) gets at the only kind of spiritual perfection
("essential integrity") available to us.

God is that which can satisfy one's needs (XIV): the dry
eucalyptus seeks salvation in moisture, and the professor seeks
it in New Haven. He looks to the objects in the ramshackle
town because there is nothing else to which he can look;
there is not much besides "the object itself" in which he can
choose to seek "god," or salvation. One can only choose the
adjective which accommodates the reality of what one sees
and at the same time satisfies the need of the ego to consider
it in a certain light. Thus it is description that makes the
object divine, derives from it salvation, quiet speech that
arrives at the description to which we respond ("the point
of reverberation"). It is not that reality is grim, but that it is
grimly seen, and may be described in a new way that makes
it seem "paradisal"; in any case, reality is never grim on the
account of the perceiver's attitude, the "human grim." The

sounds of the ramshackle town are not substitutes for salvation, but of its essence not yet perceived in the "commodious" description.

When necessary, on the other hand, Professor Eucalyptus takes refuge from "repugnant rain" (XV), in his wish for a rainless land which he constructs in a flight of imagination ("come at upon wide delvings of wings") by means of a projection of his own ego ("the self/ Of his self"). However, his desire for such a land ("heaven") had its "counterpart," its complement, in a desire for earth, the reality of New Haven, and the merry-go-round repetitions of life (the coinage, "gay tournamonde," or turn-a-world—see *LWS*, p. 699, n. 1), in which he does not exist as if in a heaven, but as he is in the real New Haven. This counterpart of heaven was a kind of antithesis set against it, a "counterpoint" registered in the irksome noise made by the rain that kept falling. The rock of reality in its wintery bareness that hangs as a shadow in spring when reality is clothed in vegetation, becomes reality glittering in the light when the vegetation dies in autumn. This bare reality is the substantial ("Ponderable") source of each insubstantial dream with which, like spring, we clothe reality, such as the dream of heaven. It is the weight of this reality that we lift with such dreams, that we lighten for ourselves with the imagination through our will to do so ("light will"), through our desire to lighten its weight, the "actual hand" of desire which is no less real than the weight of reality.

The present changes so that, among the images of time, no single one remains adequate to represent it (XVI). The present, if any image suits it, is a perpetual tragedy, "the venerable mask," because of its inevitable dissolution in the total decay ("dilapidation of dilapidations") of the past. The new day, which comes like every day has come, time out of mind ("oldest-newest"), is still the unique present; the night, though it is like all the nights of the past, does not creak by like an old ghost of the night sky ("a celestial ancientness"). It comes from the sea to the continent like sleep coming to young lovers, that of the masculine "Italian" coming from beyond the horizon to mingle with that of the "Oklahoman." But in the perfection of the present we are sometimes reminded of its tragedy, the "venerable mask," which speaks to us of the inevitable decay made of such perfection by change and, thus, of "death's poverty." The thought, in the fruition of the present, of its inevitable decay in death's poverty, should be the most affecting aspect of tragedy. It takes only a bough with its leaves fallen, and wind in the eaves that, perhaps, seems to whisper of death, to remind us of the total decay into which the living present passes, the "total leaflessness" in which the leaves are a momentary episode.

The attempt to conceive reality (XVII) is almost comic (l. 1), since reality is an inconceivable blank (l. 7). But it is not comic, because the strength of our need to do so makes the attempt too much in earnest. Perhaps it does not merely fail to become comic but rejects comedy, as serious strength rejects trifling ("pin-idleness"). The blank of reality underlies the attempts of invention to conceive it ("the trials of device"), dominates those attempts, and is "unapproachable," not to be conceived. The image ("the mirror") of the serious conception of reality is one of the blue of the imagination worked up into the symbolic colors of a precious garment that is like the presence of god's salvation in a burning bush, or that is like a fictive cloak thrown over the blank of reality, so that our pointless representations ("wasted figurations") of its meaningless processes are caught and made meaningful in a work of art (the "robe of rays"). These imaginative sayings are partly of the nature of tragedy as well as of comedy, but as the serious reflection of reality is not comic, neither is it tragic: it is composed of the commonplace caught and given value in such a "robe of rays," in a work of art.

It is looking through the window which gives on the external scene (XVIII) that makes it difficult to live in the present, and to create imaginative works with regard to the present state of the imagination ("painting"). The difficulty of living in the present stems from one's sense perception of the static external scene which seems to be the present, when in fact "the present state of things" is a state of the mind detached from the external scene and its perception by the senses. Thus, it seems that the eyes are part of the present, that what the ears perceive in the external scene affect the mind, as if life were always physical, when, on the contrary, the mind exists in a present detached from physical reality, so that "life and death" are not "ever," or always, "physical." The "life and death," the concerns of utmost importance, of one particular artificer, or "carpenter," the poet himself, depend on imaginative elaborations of a flower that do not exist in reality, "iridescences/ Of petals that will never be realized." Such imaginative perceptions are of things that will exist in reality only after they are captured in a work of art ("Things not yet true"), and which are perceived through elaboration on what does exist in reality ("perceives through truth"). This is how the artificer perceives that present which exists apart from his perception of reality, "Or thinks he does," since it is a world of thought that exists only in the mind. His present is his imaginative elaboration of reality ("a carpenter's iridescences"), artificial ("wooden"), and is the model for those who would be men of the imagination ("astral apprentices," those who learn to "star-gaze," so to speak). It is an improvisation "slapped up" for use, instrumental to fulfillment of one's needs, "like a chest of tools"; and the eccentric forms it takes in imagination may be brought about literally in time ("of which the clocks talk").

The moon (XIX), a dominant image of the imagination, orders the mind, in which each thing is touched by its radii of light ("its radial aspect"). By means of it, that which was of the external world became of the subjective world (l. 4). The moon is only an example of a "radial aspect," and there may be other such sources of order: a uniform epoch, a central human figure, a germinal symbol, or any product of the imagination that, like the poles, serves as a point with reference to which chaos may be civilized. The "radial aspect" of our time and place among the "colonies" or civilizations of which the world, a "colony/ Of colonies," is composed, the present sense of "the changing sense// Of things," is comprised in a figure "like Ecclesiast," hardy and enlightening ("Rugged and luminous"). Such a figure provides us with a point of order for our world, which, however, is not obvious, but difficult to find.

On a particular day (XX), imaginative renderings ("transcripts") are hazy or indefinite like clouds; the renderings of feeling are likewise indefinite, so that it is impossible tò distinguish one from another. It is a day when the effect of the imagination on reality languishes. Thus, the imagination does nothing to transform the town, which remains inert like the residuum of a chemical reaction, a"neuter" losing its form ("shedding shapes") in a dominant absolute, within which it loses its identity. But the renderings of the town when it was imaginatively fertile ("when it was blue") are retained by the mind: the renderings of it dictated by feeling, its personifications, persist in "a twilight" of memory. Such indefinite imaginative renderings and memories ("clouds and men") may have to do with the air or streets of the town itself, or they may be the concern of the periphery of a man's consciousness ("corners of a man") as he sits thinking in an out-of-the-way place. So separated from the town itself, the thinker may escape the real world ("the impure") for a consciousness pure of reality. But the evasion of one imaginative version of reality creates the need for another to take its place ("everything to make"), unless the thinker manages to exclude all content from his consciousness (which may therefore be described as "his nakedness"), and remains in a hypnotic state that, perhaps, resembles the extinction of consciousness in mystic nirvana or, perhaps, merely the point of inanition in revery. In such a state, he would have evaded the will to conceive reality. This state is not possible however (XXI), because he can evade neither his own will to conceive reality, nor that of other men, which results in conceptions of reality other than his own and, in fact, it is inevitable, an inescapable "given" in human nature, that he have some conception of reality ("The will of necessity"). The inevitability of forming some conception of the world is due to the operation of two factors, the two "romanzas" (or songs, from the Italian): the song of the imagination and its alternate, the song of plain reality. The first song comes from a romantic isle (Cythère), in myth sacred to Venus, which has a fanciful population ("the shepherd and his black forms," the imagination and its creations). Like a product of the imagination, it comes from an island in reality, but is not about any particular island in reality, ("not of any isle"). The alternate song comes from an isle "Close to the senses" as opposed to the imagination, and the senses render this song without taking anything from the imagination ("the senses give and nothing take"). It is the opposite of the imaginative Cythère, the reality of our place and the things around us, the isolation of which is "the object of the will," the will of necessity. This song is out of the plain things around us, not the fanciful. Such a "celestial," or extra-physical, mode as is comprised in the combination of the plain and the imaginative is paramount in conceiving reality, even if it is only a matter of branches in the rain, which is to say it is paramount even in elementary perceptions. The two songs, the distant and the near, the imaginative and the real, combine to interpret for us the nonsense sound ("boo-ha") of the wind.

The initial proposition of XXII states that the effort to isolate or conceive reality is as meaningful to us as the effort to find god, according to Professor Eucalyptus who, in XIV, is also one who seeks salvation in reality. The effort to find reality includes both the philosopher's search for the subjective exteriorized in an objective conception, and the poet's search for the objective exterior that can be made subjectively relevant. Such subjective and objective conceptions of reality are eager meditations (l. 6) that give a fresh sense of reality untouched by the mind, like the world in the cold and earliness of some archtypical beginning. But such a sense of reality is quotidian, not a predicate of philosophers or poets —creation is renewed every day at dawn, not by the creativity of isolated "wanderers." But to re-create creation, to search for a metaphorical description that transforms it, is a poetic activity. To say, in a parallel case, that the evening star is part of a reality congenial to the ego ("sleepy bosom of the real"), and that its light exists only as it is realized in the mind ("wholly an inner light"), is to find a possible metaphorical description of the star among the descriptions of it that are possible ("its possibleness"), that re-creates or shows in a fresh way even that "most ancient light."

Half the world consists of that part of it lit by the sun (XXIII). This is the "bodiless half" because it is reality beyond the self, or body. As the sun, it is an "illumination" of what is beyond the self, an "elevation" which reveals a prospect of reality; it extends into the future and includes the past, figured as fading colors shading into the darkness of obliteration represented by "the woman in black cassimere" (a variant of "cashmere"). However, the world, as represented by New Haven, is also half night. The night has not the variety of forms that the reality of day was described as including, but only one's sleep, "the single future of night." It is like a sound that is "inevitable" as sleep is inevitable at night, "coaxing" like the approach of sleep and "cozening" as sleep is an escape from the facts of reality, and maternal as the comfort of sleep. In contrast to the "bodiless" reality of day, then, night is a process of sinking back into the self and the womb-like comfort of the mind apart from reality. Thus, night, detached from the clear reality of day, brings on a unity of the self untroubled by the many-faceted consciousness ("separate, several selves") required to deal with the variety of day, a unity that is part of the single identity of night. Even in this single and unified identity the self reaches out for a sense of reality beyond the self, "disembodiments// Still keep occurring." They occur perhaps ("uncertainly") because of a desire which is sustained long enough, possibly in revery or in dream, to express itself in nostalgic conceptions of reality ("Forms of farewell") that, in comparison to vivid reality ("green ferns"), are furtive adumbrations of the real.

The consolations of "space"—reality or, perhaps, the cosmos—(XXIV) are without name, since they are exactly the destructions of inadequate specifications in preparation for others as yet nameless. It was after the derangement ("neurosis") caused by the barrenness of winter, in the fertility of summer (its "genius"), when the supernatural ideal is superfluous, that the image of Jove among his thunder clouds was destroyed. It took all day to get over the shock of his destruction, and to replace the old ideal with a new one. In the latter part of the day, when the air had been cleared of the old ideal, and before the sound of the new beginning ("Incomincia," from the Italian verb "incominciare," to begin) of the new ideal had been established, there was a time characterized by receptivity, poised for something new which was not yet specified. Whatever was to come would be different from the statue, and thus would be "An escape from repetition." It would be a new relation between reality ("space") and the self, "that touched them both at once/ And alike," a point of contact between the two, based not on a specified ideal, but on a perception by the ego of reality, like that of a town on the horizon, which brings the two into accord. The section, then, describes the moment between the destruction of an old ideal, or myth, of reality, and the crystallization of a new conception of it.

Life caught his attention (XXV) in his vagaries in artifice ("wandering on the stair of glass"), and again in his imaginative revery in which he stood "outsensing distances." It always watches him so, requiring that his thought be faithful to life. Life is personified as an hidalgo, severe and quiet, but whose serious presence is insistently felt. Only this seriousness remains constant among the metamorphoses of reality, or of the imagination, or, probably, both. The commonplace became, through the imagination, a disorder ("rumpling") of symbols ("blazons"), and the real was transformed into the imaginative, as if the plainness of reality were like a bare tree that required embellishment ("fruited red"), given in moments isolated from the mundane course of life. But the hidalgo is there as a check to fancy, reminding one that what is isolated from the mundane is not true to life. The hidalgo is an abstraction, exempt from the changes to which reality and imagination are subject, and therefore "permanent," an invention ("hatching") whose personified seriousness obliges the reciprocal seriousness that one remain faithful to the reality of life.

The first three stanzas of XXVI describe a colorful and attractive afternoon. The light on the path is effortlessly refracted into vivid colors, the capes along the Sound (probably Long Island Sound, though there are also mountains in the scene) lighten in color, and the waves change color as their green breaks against a corresponding shade of sky. The mountains of earth are a more moving sight ("appeared with greater eloquence") than the clouds in the heavens above them. The configurations of earth, so seen, are beloved, and in such a picturesque aspect the earth is commonly beloved ("of loving fame") and its repute as an inamorata wins from us further fame in this respect. But here in the proximity of New Haven the beloved picturesque quality, "the inamorata," is lost, and the earth is seen in the comparative poverty of a plain view. The inamorata shrinks to the familiar without embellishment ("naked or in rags"), and gives, not the satisfaction of the romantic lover, but the comfort of intimacy and the restfulness of the homely but sympathetic, which are the attractions of the plain view, as opposed to those of the romantic or picturesque.

XXVII is composed of several fragments supposedly left by a scholar. They concern "The Ruler of Reality" who is a personification of the imagination. The first fragment is a truism: since "The Ruler of Reality" is in fact more unreal than New Haven, he is an unreal ruler who is master of the unreal, or the imagination. The succeeding fragments are adumbrations ("draftings") of this "Ruler." He and the personification of fact are complementary. He represents the possibility latent in the imagination as dawn reveals the possibilities of the day, and she, "The Queen of Fact," represents the delimitation of possibility in fact as in sunset. Thus he has to do with the possibilities of life ("the theorist of life"), and the good therein (l. 9), not the final limitation of death. As master of the imagination he helps to inspire the beauty of poetry ("The sibilance of phrases"); the operation of the imagination, "his voice," is "audible" as an anticipation of poetry, as the anticipation of music has a meaning in the mind like the effect of the music itself. He, further, helps us to discard false conceptions of ourselves ("the regalia,/ The attributions") by enabling us to imagine ourselves accurately. Finally, he has thought out his position as master of the imagination, and continues to do so, and as a result he exists in amicable relation with the Queen of Fact: the imagination as ruler takes into account the fact in complementary relation with which it rules reality.

The initial proposition of XXVIII is that "reality exists/ In the mind" as in a monastic cell (or, since reality here is feminine, a convent cell) with its spare diet and sparse accommodations, but with indulgences granted to her by the imagination (a misericord is an indulgence in relaxation of monastic rule). If it is true that reality exists in the mind, it follows that the real and unreal exist only within the unity of the mind, are "two in one." New Haven exists in the mind, whether as one imagines it before arrival, or as one sees it after arrival. Things apprehended through the imagination, whether on a postcard, in darkness, in description, through hindered vision, or in conversation, co-exist in the mind with things apprehended clearly and immediately by the senses. Thus, since reality registers in the mind exactly like imaginative experience, all experience may be considered an "endlessly elaborating poem." The "theory of poetry"—the theory of how to create reality in the mind, as, for example, the reality of Sweden or of Rome—is, then, "the life of poetry." If one were to push the point to its extreme, the theory of poetry, of how to create reality in the mind, could be shown to be the theory of all experience, "the theory of life" as it is experienced by the ego ("As it is"), in all of the ego's metaphorical approximations of reality ("the intricate evasions of as"), in its experience of both the real and the imagined ("things seen and unseen"), and of the things created by the imagination "from nothingness," such as the worlds made by the needs of the ego through the imagination (the "Misericordia" of l. 4).

In XXIX, the natives of an earthen, autumnal land are

confronted with a bright, tropical country. They see the latter only in the perspective of their own land: it seems like their northern country inverted. The southern country seen in this perspective is the same, but the new description gives it a new aspect more significant than alterations in its aspect due to the weather. For the northerners the countrymen and each unchanging thing in the southern land are metamorphosed, because their earthen point of view had resulted in a new description of its brightness. So reality is altered by the way in which it is seen and described.

It is the end of autumn (XXX); the robins have flown south ("là-bas"), and the squirrels are prepared for winter. The wind has blown away the quiet of summer; its hushed buzzing is now beyond the horizon, or underground, beneath the disturbance of ponds which used to be smooth as mirrors and which now disclose their muddy bottoms. The wintery barrenness that appears is not the absence of summer or a nostalgia for the past season, but is itself a positive state, a revelation ("exposing") of a new season that is emerging. The new season is reflected in the change of the pines from their condition in summer to that in winter. The transparence of summer weather ("The glass of the air") becomes the more active weather of winter, in which storms and turbulence make the air a palpable element again. The summer now seems like an imaginative elaboration on the actual earth. The latter may now be seen clearly, restored, perhaps, like an original painting with overlays cleaned off. The resulting clarity is not an emptiness, but the "one mind" of winter made visible in a multitude of ways seen by "hundreds of eyes" at once. Thus the recurrence of winter is like a new and more accurate conception of reality seen clearly, without the veneer of the imagination.

The subtleties of perception in the meanings of sound (XXXI), in the shadings of experience, in the rhythm of speech, in the nuances of personality ("the inner men// Behind the outer shields"), in the music in thunder, in the implications about the night given by "dead candles at the window/ When day comes," in the play of light in a foaming sea—all these strokes of fine detail ("Flickings from finikin to fine finikin"), and the general effort to recreate them in art at whatever time and in whatever form, "from busts of Constantine/ To photographs of the late president," are approaches ("edgings and inchings") to the "final form" in which reality is successfully described through the formulation of art, which thus obliquely or immediately conceives reality. This tentative effort to conceive reality is like the evening manifesting itself through the colors of the extreme end of the spectrum only, like a philosopher trying to express himself through improvisations on the piano, or like a woman writing and destroying an approximation that does not quite capture her thought. It does not matter whether reality has any concrete substance or whether it is insubstantial. The important thing is to capture and express in the final form of art one's sense of that reality which is significant only as it is perceived by the mind.

"Angel Surrounded by Paysans" (CP, p. 496)

This poem apparently grew out of Stevens' contemplation of a painting he had bought, a still life by the French painter, Tal Coat, to which Stevens had given the name, "Angel Surrounded by Peasants." The "Angel" in the painting, according to Stevens, is a Venetian glass bowl, the "peasants," the terrines, bottles, and glasses that surround it (LWS, p. 650). Stevens writes that "the point of the poem is that there must be in the world about us things that solace us quite as fully as any heavenly visitation could" (LWS, p. 661).

The poem has the dramatic form of a biblical episode. One of the peasants has opened the door in welcome to an apparent visitor, but no visitor has presented himself. Then the angel appears for a moment and speaks. But in this case it is not one of heaven's angels, but the "angel of reality," who has none of the heavenly angel's accessories, the pale wing, the apparel of gold, the trite halo. The stars do not follow him as attendants, but are part of that reality which he represents and knows. The angel is one of the peasants, in that he is of reality rather than of heaven, and this existence as part of the reality shared in common with the peasants is all that he is and knows. Yet, though he is no more and knows no more than the peasants, he is nevertheless "the necessary angel of earth." Man needs him, as a figuration of the imagination, through which one may see "the earth," reality, afresh once more, beyond the rigidified "set" of images, or mold, in which man himself has imprisoned it. Through him, in poetry, one may distinguish the tragic in man's relation to the earth, catching the fluidity of existence in fluid articulations, the words themselves part of the fluidity of existence ("watery words awash"), so that the meanings articulated are themselves composed of the fleeting suggestions of meanings which is the nature of the reality they interpret. The angel, as part of reality, is himself merely a suggestion of meaning ("only half of a figure of a sort"), only half perceived, or perceived only fleetingly, a projection of the mind, one who appears suddenly and elusively like a ghost, so nearly invisible that at the slightest change he disappears, "too quickly," because with him disappears the illumination of reality that he brings.

"The Plain Sense of Things" (CP, p. 502)

"The Plain Sense of Things" is sufficiently unambiguous until the fourth stanza, where the crucial statement in the poem occurs: "Yet the absence of the imagination had/ Itself to be imagined." What is the "necessity," mentioned in the last line of the poem, that must be involved in this statement if it is to be read as more than a trivial verbal paradox? "After the leaves have fallen," the poem begins— that is, in autumn or in an autumnal mood (possibly provoked by advancing age)—the bare constant of reality, the "plain sense of things," is evident. (The bare earth or rock beneath the foliage as a metaphor for reality is common in Stevens; see, for example, "The Rock" CP, p. 525.) This is reality seen without the imagination, or, rather, reality known so plainly that the knowledge seems absolute and the imagination cannot act upon it, an "inert savoir." In this state of mind the vital connection between the ego and reality has been lost. The imagination, which makes that connection, cannot vitalize or give value to reality; it cannot, in other words, incorporate it into the ego. Reality therefore seems empty, lifeless, a "blank cold." This experience has not been brought about merely by a change in reality, since, if it had been, the cause of its accompanying "sadness" would be clear. The seasonal change has stimulated, but has not determined, this state of mind which primarily concerns not the sadness of autumn, but the psychological fact of depression, which autumn has provoked. The sense of reality in this state of mind is described in images of fallen splendor, dilapidation, and futility. In them the "adjective" (l. 5) so difficult to choose has been found. The "absence of the imagination" has literally been imagined in the poem, and, captured in the poem, the "plain sense" of reality is no longer alienated from and inert to the ego. Again, nothing in reality has changed, but the state of mind has changed in describing reality in a certain way. The case is now put that it was necessary to grasp the plain sense of reality, which, though it is still described as a wasted scene, is now called "The great pond." This is reality "without reflections" of the ego, desolate, existing beyond the imagination, but which is the base to which the imagination must return, and which it must incorporate. It is the gap between the ego and this alien reality, which, driven by the anguish described in the first three stanzas, the imagination must span.

"Looking across the Fields and Watching the Birds Fly" (*CP*, p. 517)

The body of this poem is discounted as one of "the more irritating minor ideas/ Of Mr. Homburg" because it is put forth as a fantastic (see stanza 13) though interesting speculation, and not as a final formulation. (Mr. Homburg's speculation has been related to Emerson and the Transcendentalists by way of Concord, and his name, suggesting such puns as Hamburg-humbug, to that movement's German background.) The thought, developed through an analogy between the mind and nature, is that the world is itself "A pensive nature" (stanza 3), a meditation of which the mind is part, and that, conversely, the mind partakes of the "mechanical" (stanza 3) quality of nature, behaving like a natural process rather than an entity with volition (stanza 11). Variations of the same idea are developed elsewhere in the late poems in connection with Ulysses (see "The World as Meditation," *CP*, p. 520, ll. 10–11, "The Sail of Ulysses," VI, *OP*, p. 102, and the two poems which derive from the latter, "Presence of an External Master of Knowledge," *OP*, p. 105, and "A Child Asleep in its Own Life," *OP*, p. 106). In this poem the idea is developed from the observation that as the mind excludes objects from its consciousness, so does the sun alter the natural world through its daily changes of light or, possibly, through gradual seasonal change (stanza 2). Therefore, the operation of nature may be like the process of thought, the world may be of "A pensive nature," except that this process of thought would be independent of man's "ghost," or spirit, would not be the product of man's aspirations like his literature and his gods, would be "mechanical" and so without reference to aspiration or choice, and thus, indifferent to man, it would be "slightly destestable" (stanzas 3 and 4). It is in any case true that we live in a somewhat alien element beyond our formulations about it, in which we are not so much at home as we are in our formulations ("that which we do for ourselves"). Reality is no longer determined for us by our assertion of a human version of it ("one of

the masculine myths we used to make"); instead, reality
has a spontaneous and formless character, like the flight of
the swallow. It consists, for us, of what we assimilate in
knowledge and feeling from the sensory data we receive; it
is what we perceive spontaneously from without ("the tumult
of integrations") as physical beings beyond the realm of
mysticism; and it includes thought, which is described as a
natural process partaking of the character of the total natural
process, "A sharing of color and being part of it," a bodily
function that is like a function of the weather, a movement
within the general movement of creation, a realization ("discovery") sharing in its general realization, and a change
sharing in its total change. This particular afternoon looks
like a source of man's spirit (and so is "Obscurest parent,
obscurest patriarch"), because it has the appearance of medi-
tating in its own quiet and tranquility. Just as natural processes are like thought, so, conversely, is thought like a natural
process. Like the changes of the sun or the wind, thought is
a response to changes in the physical world, and our expressions of thought (stanza 12) reflect those changes. A fresh
mind willing to consider possibilities in far-fetched ideas, "A
new scholar replacing an older one," considers this speculation, "this fantasia," seriously. In it he looks for a description
of the human spirit "that can be accounted for" rationally
rather than through the mysteries of the supernatural or the
metaphysical, and in Mr. Homburg's speculation he finds
that the spirit can be accounted for as a manifestation of the
natural world, as a part of it, and as a response to it. Crude
physical laws result in the integration we call mind, which,
since it is only an extreme consequence of those same crude
laws, makes but a show of being qualitatively different from
them, "an affectation of mind." The spirit is therefore a reflection of an excess or affectation of nature, a "mannerism,"
a reflection of the "blunt laws" of nature being carried to an
extreme: "A glass aswarm with things going as far as they
can." Thus, if one carries out the thought, the mind is entirely the consequence of nature, and therefore, though it

may be somewhat alienated from nature (stanzas 4 and 5), can never be completely so.

"Long and Sluggish Lines" (CP, p. 522)

The poet's mood corresponds to the winter season. His feelings are sluggish, his sensibility is barren. In his old age he has seen the things in the landscape he observes so many times before that they seem without interest, meaningless. The trees seem sad, the sound they make in the wind seems monotonous. At this point an opposition is introduced into the poem that breaks through this monotony. The poet imagines the sound of the trees in the wind, their "uproar," as an attempt to talk down a contradiction. He speculates that this contradiction might be the yellow on the side of a house that introduces a note of gaiety into the sad, monotonous landscape; or perhaps it is the first embryonic signs of spring, spring's "pre-personae," nascent, effervescent, evanescent, and "issant," the French suffix *ing* (as in "florissant"), implying process: the "first fly" of the coming season, appearing like a comic infant (but "infanta," an infant who will grow up to be, in another season, a ruler, as in Spanish royalty) against the tragic backdrop of barren winter, the first blooming of an early spring flower ("forsythia"), the first signs of bloom in the still bare magnolia, a hint of belief in the mind of the poet, as if belief, like the burgeoning of spring, were part of an organic process occurring in response to a change in the environment. The poet apostrophizes himself as "Wanderer," because in winter's "pre-history," before such changes have occurred, his mind is aimless; the life of the season has not yet begun, and correspondingly, the poem, the response to the seasonal change which would give his mind direction, is still unborn. Thus the poet's feelings had not taken shape, had not yet been born during the winter "when the trees were crystal," and, like spring, he is only now beginning to stir, to awaken ("wakefulness inside a sleep").

"Final Soliloquy of the Interior Paramour" (*CP*, p. 524)

The title character and speaker of "Final Soliloquy of the Interior Paramour" is the lover of reality within us, who, through the imagination, participates in "the intensest rendezvous" with the world. "Light the first light of evening" is an imperative that treats a common act as a ritualistic one in a ceremony in which the light is made to symbolize the power of the imagination which is, in turn, identified with God (l. 14). The light must be lit in a certain way ("as in a room") because its illumination signifies a belief, taken on faith ("for small reason"), that "The world imagined is the ultimate good." In that belief the lover of reality finds his "intensest rendezvous" with the world. Because of that idea we may find respite from all the things that are indifferent to us by passing into an imaginative state of mind, the one thing that is not indifferent, and to which we cling for exactly that reason ("Wrapped tightly round us, since we are poor"). Through the efficacy of this state of mind, its "miraculous influence," we can attain that "ultimate good" which is "The world imagined." This condition seems to be one of secular beatitude that occurs "Here, now." It is "miraculous," vital, illuminating, and efficacious (ll. 8–9). In it one loses consciousness of self and of others, and has a sense of an obscure order which is that of the imagination which determined the condition. Finally, the imagination is identified with God, without, however, asserting the reality of God. On the contrary, the reality of the experience is entirely psychological, since the power that caused it by making its presence felt, the imagination, operates only "Within its vital boundary, in the mind."[52] The point of the identification of God and the imagination is to give an idea of the magnitude of this experience by connecting it with a traditional one; the following line, "How high that highest candle lights the dark," testifies to the degree to which the imagination illuminates and orders an otherwise indifferent world. It is the power of the imagination, "this same light," as it is part of the collective mind of man ("the central mind"), that makes life in a common secular reality sufficient.

"The Rock" (*CP*, p. 525)

I. SEVENTY YEARS LATER. From the point of view of age seventy, the poet's past seems an illusion. The merest freedom of physical motion seems unreal. The very air through which one moved one's body no longer exists. The houses in which one lived ("houses of mothers," l. 2) still exist, but they are fixed, dead ("rigid"), caught in the past of memory which is itself fixed, static, and therefore empty of life, of the shadows we and they cast in the passing moment. Even their memory ("The lives these lived in the mind") seems unreal. The past does not exist, and therefore it has no existence in the present, in memory ("Were not and are not"); it is meaningless, "Absurd." So also for the poetry one has written, "The sounds of the guitar," and the words one has spoken. A passionate encounter that once took place now seems mechanical and disconnected from one's present humanity, abstract ("A theorem")—one needs a theory to account for it: it is as if the two figures are part of that nature dependent on the sun, and acting out, through nature, the sun's own purposes. It is as if the emptiness, the meaninglessness of the past, had some purpose ("a métier"), an assumption which gave it life, made it vital rather than rigid, therefore changing and impermanent, rather than static. The past one recalls may have been illusion, but it was an illusion that was required by nature, that was in the nature of things, so much so that it produced the ongoing details of existence —as opposed to "nothingness"—that clothe the basic rock of reality, details that satisfy the "métier" of existence as objects seen satisfy the faculty of sight, and vividly so, as in one who has been blind. Considered in terms of the "vital assumption" of impermanence, the ongoing detail of the past is felt as life itself in its continuity, which in turn seems part of the "gross" (big, crude, total) totality of existence.

II. THE POEM AS ICON. Part II amends the argument of the preceding part. To recognize the barren rock of reality as being fructified by the vital detail of existence still does not give us an adequate connection with that reality. Such a rapport with reality seems imposed on it ("cover the rock with leaves"), and threatens to dissolve into that feeling of meaningless disconnection described in Part I. In order to heal this division between the ego and reality, either the one or the other must change, must undergo a "cure" that is not imposed, not something merely thought of, a theory, but something that is "beyond forgetfulness." Such a cure, such a connection with the detail of existence might be provided if we made that detail, that produce ("cull") of reality, part of ourselves ("ate the incipient colorings"). "The fiction of the leaves," the necessitous "illusion," or "fiction," of a vital existence discovered in Part I, is the image of reality conceived in the poem, the "icon" of the poem through which we make the vital detail of reality, "the leaves," part of ourselves; since this image unites us with reality, it is a metaphor of "blessedness." In Christian belief man unites with the iconized god by eating his body and blood in the rite of the sacrament. But in this case the icon, the image, is of reality and, moreover, of man as part of that reality, united with it through the image of reality he projects in the poem—thus the icon also "is the man." The leaves, the seasons, the vital detail of existence are the only reality of "the poem, the icon, and the man," since there is no other reality, and this being so the three are united with reality in a "cure." The seasons, changing and derived from the sun, thus time's "copy of the sun," have their unchanging cycles manifested in the leaves (1. 17); they are the fruitful impermanence, the "vital assumption," the "métier," within the meaningless permanence of the "barren rock" of reality. The vital impermanence of the seasons do not merely clothe the barrenness of reality—they call up the vital processes of life itself. They make the palest, most tentative life come to bud; they bring about new meanings in their "engenderings" of life; they motivate the completion of the life cycle; they bring the body to life, and root the mind in that life. The language here, sometimes referring to human life, sometimes to vegetable life, sometimes applicable to both, indicates that man is part of, not disconnected from, a vital reality; conversely, the blooming of the seasons are like love, the creative force in man. The fruition of the seasons makes the year meaningful ("the year is known"), so that it seems as if its meaning ("its understanding") is the good of that fruition, the good in the pulp inside the skin of a fruit, as if that—the plenty of the natural world—were the final good ("the final found"). Within this plenty, the poem, the image of reality, conceives meaning for the meaninglessness of bare reality, which meaninglessness then "exists no more." Thus the poem ("His words," the words of man who creates the icon), in making reality meaningful, unites man and the image of reality ("the icon"), and in so doing creates the cure for the separation of man from the vital life of reality ("leaves") and, for the "ground" from which that life springs, a cure for our sense of its meaninglessness.

III. FORMS OF THE ROCK IN A NIGHT-HYMN. The third part elaborates on the nature of the rock. It is that base of man's life out of which he grows and from which he descends in death. It is the uncompromising element in which we live ("the air"). It is the reality in which we see the planets, each separately, but, from the point of view of the ego, through poetry, as a harmonious whole (rhapsodize, in an obsolete sense, means to piece a work together). In one manifestation the rock may seem "Turquoise," blue-green, blue for imaginative and green for fertile, as Stevens usually uses these colors; at sunset, it may seem a hateful red, and have an evil influence; at dawn, it may seem good ("rightness") in a way hard to discern. It is the whole of existence itself, and therefore being's only "strength and measure." It is the beginning of the process of creation, "point A," and the end, "the mango's rind" which returns to the earth to fertilize new mangoes, beginning the process again at point B. It is the field into which tranquility must be brought if it is to be realized, the bulk and strength of things ("main"), including the mind, that from which the human starts, and to which it must come back. It includes space itself; it is, for the mind, the gate to the enclosure of reality; it is the exterior fact which day illumines, and the imaginative data which night encourages: the pleasurable creations of the imagination ("midnight-minting fragrances"), including such hymns in praise of the rock as this one, realized in an intense state of the imagination, as in a dream ("vivid sleep").

"The River of Rivers in Connecticut" (CP, p. 533)

"The River of Rivers in Connecticut" develops Stevens' idea of the nature of existence. The title does not locate the river, so much as it indicates that it flows through Connecticut, as well as every place else. Rather, the river is "this side of Stygia," this side of obliteration. Stevens explained the description of the third line of the first stanza as follows: "This refers to the distortion of trees not growing in conditions natural to them and not to houses deprived of a setting of trees. The look of death is the look of the deprivation of something vital" (Poggioli, p. 185). The river, on the contrary, is vital: it does not flow mechanically to a destination, but rather it is its "mere flowing" that is desirable, "a gayety," that is itself an end. Therefore no ghost, or "shadow," walks on its banks, for it is the river of life, not of death. Like Styx, this river is "fateful": it is as impossible to escape the flow of existence as it is to escape death. No agency, like Charon, the "ferryman," is required to lead us into its current, since all things, including Charon if he existed, are by nature propelled by the current's force. The river is not an abstract essence of things, but consists of the tangible reality of common objects, such as "The steeple at Farmington," and the town of Haddam, which is described as if it were a fluent part of the "flashing" river ("shines and sways"). Hence, it is called "the third commonness with light and air," the common reality which the atmosphere of light and air contains. The river is, furthermore, a "curriculum," or a running merely, without object or qualification; it is simply an energy, "a vigor"; it is, finally, not the idea of the river, but the localized manifestation of that idea as here in Connecticut, "a local abstraction," an abstraction that exists only in the concrete. Since it has no identity except in its local and concrete manifestations, it is "an unnamed flowing" which, however, contains in it space and the changes that occur therein, as with the seasons, and the mixture of knowledge and belief, or "folk-lore," that we derive through sensation. It is like a river which flows to no destination, as a sea flows into nothing else, because there is nothing else besides it.

"The Course of a Particular" (OP, p. 96)

"The Course of a Particular" has been called by Yvor Winters one of Stevens' "greatest poems—perhaps his greatest."[53] But he notes that whereas in the original appearance in *Hudson Review* (Vol. IV, No. 1, Spring, 1951) the next to last line read "final finding of the ear," in *Opus Posthumous*, as a result of a typographical error, "ear" was printed as "air." He concludes of the poem: "In its first appearance it is comprehensible and deeply moving. In its second appearance the conclusion evaporates into vague sentiment and a masterpiece is destroyed." Samuel French Morse has confirmed this correction as well grounded.[54] The "particular" in question is the sound of the wind in the leaves, and its "course" consists of the series of modifications in meaning that it undergoes in the mind of the observer who speaks the poem. Although it is a wintery day on which the leaves make a mournful sound, its emptiness is lessened by the shades and shapes of winter scenery. But as one listens to the cry of the leaves, without projecting one's feelings into their sound, or into the winter scene ("One holds off and merely hears the cry"), one becomes increasingly isolated from the landscape. It is no longer a question of whether the wintery scene seems more or less like nothingness, for it becomes progressively plainer as the poem proceeds that the landscape exists apart from the ego, disconnected from the ego's feelings about it. Thus, though the sound of the leaves seems to indicate that it is part of a brisk activity ("It is a busy cry"), it is nevertheless a sound that concerns someone other than the listener. Though one may hold, or, at least, repeat the idea that the ego is involved in the rest of existence, it is difficult, listening to the sound of the leaves, to feel thus involved. It requires an increasing effort to project the concerns of the ego into this scene, to feel that one is part of it. Instead of a connection with the rest of existence, a sense of "being part," one feels the vitality of an irresistible given, "life as it is" without regard to the concerns of the ego. Since the cry of the leaves occurs without regard to the concerns of the ego, it signifies neither the presence of divinity communicating itself to man through nature ("divine attention"), nor an ephemeral evocation of a more than human ideal ("the smoke-drift of puffed-out heroes") read into the sound of the wind, nor any sound that can be construed in human terms. It is the cry of leaves that, without fantasy, cannot be interpreted as being anything other than what they are ("that do not transcend themselves"), that signify nothing beyond the sound they make ("the final finding of the ear"), beyond their physical reality ("the thing/ Itself"). Since the leaves signify nothing beyond their physical reality, their sound not only does not concern the listener, but has absolutely no meaning in human terms, and so "concerns no one at all." The poem, then, is about the discovery of an absolute reality beyond the mind. As one becomes isolated from the landscape, the landscape takes on increasingly the character of an indifferent, alien reality. The ego must be projected into reality for reality to be involved in its concerns, and as the ego recedes, both the nature of reality and its indifference become more evident.

"Reality Is an Activity of the Most August Imagination" (*OP*, p. 110)

"The Most August Imagination" is that of reality itself. The "big light of last Friday night" was that of the moon mentioned in the final line. The night was not one of a traditional and outworn artifice, such as might be seen in Vienna or Venice—it was not a traditional reality that has come to an end, static, like an artifact from a glassworks, but a reality strongly in process, on the forward edge of time, as the evening star marks the revolution of the earth. It has the strength of splendor and magnificence (not merely their appearance as in Vienna or Venice), a "glory" that is felt in the self ("a glittering in the veins") as the landscape emerges out of the darkness toward the car, moves through the field of vision, and dissolves behind, either in the distance, or in the change of the scenery, or into nothingness, as it passes from that immediate apprehension in the present by which we perceive existence itself. These "transformations" are "visible": it is reality itself, not the imagination, that creates these metamorphoses. Reality approaches, silvery in the light of the moon, at first not clearly discerned, and, as we are on the point of capturing its substance, dissolves away into nothingness. The landscape, reality, is something that surges toward us as we move through it, and recedes away from us—the "solid" is "insolid," a process rather than something static. "Reality Is an Activity" that, in its fluidity, resembles the fluidity of the imagination ("moonlight") in its metamorphoses. This fluidity ("lake") is composed not of water or air, but of reality itself.

"Solitaire under the Oaks" (*OP*, p. 111)

The only possible difficulty of the statement itself in this poem is in lines six and seven: "One knows at last what to think about// And thinks about it without consciousness." This, obviously, does not mean that one is unconscious of what one thinks about, but that one is unconscious of the act of thinking, because the thought itself is so absorbing. The poem says that when one is absorbed in a card game one forgets everything but the principles of the game, including one's surroundings, and even the cards themselves. In this state one escapes from fact to meditation, the contemplation of "pure principles." So absorbed in the contemplation of principle, one is "completely released" from the pressure which the facts of reality exert on the mind. This poem, then, represents a radical experience in meditation. It demonstrates a statement Stevens made about the function of poetry in one of his essays:

> . . . how is it possible to condemn escapism? The poetic process is psychologically an escapist process. The chatter about escapism is, to my way of thinking, merely common cant. My own remarks about resisting or evading the pressure of reality mean escapism, if analyzed. (NA, p. 30.)

The point of the experience described in the poem is "release," and though it is achieved through contemplation of principle, the principle is unimportant so long as it is instrumental in bringing about this release. What is desired is a state of mind, a psychological equilibrium without any particular intellectual content, in which one is relieved of the pressures of reality. (Compare the beginning of the poem, "Artificial Pouplations," OP, p. 112: "The center that he sought was a state of mind,/ Nothing more.")

"Local Objects" (OP, p. 111)

The word, "local" in "Local Objects" is used in the sense in which it is opposed to central. In this poem it is in contrast with "foyer" which, in French, means the hearth, the center of the home. Thus, the subject of the poem was a spirit without a center, or, better, without a central focus, a guiding idea or belief. Knowing this, he knows that things that can be valued without reference to such a central ideal, "local objects," are more precious than things that must be so referred, the "objects of home" valuable with reference to the hearth as the center of the life lived there. Such "local objects" are the precious things in a world that has no "foyer," no central focus or belief, a world, furthermore, that since it has no such belief has no tradition ("remembered past") that is alive to the present ("a present past"), and that has no ideal on which the present may form the future ("a present future, hoped for in present hope"). In such a world valuable things occur at random, not by provenance of an order (compare "July Mountain," *OP*, p. 114); hence, they are not anywhere "present as a matter of course," and there are few that by nature belong to "that sphere," the world without central belief. These few things were to him the important things for which, since they were important, fresh names would suggest themselves as the older ones grew stale, as if by describing them he could catch them in final form ("make them") in order to preserve them. These things that are valuable in themselves include that which is discovered by insight, and unifications or harmonizations of the feelings. In other words, the intrinsically valuable things are fortuitous, since there is no ideal beyond the ego by which value may be inferred. They come without being sought, "of their own accord," because, though desirable, the ideal conditions of whose fulfillment they are reflections are unknown in the absence of a central focus, a belief: "he desired without knowing quite what." These insights and moods were the only manifestations of the ideal, "the classic, the beautiful," that he knew. They were that ideal state of mind, "that serene," that he had always been approaching as if it were an absolute ideal that could be established objectively, on the basis of the fact of reality, rather than on that of the imaginative or sentimental, or "romance." It is this "serene" that he has always desired, and that he now treats as the only possible ideal.

"Artificial Populations" (*OP*, p. 112)

"The center" in question here is a spiritual focus, a composing of the ego. The poem begins by defining it as a state of mind that has the clarity and composure of "weather after it has cleared." The poem goes on to qualify that definition: the "center" is more than a static state of mind; it is a state of mind that sustains itself to create an ambiance, an imagery. It is like weather that has clarity and composure and sustains them, producing a climate which in turn produces a population appropriate to that climate (one that is "rosy," happy in disposition in response to such weather.) Just as the climate produces its appropriate population ("artificial" both because it is a hypothesis of the imagination and something created), so also the central state of mind creates an imagery appropriate to itself which reconciles the mind with reality, and consequently heals its "sickness." Angels imagined on steeples by a religious sensibility, or, in contrast, humanity seen mirrored in configurations of leaves, are appropriate projections of the mind as artificial populations are appropriate projections of the weather; the climate produces a population that is harmonious with it as the mind images a reality that is harmonious with the mind. The "faces in a summer night" are, perhaps, such images created in response to a season and a time fertile for the imagination. Finally, there are also populations (or kinds of imagery) that are appropriate to various kinds of weather (or states of mind), as well as kinds of imagery appropriate to dream ("late sleep"), and to enduring poetry (or any art resembling poetry for which "music" might stand).

"A Clear Day and No Memories" (*OP*, p. 113)

The experience described in "A Clear Day and No Memories" is one of composure without content, of composure through exclusion of content. There is no one in the mind's prospect who is involved in the struggles of life, "No soldiers in the scenery," nor is the attention directed to memories of those from the past. The mind has withdrawn from reality, "the weather," into itself. What surrounds one, "the air," yields no perception other than its immateriality to the mind so withdrawn. To the mind so disconnected from it, the external world has no meaning. That world seems remote to the point where it seems that no one has any memory of it, nor any present connection with it, that one is absent from it. As the mind withdraws, what is beyond it becomes unreal, an unconvincing performance, an activity imperceptible to it, not a reality at all but a "sense," a faculty of the mind. What is described, then, is a composed disengagement of the ego from its life in reality.

"As You Leave the Room" (*OP*, p. 116)

Samuel French Morse notes in his introduction to *Opus Posthumous* (p. xvii) that "As You Leave the Room" grew out of an earlier version called "First Warmth" (*OP*, p. 89), which dates from 1947. He says of the later poem that it "must be one of the very last poems he wrote." Among the other additions to and modifications of the earlier poem, the addition of the contentious initial statement by a third person calls for more of an argument than is presented in the first version, and therefore allows the second to become more assertive, more of an apologia. The argument is carried on in a reflection as the first speaker leaves the room. He has said that he who dominates the contemporary scene, "Today's character," is not one separated from sensuous life, like a skeleton escaped from its death chamber. But, the argument goes, the writer's poems (they seem identifiable poems of Stevens') are about the concerns of life, not those of someone separated from life, "not what skeletons think about." Is he one who, not accepting the realm of the real as "a disbeliever in reality," has lived apart from reality as one dead to life, "A countryman of all the bones in the world?" Proof that this is not so is provided in the experiénce which now occurs, and which, presumably, is to be taken as a paradigm of his past experience. The snow, to which his attention now returns, seems to be part of an important, or "major," reality because he suddenly appreciates it as a part of reality, and since he does so appreciate it, since he discovers something meaningful in it, he undergoes an exaltation of mood, "an elevation." (The snow has also become an addition to reality, as Roy Harvey Pearce points out in his reading of the word "appreciation.")[55] The relation thus formed with reality is an intensely sensuous one, so that it is as if he left this experience (or, perhaps, as if he were leaving life itself) not merely with something to be formulated in words, but with something he could "touch, touch every way." This relation is formed through the kind of modification of mind and feeling of which his poems consist, which occurs not in the realm of the real but in that of the unreal, the ego. Nothing has altered in reality, but this modification of unreality, far from being divorced from reality, is a way of reaching the latter, of getting a sense of reality.

"Of Mere Being" (OP, p. 117)

"Of Mere Being" sets up existence itself as the goal of desire. One senses existence beyond thought as a palm "In the bronze distance," as though it were a goal sought for in an ideal, hence brazen, atmosphere. It is, perhaps, present "at the end of the mind" not only because it is beyond thought, but also because it is what the mind desires. But, the point of existence, the song of the golden bird in the palm, is alien to humanity and, since it is without human meaning or feeling, is not available to thought or desire. Therefore, fulfillment of desire or its frustration, happiness or unhappiness, does not depend on the reason; it makes no difference what we think, or what we want. The bird goes on singing, its feathers shining, without regard to us. The palm does not exist for us and is as remote from us as it can be, "on the edge of space." Yet to us and, no doubt, especially to an old man close to death, existence itself seems as dazzling as the bird and as tantalizing as the palm's slowly moving branches and the bird's dangling feathers. The bird does not sing for us, and will continue singing without us, but it is its song that we above all want to hear, the sense of mere existence that we most want to sustain.

NOTES

1 Samuel French Morse finds that "echoes of Pope's rhetoric and tone and even prosody abound in 'The Comedian as the Letter C' and 'Le Monocle de Mon Oncle,' and in *Harmonium* as a whole." "Wallace Stevens: Some Ideas About the Thing Itself," *Boston University Studies in English*, II (Spring 1956), 59–60.

2 Frank Kermode, *Wallace Stevens* (New York, 1961), p. 44. So also for the "interior paramour"—see Eugene Paul Nassar, *Wallace Stevens: An Anatomy of Figuration* (Philadelphia, 1965), p. 139. If one must resort to mythology here, the imagery seems to suggest Hera or Juno at least as much as Aphrodite or Venus. However, any such search for an allusion is probably superfluous. Stevens writes: "My recollection is that the Mother of Heaven was merely somebody to swear by, and that the reference was not symbolic" (*LWS*, p. 251).

3 Compare Kermode, p. 44: the apple "was also the cause of unreasonable passion, and comes to be moralized only when the moralist is too old to be passionate."

4 Stevens' comment (in *LWS*, p. 251), identifying the "rose rabbi" with youth—which he apparently made without a text at hand—has no meaning in context, except, possibly, the tenuous one that the "rose rabbi" represents a stage of youth succeeding the "dark rabbi" stage, and which carried over into the present of middle age.

5 J. V. Cunningham, "Tradition and Modernity: Wallace Stevens" (formerly published in *Poetry*, LXXV [Dec. 1949], 149–65), *Tradition and Poetic Structure* (Denver, 1960), p. 112.

6 " 'The Comedian as the Letter C': Its Sense and Significance," *Southern Review*, V (Winter 1940), 467.

7 See Joseph N. Riddel, *The Clairvoyant Eye: The Poetry and Poetics of Wallace Stevens* (Baton Rouge, 1965), pp. 94–95.

8 Simons, " 'The Comedian as the Letter C': Its Sense and Significance," p. 456.

9 See, for example, R. P. Blackmur, "Examples of Wallace Stevens," *Form and Value in Modern Poetry* (Garden City, New York, 1957), pp. 207–8: "Moonlight is imagination, a reflection or interpretation of the sun, which is the source of life." Simons' interpretation, p. 458, in which the moonlight stands for the "romantic" imagination and the sun for matter-of-fact realism, is more satisfactory—though the realism is more likely that of Yucatan than matter-of-fact.

[10] See George McFadden, "Probings for an Integration: Color Symbolism in Wallace Stevens," *Modern Philology*, LVIII (Feb. 1961), 186–93, for an attempt to work out a key to Stevens' use of colors.

[11] "Often I have to let go, in the most insignificant poem . . . the most skyey of skyey sheets." Stevens, in a letter to Harriet Monroe, Oct. 28, 1922 (*LWS*, p. 231). Stevens had been working on the poem during the summer preceding the date of the letter.

[12] Yvor Winters, "Wallace Stevens, or the Hedonist's Progress," *In Defense of Reason* (Denver, no date), pp. 442–43. Francis Murphy, " 'The Comedian as the Letter C'," *Wisconsin Studies in Contemporary Literature*, III (Spring–Summer 1962), 93, reads this passage in a similar way, as against Winters.

[13] Daniel Fuchs, in *The Comic Spirit of Wallace Stevens* (Durham, N. C., 1963), pp. 58–59, counts the cabin as phylactery because it reminds Crispin of his obligation to keep "the law of natural reality."

[14] Frank Doggett, *Stevens' Poetry of Thought* (Baltimore, 1966), pp. 127–28.

[15] For a brief summary of the many conflicting interpretations of this poem (followed by a rather perverse reading) see Taylor Culbert and John M. Violette, "Wallace Stevens' Emperor," *Criticism*, II (Winter 1960), 38–47.

[16] Riddel, p. 68, notes this separation as a fortunate one, since it gives birth to imagination, but for Stevens the separation is obviously anguished.

[17] W. R. Keast's interpretation of the poem—" 'Thirteen Ways of Looking at a Blackbird,' " *Chicago Review*, VIII (Winter–Spring 1954), 48–63—as the unified experience of an assumed speaker, which he gives hesitantly, only makes the separate sections harder to explicate, because one must then additionally explain them in relation to that hypothetical experience. The hypothesis makes for strained interpretation.

[18] See Part I, n. 10. The resemblances to traditional oriental poetry, particularly to the *haiku*, in this and similar Stevens poems, have long been widely noted.

[19] VII (Nov. 1948), Item 18.

[20] See Marcel Raymond, *De Baudelaire au Surréalisme* (Paris, 1933), pp. 32–33; and Guy Michaud, *Message Poétique du Symbolisme*, III (Paris, 1947), 572.

[21] Michaud, III, 560.

[22] Riddel, pp. 117–18, finds the theory sufficiently parallel to feel that the poem "might have been written to confirm" a passage from the critic's essay, "Of Philosophical Criticism." Stevens' comment about the name: "I used two every day names. As I might have expected, they turned out to be an actual name." See Kimon Friar and John Malcolm Brinnin, eds., *Modern Poetry, American and British* (New York, 1951), p. 538; also, *LWS*, pp. 798 and 823, where Stevens accompanies his denials of any reference to the real Fernandez with acknowledgments that he knew of him and had read some of his writings.

[23] Stevens wrote of Mario Rossi: "A young Italian philosopher who taught at Naples. I exchanged a few letters with him many years ago. He knows English. He made a trip to the west of Ireland and wrote a

little book about the trip which was of particular interest to me as reflecting what a man brought up in the light and color of Naples would feel in the mist and general dimness of the west of Ireland." Quoted in Friar and Brinnin, p. 537. Stevens uncertainly recalled the epigraph as being from "something in the *London Mercury*" (*LWS*, p. 347).

24 Stevens, quoted by Samuel French Morse from a jacket note on *The Man with the Blue Guitar*, in "The Motive for Metaphor," *Origin* V, II (Spring 1952), 16.

25 Ibid.

26 On the resemblances of Stevens to Monet and modern French painting, see Michel Benamou, "Wallace Stevens: Some Relations Between Poetry and Painting," *Comparative Literature*, XI (Winter 1959), 47–60.

27 Many of Stevens' glosses in Poggioli (of sections III, IV, VI—two comments—XVI, XVII, XIX, XXI, XXIII, XXV, XXIX,XXVII, XXX—two comments) are not included in *LWS*.

28 *LWS* reads "role" instead of "robe," but the poem speaks of the "robe" of the actor and the latter word makes more sense in context. There are many minor differences between the letters as printed in Poggioli and in *LWS*. Some seem to be the consequence of foreign printers, and others are presumably that of different readings of Stevens' handwriting; there are plainly some differences in transcription as well.

29 Doggett, p. 74: "time as a pregnancy, deep in the dark of its own mystery of process."

30 Hi Simons, "Wallace Stevens and Mallarmé," *Modern Philology*, XLIII (May 1946), 243.

31 "On the Grammar of Wallace Stevens," in Roy Harvey Pearce and J. Hillis Miller, eds., *The Act of the Mind* (Baltimore, 1965), p. 183.

32 Simons, "Wallace Stevens and Mallarmé," p. 243.

33 This interpretation of XXXI is that of J. V. Cunningham, written on an earlier draft, and slightly reworded here. Cunningham's reading is published in his recent article, "The Styles and Procedures of Wallace Stevens," *The Denver Quarterly*, I (Spring 1966), 10.

34 Doggett, p. 98, n., points out that the phrase "the act of the mind" was apparently taken from Samuel Alexander's *Space, Time, and Deity*, quoted in *OP*, p. 193, or misquoted, since Alexander's phrase is "the act of mind."

35 Robert Pack's interpretation of this section in *Wallace Stevens* (New Brunswick, N.J., 1958), pp. 37–38, and that of Roy Harvey Pearce in *The Continuity of American Poetry*, corrected and revised (Princeton, 1965), p. 401, become confused because of the assumption of the moon as a symbol for the imagination. Such assumptions of constant meanings for Stevens' images are always dangerous, even in the cases of those that are commonly used as symbols.

36 "Wallace Stevens: Some Ideas About the Thing Itself," p. 62.

37 "I follow his chain of reasoning with the secret uneasiness that one feels in the presence of some lunatic logician. And I observe that he has the inspired face of a madman. But in all that he says, he is driven by one basic idea which is not the idea of a madman: 'We did not

create the Revolution to come to this'" [i.e., to the betrayal of the Revolution]. Victor Serge, *Memoirs of a Revolutionary, 1901–1941*, trans. from the French by Peter Sedgwick (Oxford, 1963), p. 204. Obviously Stevens has changed the sense of Konstantinov's "one basic idea" to suit his own purposes.

38 Stevens has written that, "If you take the varnish and dirt of generations off a picture, you see it in its first idea" (*LWS*, pp. 426–27; see below, n. 41). In speaking of the unsystematic character of the connections between the poems in "Notes," Stevens says that he began by trying to follow a scheme, but dropped it because such systematic development was leading him to produce "something that did not come off in any sense, not even as poetry" *LWS*, p. 431. *It Must Be Abstract* bears traces of schematic development, though VII seems to express impatience with such systematization. It may be, in part, the vestiges of a poorly realized scheme that makes *It Must Be Abstract* hard to follow: the rest of "Notes" is more clearly improvisatory in its sequence and its terminology.

39 Louis L. Martz, "The World of Wallace Stevens," *Focus Five*, ed. B. Rajan (London, 1950), pp. 99–100, gives another possible reading: "'Its late plural' is the varied manifestation of that essence ['ever-early candor'] as now exhibited in the world about us—often a sorry assortment of objects encrusted with the dirt of time, but, seen in their first idea, radiant." Bernard H. Heringman, "Wallace Stevens: The Use of Poetry," *ELH*, XVI (Dec. 1949), 331, also reads it this way: "the idea and its descendant manifestations." (The Heringman essay is republished in Pearce and Miller, pp. 1–12.) However, Stevens uses the word "plural" to mean the two members of a couple in the second part of "Notes," IV (*CP*, p. 392).

40 N. P. Stallknecht comments that the point that the first idea is not our own "transposes *Cogito ergo sum* into the more humble *Sum ergo cogito*." "Absence in Reality," *Kenyon Review*, XXI (Fall 1959), 548.

41 In a letter to Henry Church dated Oct. 28, 1942, Stevens wrote as follows: "Some one here wrote to me the other day and wanted to know what I meant by a thinker of the first idea. If you take the varnish and dirt of generations off a picture, you see it in its first idea. If you think about the world without its varnish and dirt, you are a thinker of the first idea" (*LWS*, pp. 426–27).

42 Riddel, p. 173, finds a difficulty in this passage because he identifies "the pensive giant" with "the first idea." There is no good reason for this identification: the "pensive giant" is the "major man" who thinks "the first idea." See quote from Stevens, n. 41.

43 Roy Harvey Pearce, pp. 396–97, says that major man is "man imagining," that he discovers a supreme fiction, and that the supreme fiction is major man. This seems to me confused. He is correct in stating that major man is the poet. Major man, as an elusively possible abstraction, is much like the "impossible possible philosophers' man" in "Asides on the Oboe" (*CP*, p. 250), who has had "the time to think enough," the "central man" who "sums us up."

44 Harold Bloom, "*Notes toward a Supreme Fiction*: A Commen-

tary," in Marie Borroff, ed., *Wallace Stevens: A Collection of Critical Essays* (Englewood Cliffs, N.J., 1963), pp. 82–83, fails to see this distinction between "major man" and "the major abstraction," the "idea of man," and thus misreads the tramp-like figure of stanzas 5 and 6 as "major man." Merle E. Brown, "Concordia Discors in the Poetry of Wallace Stevens," *American Literature*, XXXIV (May 1962), 255, makes this distinction.

45 Riddel, p. 175, and Nassar, p. 199, note the pun on "bee" and "be" in this section; it is, of course, relevant to the following section.

46 *The Shaping Spirit* (Chicago, 1950), p. 72.

47 Bloom, p. 88, relates the wind to the Romantic image of the west wind.

48 Pearce, p. 399, sums up II with the statement, "What is needed is the pleasure of things-in-themselves." Stevens says of it: "One of the approaches to fiction is by way of its opposite: reality, the truth, the thing observed, the purity of the eye. The more exquisite the thing seen, the more exquisite the thing unseen" (*LWS*, p. 444).

49 Brown, p. 259.

50 Pearce, p. 399, followed by other critics, considers V–VII "the parable of the canon who would impose an alien order on reality." But "He" of VII is not demonstrably Canon Aspirin, the problems concerning whom have, on the contrary, been resolved in VI.

51 Pack, p. 107, reads this phrase the same way.

52 The period at the end of l. 12 in *CP* seems an obvious typographical error. In the poem's first appearance in *Hudson Review*, IV (Spring 1951), and in the Faber *Selected Poems*, the line ends with a comma, but, as with "air" for "ear" in *OP*'s "The Course of a Particular," the apparent error is carried over to the Vintage selection.

53 "Postscript, Written in 1958," to "A Hedonist's Progress," in Winters' *On Modern Poets* (New York, 1959), p. 35.

54 In a letter to me. He noted, however, that in the original typescript from which he took his copy, "air," not "ear," appeared in the last stanza.

55 "Wallace Stevens: The Last Lesson of the Master," Pearce and Miller, pp. 133–34.

III.
A Guide
to Stevens' Collected Poetry

The following guide covers the complete *Collected Poems,* plus all the poems in *Opus Posthumous* that are of importance. The numbers refer by page to apposite material in the body of this book; the letters a–d pertain to the first through fourth quarters of a given page. An asterisk signifies that the poem is paraphrased on the page indicated.

ACADEMIC DISCOURSE AT HAVANA. "Rouge-Fatima": Stevens has noted that Fatima was one of the most beautiful women in the world, adding that he supposed he put the Rouge on to touch her up.[1] 5c–6c, 107b–108a

ADD THIS TO RHETORIC. 19d, 26b–c

ADULT EPIGRAM. Precision reaches toward the truth of abstraction, of permanence within impermanence. 5b–c

THE AMERICAN SUBLIME. "The mickey mockers/ And plated pairs": cynics with their money grubbing ("plated pairs" for coins). 1a–b, 29b, 30a–b

ANALYSIS OF A THEME. Novel forms exist in time as pure potential, to be realized by the imagination in its inventions and discoveries. The name Blandina figures in Stevens' geneology as an ancestor born in 1743 (*LWS*, p. 405).

*ANATOMY OF MONOTONY. 78

ANECDOTE OF CANNA. The antidote to the solipsism of the purely imaginary is acute observation of the real. Stevens glosses "Now day-break comes" as the return of reality. He wrote the poem while walking around the Capitol in Washington (*LWS*, p. 464).

ANECDOTE OF MEN BY THE THOUSAND. 54a–c

ANECDOTE OF THE JAR. "Of a port in air" may be read to mean, of the nature of an evanescent entry ("port" for portal) to order in a scene of disorder. 73c–74a

ANECDOTE OF THE PRINCE OF PEACOCKS. The "Berserk" chaos of reality threatens the beauty of the imagined, realm of "The Prince of Peacocks."

*ANGEL SURROUNDED BY PAYSANS. 186

ANGLAIS MORT À FLORENCE. Stevens writes: "Most people stand by the aid of philosophy, religion and one thing or another, but a strong spirit . . . stands by its own strength. Even such a spirit is subject to degeneration. . . . If men have nothing external to them on which to rely, then, in the event of a collapse of their own spirit, they must naturally turn to the spirit of others" (*LWS*, p. 348).

ANOTHER WEEPING WOMAN. Death reduces the power of the imagination so that the mourning woman is left, with no defense against grief, confronting a meaningless reality.

ANYTHING IS BEAUTIFUL IF YOU SAY IT IS. The "concubine" is alienated from her environment, Hans is not.

THE APOSTROPHE TO VINCENTINE. A human context transforms "Monotonous earth." 141c–d

ARCADES OF PHILADELPHIA THE PAST. The poem refers to the ancient Palestinian city of Philadelphia. The inhabitants of the Apennine Vallombrosa (of monastic reputation as the former site of a monastery) do not use their five senses and thus can apprehend neither the past nor the present. This sensory impoverishment prevents them from responding to the world or to themselves imaginatively (sounds, speech; i.e., poetry). In face of the sensuous wealth of the present, the past seems fake.

ARRIVAL AT THE WALDORF. 10b–d

*ARTIFICIAL POPULATIONS. 202

*AS YOU LEAVE THE ROOM. 203

*ASIDES ON THE OBOE. 108

ATTEMPT TO DISCOVER LIFE. An attempt to discover the life that the place and the flowers imply by imagining it in terms of the two figures. One should then add Stevens' comment that the poem prompts the question of "whether the experience of life is in the end worth more than tuppence: dos centavos." Hermosas are a variety of roses, San Miguel de los Baños is a Cuban spa (*LWS*, p. 540).

THE AURORAS OF AUTUMN. The title refers to the aurora borealis, which Stevens could sometimes see from Hartford, and which symbolized for him "a tragic and desolate background" (*LWS*, p. 852). "Serpent": the flux of time. "Farewell to an idea": the dissolution of a given idea of reality. "Mother": nature, reality. "Father": the cosmic imagination, the creative source. "Innocence": the character of that existence with which we must be reconciled, neither false nor malicious. "Cabin," "room," "house," "festival," "Danes in Denmark": given imaginative integrations of reality. 5d–6c, 9d–10b, 35a–b

AUTUMN REFRAIN. The desolate mood of the autumnal day remains at night to contradict night's poetic associations. 9d–10b

THE BAGATELLES THE MADRIGALS. Trivial thoughts of life's imperfection ("Bagatelles") formed into a poem concerned with abstract generalization ("Madrigals").

BANAL SOJOURN. "The mildew of any late season, of any experience that has grown monotonous as, for instance, the experience of life" (Stevens, *LWS*, p. 464). 7b–8a

BANJO BOOMER. Life figured in the mulberry against the ground of death—an expression of desire for a little longer to live.

*BANTAMS IN PINE-WOODS. 67

THE BED OF OLD JOHN ZELLER. John Zeller was Stevens' maternal great grandfather (*LWS*, pp. 4, 469). 10b–11c

THE BEGINNING. 7d–8a

THE BIRD WITH THE COPPERY, KEEN CLAWS. "Pip" means speck or spot; also the chirping of a bird. "Mort" would here mean both dead, and a great quantity. An "alguazil" is a justice, here a law-giver. The parakeet represents the principle of existence. As pure principle, he lives a more vital life than does the mortal and transitory existence whose inscrutable, perhaps meaningless laws he applies with his blind, inexorable will.

THE BLUE BUILDINGS IN THE SUMMER AIR. 5d–6b, 125c–126a

BOTANIST ON ALP (NO. 1) AND (NO. 2). (No. 1), 6c. "Claude": Claude Lorrain, the seventeenth-century French painter. (No. 2), its answer, 66b–67a

THE BOUQUET. An object seen through the proliferating imagination.

BOUQUET OF BELLE SCAVOIR. "She" is nature. 171d–172b

BOUQUET OF ROSES IN SUNLIGHT. 26c, 27a–b

THE BRAVE MAN. Dawn as a major statement of confrontation with secular reality.

BURGHERS OF PETTY DEATH. 78a–c

THE CANDLE A SAINT. The night is "green," fertile to the imaginative "madness" of the poet who conceives its abstract image. The "candle" by which the poet works, the imagination, is thus a "saint."

CELLE QUI FÛT HÉAULMIETTE. Representing the return of meaningfulness to the year, "she" is the child of the moon, an imagination as yet incapable, and of the sun, a potent reality. The title refers to Villon's faded *"fille de joie,"* who, in this poem, is seasonally reborn.

CERTAIN PHENOMENA OF SOUND. Poetry, "the word," creates its own world.

CHAOS IN MOTION AND NOT IN MOTION. Richter: German painter and book illustrator, 1803–1884. His world and art have become chaotic. 5d–6b, 9d–10a

A CHILD ASLEEP IN ITS OWN LIFE. The old man of (l. 9 exists within the meditation of the old man's universe he has himself imagined. 189b

CHOCORUA TO ITS NEIGHBOR. 94c, 143b–144c

*A CLEAR DAY AND NO MEMORIES. 202

COLLOQUY WITH A POLISH AUNT. "Imagination is the will of things": 151d–152c. "Voragine": Jacobus de Voragine, thirteenth-century hagiographer, author of the *Legenda Aurea.*

*THE COMEDIAN AS THE LETTER C. 46

THE COMMON LIFE. A scene that resists the imagination. 129c–d

A COMPLETELY NEW SET OF OBJECTS. A summoning of youthful friends and ancestral figures. The place names are in Pennsylvania. Annual festivals were held on the Schuylkill with canoes and boats lighted at night with Chinese lanterns.[2]

*CONNOISSEUR OF CHAOS. 104

CONTINUAL CONVERSATION WITH A SILENT MAN. Existence as a chain of interaction. "Turquoise": Imaginative abstraction.

CONTRARY THESES (I). 7d–8a

CONTRARY THESES (II). A vision of the order beyond the transitory seasons.

CONVERSATION WITH THREE WOMEN OF NEW ENGLAND. 25c–d, 170a–c

CORTÈGE FOR ROSENBLOOM. Death is dealt with in a ceremonious assertion of its matter-of-fact nature. Stevens comments: "From time immemorial the philosophers and other scene painters have daubed the sky with dazzle paint. But it all comes down to the proverbial six feet of earth in the end. . . . The ceremonies are amusing. Why not fill the sky with scaffolds and stairs, and go about like genuine realists?" (LWS, p. 223). 63b

COUNTRY WORDS. 163d–164b

THE COUNTRYMAN. Swatara: a stream above Harrisburg, Pennsylvania. 196b–197a

*THE COURSE OF A PARTICULAR. 197

THE CREATIONS OF SOUND. 135c–d

CREDENCES OF SUMMER. Reality in a phase perfectly adequate to the desires of the ego. "Oley" is a valley in eastern Pennsylvania. 10d–11b, 134b–135b

CRUDE FOYER. "Thought" as opposed to "vital metaphor." "Ignorant" here refers to a dearth of imagination, which leaves one at the mercy of reality. 106b–107a

THE CUBAN DOCTOR. The "Indian" is the transitory flux of existence, and, ultimately, death.

CUISINE BOURGEOISE. When general belief collapses we must feed upon our own minds. 5d–6c

THE CURTAINS IN THE HOUSE OF THE METAPHYSICIAN. 9d–10a, 12c–13a

CY EST POURTRAICTE, MADAME STE URSULE, ET LES UNZE MILLE VIERGES. The sensual, as well as the aesthetic, is a worthy aspect of creation.

DANCE OF THE MACABRE MICE. 5d–6b

DEATH OF A SOLDIER. 18b

DEBRIS OF LIFE AND MIND. "Bright red woman": the sun.

DELIGHTFUL EVENING. "Wormy": earthy, natural. 30d–31b

DEPRESSION BEFORE SPRING. 7d–8a

DESCRIPTION WITHOUT PLACE. A major statement of Stevens' poetics. 16a–18a, 25c–26c, 178d–179a, 184b–d

DESIRE & THE OBJECT. Does desire have its origin within or without, or both?

THE DESIRE TO MAKE LOVE IN A PAGODA. The virtue of change; the title is apposite. 151d–152c

DEZEMBRUM. Re-imagining heaven as appropriate to the contemporary.

DINNER BELL IN THE WOODS. Not ideas about the thing but the thing itself. 14a–c

A DISCOVERY OF THOUGHT. 26d–27a

A DISH OF PEACHES IN RUSSIA. The imagination re-creates the Russian's past life, and tears it away from the present.

DISILLUSIONMENT OF TEN O'CLOCK. The vividness of the imagination in the dullness of a pallid reality.

THE DOCTOR OF GENEVA. "Lakes are more reasonable than oceans"—Esthétique du Mal, XIV. 133b–134a

*DOMINATION OF BLACK. 38

THE DOVE IN THE BELLY. 134b–c

THE DOVE IN SPRING. The coming season neither exists as yet nor is totally imaginary.

DRY LOAF. The sense of a time expressed in a metaphor of a place.

*DUTCH GRAVES IN BUCKS COUNTY. 117

THE DWARF. The dwarf is the ego contracted to its barest self in winter. 7d–8a

EARTHY ANECDOTE. The "clattering" of the animals ordered

by confrontation with the "firecat," representing a given principle of order.

*THE EMPEROR OF ICE-CREAM. 62

*ESTHÉTIQUE DU MAL. 122

*EVENING WITHOUT ANGELS. 80

EXAMINATION OF THE HERO IN A TIME OF WAR. 143b–d; 143d–144c, especially for XII, XV; 108b–110c, especially for XIV.

EXPLANATION. The imagination is concerned with real adornment of reality, not romantic day dreams.

*EXTRACTS FROM ADDRESSES TO THE ACADEMY OF FINE IDEAS. 110

EXTRAORDINARY REFERENCES. Items of a tradition through reference to which one may gain composure. "Jacomyntje": a figure from Stevens' geneology (*LWS*, p. 4). "Tulpehocken": an area of Pennsylvania where Stevens' ancestors, the Zellers, lived (*LWS*, p. 470).

FABLIAU OF FLORIDA. An embarcation of the imagination on a voyage that seems endless.

A FADING OF THE SUN. The saving power of the imagination "within." Stevens comments: "instead of crying for help to God or to one of the gods, we should look to ourselves for help" (*LWS*, p. 295).

FAREWELL TO FLORIDA. Leaving the exotic as subject matter for the hard social fact of "men in crowds."

FAREWELL WITHOUT A GUITAR. His poems are left as a final record of his experience of "male reality" and the female imagination which embodies what the ego desires of reality.

*FINAL SOLILOQUY OF THE INTERIOR PARAMOUR. 192

First Warmth. 203c–204b

A FISH-SCALE SUNRISE. A shift from the imagination to a sensuous apprehension of reality itself. The names are those of friends of Stevens, to whom he wrote that the poem would be a souvenir of the state in which a "bat" they went on left him (*LWS*, p. 301). 30d–31a

FLORAL DECORATIONS FOR BANANAS. The need for an earthy harmony in which image suits image, decor suits person—an ideal of the good for the secular here-and-now.

FLYER'S FALL. 28a

FORCES, THE WILL, & THE WEATHER. The metaphors for the sensuous reality of the season enhance it: the girl and dog, the nougats, the waiter. This despite lack of abstract ideas about the season. "Peer yellow": the sun.

FROGS EAT BUTTERFLIES. . . . As in the title, the poem describes a nature in which one thing feeds on another in an intradependent whole. For a parallel in poetic method, 38a–b

FROM THE MISERY OF DON JOOST. The death of the body. 34d

FROM THE PACKET OF ANACHARSIS. "Puvis" (the painter, Puvis de Chavannes): the clarity of the idea; "Bloom": the particularity and variety of the world.

GALLANT CHÂTEAU. The order of the "prim" curtains as opposed to the potential disorder of the wind blown ones. 11c–13a

GHOSTS AS COCOONS. Stevens: "The bride is literally 'sun and music' etc.; not so literally, love and happiness. The butcher, seducer, etc. is literally the inept politician, and that sort of thing, and again, not quite so literally, evil and unhappiness. When *Ghosts* was written there was the same profound desire to be released from all our misfortunes that there is today. 'Those to be born': 'the grass is in seed': the people of the future who need to know something of the happiness of life." (*LWS*, p. 347).

GIGANTOMACHIA. The effect of an "idea of man." 144d–145b

GIRL IN A NIGHTGOWN. Impending social chaos disturbs the peace of time and season (published in 1942).

THE GLASS OF WATER. The imaginative, or metaphysical has its fluctuating states, parallel to the chemical states of the physical, but in the former, the realm of ideas, we may discover what is central to our lives.

GOD IS GOOD. IT IS A BEAUTIFUL NIGHT. A flight of the imagination, here "brown bird."

A GOLDEN WOMAN IN A SILVER MIRROR. Our lives are the reflections of our egos that we see in reality; but the images thus projected in poetry endure beyond our lives.

THE GOOD MAN HAS NO SHAPE. The idea of the good man in a secular world is made a mockery by death, "Lazarus."

GRAY STONES AND GRAY PIGEONS. Not monuments, but the human imagination, vivifies the religious institution. In the absence of the archbishop, who embodies the idea of the church, the church building is empty of meaning. (Compare *LWS*, pp. 347–48.)

THE GREEN PLANT. The idea of reality endures beyond the decaying season.

GUBBINAL. The world is oppressive beyond any relief the imagination can offer. Gubbins: a contemptuous name formerly given to inhabitants of a certain district in England, said to have been absolute savages.

THE HAND AS A BEING. "Mi-bird": the ego, which flies to its sanguine ("ruddier") encounter with reality. 159a–d

THE HERMITAGE AT THE CENTER. The "end" represented by the wind, and the "beginning" represented by "the desired," come together in the cyclic nature of reality, in which the end is part of the beginning.

HIBISCUS ON THE SLEEPING SHORES. The mind seeks the beauty of the flowers to pass a dull time.

A HIGH-TONED OLD CHRISTIAN WOMAN. Through the imagination one can just as well conceive a universal vision based on pleasures as one based on morality.

HOLIDAY IN REALITY. 168c–169a

HOMUNCULUS ET LA BELLE ÉTOILE. Stevens: "there is a center for every state of confusion. A number of such states are described in the early verses of the poem" (*LWS*, p. 306). The "ultimate Plato" focuses, tranquilizes, rather than resolves. 53d

THE HOUSE WAS QUIET AND THE WORLD WAS CALM. A major discovery of spiritual order. 31d–32a

HOW TO LIVE. WHAT TO DO. 195c–196a

HUMAN ARRANGEMENT. An abstract idea of a center from which the flux of existence proceeds. 5b–c

HYMN FROM A WATERMELON PAVILION. Both reality, "day," and dream, that of the "dark cabin" of the mind, "night," are products of the imagination; both are dreams. Why not, then, since "rising will not waken," choose the more tangible and various dream of reality, the real watermelon, rather than the imaginary one that is "always purple"?

*THE IDEA OF ORDER AT KEY WEST. 78

IDIOM OF THE HERO. "Clouds": that which is open to imaginative interpretation.

IMAGO. The imagination creates the national myth. 170b–c

IN A BAD TIME. An apostrophe to the muse of tragedy, that her art make us see the tragic nature of life as it is, and not merely the trappings of tragedy.

IN THE CAROLINAS. 7d–8a

IN THE CLEAR SEASON OF GRAPES. The meaninglessness of the sea does not negate human values; sea, land, and mountains co-exist in a meaningful integration (for example, each man contains the sea within him).

IN THE ELEMENT OF ANTAGONISMS. The world is without presiding spirit, god ("genius"), but an image of man to replace god also seems a mockery.

INDIAN RIVER. The flux of reality in Florida begets no seasonal change.

INFANTA MARINA. The spirit of the sea. "Sleights of sails": "the passing of a sail at a distance on the sea, in sight and out of sight . . . like sleights of hand" (LWS, p. 785).

INVECTIVE AGAINST SWANS. The dying summer makes out its testament, while the soul, yearning for something more permanent than ephemeral nature imagery, flies beyond the decaying season to the sky.

THE IRISH CLIFFS OF MOHER. 195c–196a

THE JACK-RABBIT. The buzzard as reminder that life is subject to death.

JASMINE'S BEAUTIFUL THOUGHTS UNDERNEATH THE WILLOW. Immediate pleasure in experience, beyond the artificiality of convention, and therefore "idiosyncratic," eccentric, subjective. The "love" here seems sensual, Jasmine enjoying her "titillations" as she "rocks" under Willow, feeling the "fugues and chorals" of her pleasure.

JOUGA. "Ha-eé-me" is the wind who plays his guitar, the sea. After the wind stops, the sea will be like a "great jaguar" making "a little sound," since the wind will no longer be playing on it.

JULY MOUNTAIN. 185d–186b, 200d–201d

JUMBO. A generalized abstraction representing the imaginatively perceiving ego.

THE LACK OF REPOSE. The young man reads his own tradition into the poet's nontraditional book.

LANDSCAPE WITH BOAT. 10b–11b, 172c–d

*LARGE RED MAN READING. 163

LAST LOOKS AT THE LILACS. 57d–58a

LATE HYMN FROM THE MYRRH-MOUNTAIN. "Snood": foliage of summer; "Neversink": mountain near Reading, Pennsylvania; "external world": the unadorned reality of winter. "Madanna," in l. 1, is probably a variation on "madane," an obsolete form of "maiden."

THE LATEST FREED MAN. Vidal bought books and paintings in Paris for Stevens and was an amateur painter. Stevens had a self-portrait of Vidal's. Samuel French Morse has indicated that the French phrase is probably from a Vidal letter and in description of his paintings.[3] 10b–11b, 14d–15a

LEBENSWEISHEITSPIELEREI. The death of autumn, the approach of death, reduces people to the essentially human.

LESS AND LESS HUMAN, O SAVAGE SPIRIT. 10b–11b, 124a–125b

LIFE IS MOTION. We live in a present of constant change, of which motion is the essence.

LIKE DECORATIONS IN A NIGGER CEMETERY. A "litter" (see LWS, p. 272) of observations dealing with the conditions of life on Stevens' naturalistic assumptions, the world bare of myth, man's only resort the "decorations" of the imagination. In form, of the variations-on-a-theme type of "Thirteen Ways of Looking at a Blackbird." 71c–72a, 23b–d, 6d–7a Stevens comments on twelve of the fifty sections in LWS, pp. 348–50.

LIONS IN SWEDEN. "Dufy's Hamburg": Dufy's illustration of a lion for Apollinaire's "Le Bestiaire ou le Cortège d'Orphée," 1911;[4] Apollinaire's lions are described as unfortunate images, since we now usually associate them merely with zoos. 5d–6c

THE LOAD OF SUGAR-CANE. Each element like another, in a chain of resemblances within the intradependent whole of nature. For a parallel in poetic method, see 38a–b.

*LOCAL OBJECTS. 200

LONELINESS IN JERSEY CITY. Confrontation with a world incapable of distinguishing between the grace of the deer and the comic clumsiness of the dachshund.

*LONG AND SLUGGISH LINES. 191

*LOOKING ACROSS THE FIELDS AND WATCHING THE BIRDS FLY. 189

A LOT OF PEOPLE BATHING IN A STREAM. 35a–b, 196b–197a

LUNAR PARAPHRASE. The light of the moon gives the comforting, but pathetic, illusion of a return to a more peaceful season, a more tranquil era.

LYTTON STRACHEY, ALSO, ENTERS INTO HEAVEN. Understanding such a figure as Lenin, who cannot be understood without the passionate misunderstandings of life, troubles the biographer.

MADAME LA FLEURIE. Death shows that one is not part of, but separate from, nature.

MAN AND BOTTLE. 8a–b

*MAN CARRYING THING. 135

*THE MAN ON THE DUMP. 102

THE MAN WHOSE PHARYNX WAS BAD. An expression of desire to break out of a depressing emotional stasis, caused by an indifferent quotidian, through a discovery of some final principle beyond the quotidian, beyond time which, however, "will not relent." 5b–c

*THE MAN WITH THE BLUE GUITAR. 82

MARTIAL CADENZA. 8d–9a

MEDITATION CELESTIAL & TERRESTRIAL. 7d–8a

MEN MADE OUT OF WORDS. 24d–25a

THE MEN THAT ARE FALLING. The dreamer envisions one engaged in the Spanish Civil War (LWS, p. 798) who, being more than the mythical Christ whose facial impression was miraculously left on the "sudarium," is like the historical Christ who died for love of earth, not heaven. 66c–67c

METAMORPHOSIS. The metamorphosis of summer into

autumn with appropriate deformations and disintegrations of the month names in what Stevens calls a "poem of disintegration" (*LWS*, p. 753).

METAPHOR AS DEGENERATION. Metaphor creates our images of both generation and degeneration, existence, and nonexistence. "Swatara": river above Harrisburg, Pennsylvania. 164c, 196b–197a

METAPHORS OF A MAGNIFICO. 50d–51b

*LE MONOCLE DE MON ONCLE. 38

MONTRACHET-LE-JARDIN. An attempt at an ideal of man dissolves into the particulars of reality. 143b–d

THE MOTIVE FOR METAPHOR. The imagination's metamorphoses vitalizes reality's "primary noon." 129b–130a, 151d–152c

MOUNTAINS COVERED WITH CATS. In contrast with the sameness of the mass, the impotent outcasts, the originals, the innovators, were not at all impotent, as they had seemed to be.

MOZART, 1935. 107b–108a

MRS. ALFRED URUGUAY. The necessity of imagination for a positive rapport with reality. 16a–17b

MUD MASTER. The sun, master of nature, is also master of the mind, which is part of nature.

NEGATION. The initially cheerful tone of this assertion of pointless imperfection is an ironic way of approaching a somber truth which we can do no more than bear.

NEW ENGLAND VERSES. 23c–d

THE NEWS AND THE WEATHER. I. Spring. II. "The deep breath": physical contact with reality. 171d–172b

*NO POSSUM, NO SOP, NO TATERS. 120

NOMAD EXQUISITE. The speaker is the "Nomad," wanderer, traveler; in this case, probably he is a tourist. The effect of Florida on his imagination is like the effect of the climate on the proliferating vegetation of Florida.

NOT IDEAS ABOUT THE THING BUT THE THING ITSELF. A major statement of the importance of contacting a solid reality beyond the mind. 14a–15d

NOTE ON MOONLIGHT. The imagination, "moonlight," projects the feelings of the ego into reality, creating a subjective variety within its apparent objectivity. 16a–17b

*NOTES TOWARD A SUPREME FICTION. 136

THE NOVEL. The lines of italics in the third and fourth stanzas are taken from a letter to Stevens from José Rodríguez-Feo; that in stanza six is from Lorca's "Martirio de Santa Olalla," which was quoted by Thomas McGreevy in a letter to Stevens (*LWS*, p. 617). Varadero is a Cuban beach resort that was frequented by Rodríguez-Feo. The imagination, the "novel," adds its intense reality to the reader's (José's) decaying autumnal scene as he reads it and empathizes with the reader of the novel by Camus. Rodríguez-Feo was at Princeton at this time and thus is pictured as facing a northern autumn while remembering Cuba.

NUANCES OF A THEME BY WILLIAMS. 50d–51a

NUDITY AT THE CAPITAL; NUDITY IN THE COLONIES. Artlessness conceals; artfulness conceals (see *LWS*, p. 347).

NUNS PAINTING WATER-LILIES. The nuns, through the images ("sproutings") of reality they create, become united with reality. 194a–c

O FLORIDA, VENEREAL SOIL. The spirit of Florida pure ("virgin") of "boorish births," should breed ("Venereal") a few things beautiful in themselves.

OAK LEAVES ARE HANDS. "Flora Lowzen" represents the principle of metamorphosis which in past times had been figured as "Flora," the seasonal cycle of vegetation, and as the Fates ("Mac Mort," son of death), their twelve limbs resembling a single spider as they weave the course of men's mortality. As the acorn contains the principle of oaks beyond any actual oaks ("unreal"), so she contains the principle of change which informs past and future events.

OF BRIGHT & BLUE BIRDS & THE GALA SUN. 106b–107a

OF HARTFORD IN A PURPLE LIGHT. 151d–152c

*OF HEAVEN CONSIDERED AS A TOMB. 61

*OF MERE BEING. 204

*OF MODERN POETRY. 107

OF THE SURFACE OF THINGS. The "Surface of Things" is the particulars of reality. "The gold tree is blue": the real tree is imaginary. The moon stands for imagination. The subject is the fluctuation between the imagined and the real.

THE OLD LUTHERAN BELLS AT HOME. The bells are aesthetically meaningful, but as symbols of a "truth," a "sect," seems jangling and meaningless.

AN OLD MAN ASLEEP. The external, as well as the internal, is part of the individual consciousness.

ON AN OLD HORN. The music of poetry is the mind's defense against chaos. (See Stevens' paraphrase, *LWS*, p. 403.)

ON THE ADEQUACY OF LANDSCAPE. The "Landscape," as opposed to discursive thought about it ("owl"), is adequate for the ego. 134b–d

*ON THE MANNER OF ADDRESSING CLOUDS. 61

ON THE ROAD HOME. 10b–11b

ON THE WAY TO THE BUS. 185b–c

ONE OF THE INHABITANTS OF THE WEST. A human meaning read into nightfall: one associates the dying of day with the yearly death engendered by autumn.

*AN ORDINARY EVENING IN NEW HAVEN. 167

THE ORDINARY WOMEN. The refreshment that art, in its palace, gives to reality.

OUR STARS COME FROM IRELAND. Tom McGreevy: an Irish poet with whom Stevens corresponded. Part I contains references to his poetry (*LWS*, p. 608). Swatara and Schuylkill are rivers in Pennsylvania. Mal Bay, Tarbert, and Kerry are places on the western coast of Ireland. Stevens wrote McGreevy in connection with I, "When we look back, at least when I look back, I do not really remember myself but the places in which I lived and things there with which I was familiar" (*LWS*, p. 608).

THE OWL IN THE SARCOPHAGUS: AN ATTEMPT TO CONTAIN DEATH WITHIN THE MODERN IMAGINATION. The "third form": the last fleeting knowledge of life's flux, of which death is part. Compare 127d–128b.

OWL'S CLOVER. 5d–7a. (See Stevens' long gloss of this poem, *LWS*, pp. 366–75.)

PAGE FROM A TALE. Substituting for Yeats's secure cabin the vision of Stevens' problematic universe.

PAISANT CHRONICLE. Stevens writes of this poem that "we have to fix abstract objectives and then to conceal the abstract figures in actual appearance" (*LWS*, p. 489). 143b–d

PALACE OF THE BABIES. The imagination dead to an imagery in which it cannot believe.

*THE PALTRY NUDE STARTS ON A SPRING VOYAGE. 37

PAROCHIAL THEME. 8c–9a

THE PASTOR CABALLERO. The figure becomes a transcendent form through the improvisation of the imagination.

A PASTORAL NUN. Both "poetry" and "apotheosis" are creative in conceiving "favorable transformations" of reality.

THE PEDIMENT OF APPEARANCE. 10b–c

*PETER QUINCE AT THE CLAVIER. 69

PHOSPHOR READING BY HIS OWN LIGHT. Phosphor, who projects his ego onto reality, therefore sees nothing of reality and is not a realist. The realist, open to reality, thinks it is the product of his ego after he has perceived it. "Fusky": dark, mysterious.

PIECES. The "sense in sounds" is what they suggest to the imagination because of what we feel about them. 19d–20b

THE PLACE OF THE SOLITAIRES. About the continuous iteration of the cyclic processes of reality, including the "restless iteration" of the mind in its lonely meditation of these processes in "the place of the solitaires." The poem is itself a cycle.

*THE PLAIN SENSE OF THINGS. 187

THE PLANET ON THE TABLE. His poems were alive to him because they had captured the sense of his existence.

THE PLEASURES OF MERELY CIRCULATING. Stevens comments: "The spectacle of order is so vast that it resembles disorder. . . . But for all the apparent fortuitousness of things, they hold together" (*LWS*, p. 348). Mrs. Anderson's baby: it is the process, not the result, that matters. 158c–d

THE PLOT AGAINST THE GIANT. Brute reality undone by the beauty of art.

PLOUGHING ON SUNDAY. The poet, on the day devoted to faith, works like Uncle Remus to compose the myths of the continent.

LES PLUS BELLES PAGES. The works of the Saint survive because they do not exist in isolation from the human. (See *OP*, p. 293 for Stevens' explication.)

THE POEM THAT TOOK THE PLACE OF A MOUNTAIN. 11c–12a

POEM WITH RHYTHMS. The imagination projects the ego into the world.

POEM WRITTEN AT MORNING. 11d–12a, 25c–d

THE POEMS OF OUR CLIMATE. 130d–131d

POESIE ABRUTIE. The greenhouse and the flowers "speak" of the coming strength of the sun. 7d–8a

POETRY IS A DESTRUCTIVE FORCE. Misery, given figuration in poetry, becomes potent. It is like having the strength of a dumb brute at heart ("Corazon"—thus the animal's blood is his, and he tastes it rather than his own spit), which, if it expressed itself, would do so with destructive violence.

POLO PONIES PRACTICING. 8d–9a

A POSTCARD FROM THE VOLCANO. The poet's words of the existence that continues after his severance from it in death, continue to shape our image of that existence.

THE PREJUDICE AGAINST THE PAST. Images seem dead "relics" until they are seen, not as hypotheses about reality, but as projections of the ego.

PRELUDE TO OBJECTS. 144d–145b

PRESENCE OF AN EXTERNAL MASTER OF KNOWLEDGE. A condensation out of "The Sail of Ulysses." 189b

A PRIMITIVE LIKE AN ORB. Minor variation on "Notes toward a Supreme Fiction."

PROLOGUES TO WHAT IS POSSIBLE. I. Approaching the moment of poetic truth in the "boat" of imagination which transcends the "stones" of reality. II. is a description of such a moment. 16a–17b

THE PUBLIC SQUARE. A vision of nothingness. 9d–10a

PUELLA PARVULA. The title: "young girl"—as opposed to "wild bitch." 13b–14a

THE PURE GOOD OF THEORY. I. 143b–d. II. 106d–107a. III., IV. 24d–26c. IV. Lines 7–15: the efforts of the ego, through the imagination, to contact reality, its "element." 85d–86c

QUESTIONS ARE REMARKS. The child sees the freshness of

the world beyond rhetoric. "Red horse": the mother's description of the newly risen sun. 10b–c

A QUIET NORMAL LIFE. The "candle" of imagination, itself a reality, illuminates the reality of here and now. 203d–204b

A RABBIT AS KING OF THE GHOSTS. The rabbit is the expansive ego, the cat, potentially dangerous reality.

THE READER. 9d–10a

*REALITY IS AN ACTIVITY OF THE MOST AUGUST IMAGINATION. 199

THE RED FERN. The "fern" is the sunrise; the sun is considered as the creative principle beyond its physical manifestations.

THE REGION NOVEMBER. A contemplation of meaningless annihilation perceived in the destroying wind of autumn that is the "critic" of anything meaningful in the "waste" of existence. 9d–10a

REPETITIONS OF A YOUNG CAPTAIN. "Major men": "the pick of young men" (LWS, p. 489). "Giant": the fictive abstraction. 26d–27a, 114b–d

REPLY TO PAPINI. The poet does not proceed by systematic belief, like the Pope; he rather "shares the confusions of intelligence" which are "appropriate to/ The complexities of the world." 24b–d

RE-STATEMENT OF ROMANCE. Ego in relation with responsive ego transcends alien reality.

THE REVOLUTIONISTS STOP FOR ORANGEADE. The need for the artificial in art. 131a–b

*THE RIVER OF RIVERS IN CONNECTICUT. 196.

*THE ROCK. 193

SAD STRAINS OF A GAY WALTZ. "See Tea at the Palaz of Hoon. 6c"

SAILING AFTER LUNCH. The poet, an "inappropriate man" in an "unpropitious place," must rid himself of the stale romantic for the fresh romance of confrontation with the actual. (Compare LWS, p. 277.)

THE SAIL OF ULYSSES. The mind in search of the fiction is figured as Ulysess. 157a–158a, 189b

ST. ARMORER'S CHURCH FROM THE OUTSIDE. 119a–120b

*saint john and the back-ache. 165

sea surface full of clouds. The seascape is: I. calm; II. threatening, windy, then clearing; III. seen at night, then dawn; IV. ominous, then clearing; V. changeable, and again clearing. Each mood of the sea evokes a mood in the viewer, the expression of which culminates in the line of French. 25c–26a, 71d

the search for sound free from motion. The world repeats its sounds, which yet are nicely turned to express its own, nonhuman intelligence, in a way quite equal to the way the "self" uses "the word."

*the sense of the sleight-of-hand man. 106

six significant landscapes. 72c–73b. In method, parallel to "Thirteen Ways of Looking at a Blackbird."

sketch of the ultimate politician. Major man. 143b–d, 144d–145b

snow and stars. 7d–8a

the snow man. The listener beholds "the nothing" that is there. Stevens explains the poem as "an example of the necessity of identifying oneself with reality in order to understand it and enjoy it" (*LWS*, p. 464). 9d–10c

*so-and-so reclining on her couch. 121

*solitaire under the oaks. 199

some friends from pascagoula. A "sovereign image." See the poem "Lions in Sweden." Such images give "ideas of a new and noble order" (*LWS*, p. 349).

somnambulisma. Without the incompletion inherent in change, life would be static, dead, without particularity for the man of imagination ("scholar"). 65c–66b

sonatina to hans christian. The first "mother": hostile nature; the second: the chaos to which all must return. 9d–10a

song of fixed accord. The dove is permanently attuned to the ordinary processes of reality. 158c–d

stars at tallapoosa. The unearthly abstraction of the stars has its parallel in abstraction in the mind, whose clarity can refresh reality.

study of images i. It does no good to contrive images; they occur as our normal manner of perception. 168c–169a

STUDY OF IMAGES II. Things must be joined with their appropriate images to be adequately perceived.

STUDY OF TWO PEARS. 102d–103b

THE SUN THIS MARCH. The end of winter brings reminiscences of spring that make the adjustment to winter more difficult. The rabbi appealed to Stevens as a figure "devoted in the extreme to scholarship and at the same time to making some use of it for human purposes" (LWS, p. 786).

*SUNDAY MORNING. 63

THE SURPRISES OF THE SUPERHUMAN. The superhuman would surprise us by making things right.

TABLE TALK. 200d–201d

TATTOO. Reality is tattooed on our flesh through the medium of light; and our vision is tattooed on reality.

TEA. A dominance of the imaginative.

TEA AT THE PALAZ OF HOON. Hoon conceives reality as a projection of the imagination.

THEORY. 54b

THINGS OF AUGUST. An attempt to develop a fiction appropriate to August. 55, note 5; 26d–27c

THINKING OF A RELATION BETWEEN THE IMAGES OF METAPHORS. 5b–c

*THIRTEEN WAYS OF LOOKING AT A BLACKBIRD. 71

*THIS SOLITUDE OF CATARACTS. 164

A THOUGHT REVOLVED. 143b–145b

THUNDER BY THE MUSICIAN. The music would have been more appropriate to our time had it ended in groping uncertainty rather than triumphant assurance.

TO AN OLD PHILOSOPHER IN ROME. For the dying Santayana, the imagination transforms Rome into a vision of heaven which yet remains an imaginative version of the real Rome. xi, c.

*TO THE ONE OF FICTIVE MUSIC. 68

TO THE ROARING WIND. The wind and the poet hover at the point of articulation.

TWO AT NORFOLK. The feeling of the lovers lives beyond death in the feeling of the summer night.

TWO FIGURES IN A DENSE VIOLET NIGHT. "Violet" as allied with the blue of imagination. The woman demands that her companion's love-making be imaginative, rather than merely physical.

TWO ILLUSTRATIONS THAT THE WORLD IS WHAT YOU MAKE OF IT. I. Winter is the image he gives to it; II. such transformations are transitory.

TWO LETTERS. I. 28c–29d; II. 154c–155a

TWO TALES OF LIADOFF. Liadoff's music expresses the town, I. in a flight of fancy, II. in a return to the reality of the town.

TWO VERSIONS OF THE SAME POEM. The slippery "eel" of the ocean, reality (I), refuses to be fixed by the "mould" of the mind (II). Zeller was the family name of Stevens' mother.

THE ULTIMATE POEM IS ABSTRACT. 5b–c

UNITED DAMES OF AMERICA. The aristocratic idea of the singular man, as opposed to the collective "man of the mass" who will "declaim" our collective purpose. 144d–145b

VACANCY IN THE PARK. The reality of the past winter is at an end, and that of the expected spring (l. 2) has not appeared, leaving a vacancy in the present. 7d–8a

VALLEY CANDLE. The candle orders the world, but both as artifact (l. 1) and thing of imagination ("image"), is transitory. 73c–74a

VARIATIONS ON A SUMMER DAY. In form like "Thirteen Ways of Looking at a Blackbird." 18c–19b, 25d–26a

THE VIRGIN CARRYING A LANTERN. The "negress" projects her own imaginative version of the "pious" virgin's situation.

WAVING ADIEU, ADIEU, ADIEU. "Death is absolute" (CP, p. 97—see "The Death of a Soldier"). This being so, we turn to the "ever-jubilant weather" of which Stevens writes: "We are physical beings in a physical world; the weather is one of the things that we enjoy, one of the unphilosophical realities" (LWS, pp. 348–49).

A WEAK MIND IN THE MOUNTAINS. A time of inadequate imagination.

THE WEEPING BURGHER. The "burgher," a ghost, "distorts the world" through "excess," thus cloaking the "sorry verities"; yet this makes him yearn more for life, from which he is severed, and so is "a strange malice" because it is against himself, making him weep.

THE WELL DRESSED MAN WITH A BEARD. 128b–129a

WHAT WE SEE IS WHAT WE THINK. As reality becomes less adequate, imagination becomes more necessary.

WILD DUCKS, PEOPLE AND DISTANCES. In a secular world people, like the weather, comprise an element in which we live.

THE WIND SHIFTS. We read into reality our own human feelings.

WINTER BELLS. A sufficiency of secular good, including that offered by the solemnity and propriety of the church, makes metaphysical speculation ("further thought") superfluous. Stevens says that l. 12 alludes to Descartes (compare Stevens' gloss, *LWS*, p. 348).

THE WOMAN IN SUNSHINE. The woman as image for the day.

WOMAN LOOKING AT A VASE OF FLOWERS. The inhuman forces of reality are productive of that which is sympathetic to the human. "Owl within": her wisdom.

A WOMAN SINGS A SONG FOR A SOLDIER COME HOME. Integration with the present requires communion with the reality of the present. "His wound": his isolation.

A WORD WITH JOSÉ RODRÍGUEZ-FEO. The "grotesque" is the imaginative version of things, not "apparition," but the way they actually appear to the ego. The person named in the title was a literary friend with whom Stevens maintained an important correspondence. 25c–d

THE WORLD AS MEDITATION. The coming of Ulysses in her meditation merges with the coming of the sun in the larger meditation of nature. 189b

WORLD WITHOUT PECULIARITY. Reality is alien until humanized as, in this poem, is the day (ll. 17–18), and the earth in its personification as "humanity."

THE WORMS AT HEAVEN'S GATE. An ironic resurrection of the body.

YELLOW AFTERNOON. "Face/Without eyes": consciousness of a responsive reality. For a parallel relation with reality, see 54a–c.

NOTES

[1] Kimon Friar and John Malcolm Brinnin, eds. *Modern Poetry, American and British* (New York, 1951), p. 537.

[2] *Historical Review of Berks County*, XXIV (Fall, 1959), 108 (caption).

[3] Daniel Fuchs, *The Comic Spirit of Wallace Stevens* (Durham, N.C., 1963), p. 150, n. 22.

[4] Ramon Guthrie, "Stevens' 'Lions in Sweden,'" *Explicator*, XX (Dec., 1961), Item 32.

Selected Stevens Criticism

Baird, James. "Transvaluation in the Poetics of Wallace Stevens," in Richard Beale Davis and John Lievsay (eds.), *Studies in Honor of John C. Hodges and Alwin Thaler.* Knoxville: University of Tennessee Press, 1961, pp. 163–73.

Benamou, Michel. "Jules Laforgue and Wallace Stevens," *Romanic Review,* L (April 1959), 107–17.

Borroff, Marie (ed.). *Wallace Stevens: A Collection of Critical Essays.* Englewood Cliffs, N.J.: Prentice-Hall, 1963. See especially essays by Zabel, Quinn, Frye, Martz (also in the Brown and Haller collection), and Pearce (appearing in different form as part of his study of Stevens in his *The Continuity of American Poetry*).

Brown, Ashley, and Robert S. Haller (ed.). *The Achievement of Wallace Stevens.* Philadelphia: J. B. Lippincott, 1962. A collection of 19 essays, arranged historically, many of them essential to the body of Stevens criticism. Note especially essays by Blackmur, Baker, Cunningham, Bewley, Jarrell, Morse, Martz (also in the Borroff collection), Benamou, and Moore.

Buttel, Robert. *Wallace Stevens, The Making of Harmonium.* Princeton: Princeton University Press, 1967.

Cunningham, J. V. "The Styles and Procedures of Wallace Stevens," *The Denver Quarterly,* I (Spring 1966), 8–28.

Doggett, Frank. "Wallace Stevens' Later Poetry," *ELH: A Journal of English Literary History,* XXV (June 1958), 137–54.

Howe, Irving. "Another Way of Looking at the Blackbird," *New Republic,* CXXXVII (November 4, 1957), 16–19.

Morse, Samuel French. "Introduction," in *Poems by Wallace*

Stevens, selected by Samuel French Morse. New York: Vintage, 1959, pp. v–xx.

Morse, Samuel French, Jackson R. Bryer, and Joseph N. Riddel. *Wallace Stevens Checklist and Bibliography of Stevens Criticism.* Denver: Allan Swallow, 1963.

Nemerov, Howard. "The Poetry of Wallace Stevens," *Sewanee Review,* LXV (Winter 1957), 1–14.

Pearce, Roy Harvey, *The Continuity of American Poetry.* Princeton: Princeton University Press, 1961; corrected and revised, 1965. Chapters 9 and 10.

Pearce, Roy Harvey, and J. Hillis Miller (ed.). *The Act of the Mind: Essays on the Poetry of Wallace Stevens.* Baltimore: The Johns Hopkins Press, 1965. Contains important essays by Benamou, Pearce, Miller, and Riddel, which are also included in the special Stevens issue of *ELH: A Journal of English Literary History,* March, 1964.

Riddel, Joseph N. *The Clairvoyant Eye: The Poetry and Poetics of Wallace Stevens.* Baton Rouge: Louisiana State University Press, 1965.

Stallknecht, Newton P., "Absence in Reality: A Study in the Epistemology of the Blue Guitar," *Kenyon Review,* XXI (Autumn 1959), 545–62.

Williams, William Carlos. "Comment: Wallace Stevens," *Poetry,* LXXXVII (January 1956), 234–39.